Internet File Formats

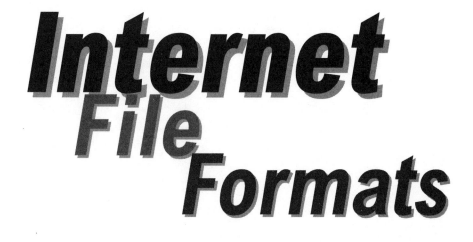

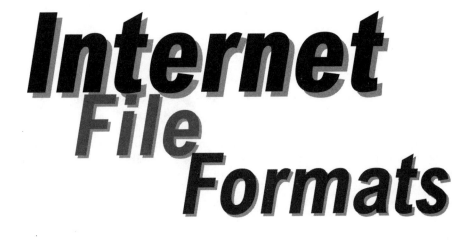

Internet File Formats

Tim Kientzle

CORIOLIS GROUP BOOKS

Publisher	Keith Weiskamp
Editorial Director	Jeff Duntemann
Managing Editor	Ron Pronk
Editor	Diane Cook
Cover Design	Gary Smith and Bradley Grannis
Interior Design	Tim Kientzle
Layout Production	Tim Kientzle
CD Production	Anthony Potts

This book was produced using LaTeX 2_ε and dvips typesetting software on FreeBSD 2.0R. The text fonts are Adobe Garamond and Computer Modern Typewriter; headings are in Adobe Helvetica and Monotype Arial.

Library of Congress Cataloging-in-Publication Data
Kientzle, Tim
    Internet File Formats/Tim Kientzle
        p.   cm.
    Includes bibliography and index.
    ISBN 1-883577-56-X: $39.99

Printed in the United States of America

10 9 8 7 6 5 4 3 2 1

TO BETH

Acknowledgments

Many people have generously contributed to the production of this book, among them: Jeff Duntemann and Keith Weiskamp suggested the idea for this book. Tom Lippincott read and critiqued some of the early chapters. Diane Cook's watchful red pen corrected many slips and blunders. Anthony Potts' enthusiastic gathering made the accompanying CD-ROM a useful accompaniment. The staff at Dr. Dobb's gave me the time and encouragement to finish. But most importantly, Beth brought me innumerable ice cream sandwiches when I needed them most.

Contents

Part Two   Graphics Formats

Part Three   Compression and Archiving Formats

Part Four   Encoding Formats

Part Five   Sound Formats

Part Six   *Movie Formats*

Appendices

The Great Melting Pot

1

New York has built a reputation as a place where people from many different cultures live and work together. Much of current American culture was shaped by the immigrants of the early 1900s, and today's immigrants will doubtless shape future American culture. Similarly, the Internet is a place where different technologies and computer cultures meet. Hopefully, the best ideas from each will form a sound technological basis for tomorrow's networked society. In the meantime, the overabundance of different approaches and standards is creating a lot of confusion.

Internetworking

In the early 1970s, many people were experimenting with different ways to connect computers. At one end of the spectrum, the Xerox Palo Alto Research Center (PARC) was developing the precursor of today's high-speed Ethernet. At the other end, the University of North Carolina and nearby Duke University were using slow dial-up modem connections for what later grew to be the Usenet news system. The various networking ideas and approaches were far from compatible, which made it all the more remarkable when the Advanced Research Project Agency (ARPA) and the Defense Advanced Research Project Agency (DARPA) set out to connect the computerized islands at various universities and research agencies.

The approach used to build ARPAnet and DARPAnet was dubbed *internetworking*. Rather than try to convert all of the participating companies and organizations to the same kind of network, they fostered the development of *gateways* to bridge the different networks. These gateways used a common software protocol appropriately dubbed the *Internet Protocol* (IP).

The resulting conglomerate grew in many directions. As IP became more standardized, it was used for local networks as well, which led to new services being built on top of IP. Services built on IP could be accessed not only within the local network, but also from computers at other companies, which continued to foster the adoption of IP as a fundamental networking technology. The growing standardization and improving services attracted many new users, and the number of computers with direct or indirect access to these services grew steadily. Eventually, users began to think of this loosely connected group of computers as a single entity, the *Internet*.

Bulletin Board Systems

While university and corporate researchers were laying the foundation for today's Internet, microcomputer hobbyists took a slightly different track. The availability of inexpensive modems allowed them to connect their computers over the phone lines to exchange programs and information. Dedicated computers were set up as *electronic bulletin board systems* (BBSs), which answered the phone and allowed the caller to copy files to and from the system, and to read and exchange messages.

Each BBS was set up by a single person, and usually reflected the interests of that person. Most BBSs only stored programs and data files for users of a particular kind of computer. Macintosh BBSs and IBM PC BBSs often had little in common.

This isolation weakened as BBSs began to relay messages to one another. The most successful relay system was *Fidonet*. Fidonet is a loose affiliation of BBSs that periodically exchange data over normal dial-up telephone connections. Fido-compatible BBS software is widely available and fairly easy to use. As a result, Fidonet is remarkably widespread. In some parts of the world, it's the predominant form of networking.

The growth of BBSs and Fidonet had much in common with the early growth of the Internet. BBSs have traditionally been improved by amateurs, who develop new services and approaches not for commercial gain, but simply out of personal curiosity. Similarly, many Internet services were developed at universities and research establishments as tools for sharing information with colleagues or experimenting with new ideas.

Greater Internetopolis

Today, these networking services are merging. The term "Internet" now commonly refers not only to the system of computers connected by IP but also to the much larger universe of computers that can access such basic services as *electronic mail* (email). This larger Internet subsumes ARPAnet and Fidonet, as well as many non-Fidonet BBSs and major online services. The "core" Internet—the part connected by IP—is also growing rapidly, as the "fringe" Internet becomes more tightly interconnected.

As a result of this consolidation, the walls between computing communities are slowly dissolving. The Internet of the 1990s is a melting pot, where users of Macintosh, Unix, MS-DOS, Amiga, Atari, OS/2, BSD, VMS, Windows, Apple II, and TSO, are exposed, if not to one another's ideas and viewpoints, at least to their files. One of the most common questions asked on Internet newsgroups is how to handle a particular kind of file. Such questions come from PC users unfamiliar with Unix files and from Macintosh users trying to extract data from Amiga files.

These problems are not unique to the Internet. The Internet is just the most visible way that people exchange files between different types of computers. Diskettes and modems are still widely used. Whether you're downloading files from an Internet archive on another continent or handing a diskette to your next door neighbor, you need a basic understanding of the various file formats and what they mean.

The variety of file formats causes problems even for experienced users. One long-time user and programmer of IBM PC systems confessed to me that shortly after he got an Internet email connection, he was stumped by a uuencoded gzipped tar file, a mixture of three formats of which he'd never heard, much less seen.

Sticking to the Big Streets

In practice, the concerns of file portability have led to the dominance of a handful of file formats. Formats popular on the Internet as a whole are formats that can be easily manipulated on a wide variety of systems. People who pull files from Internet archives, or who exchange files on diskettes, usually deal with only a small fraction of the file formats that exist.

Different formats serve different needs, even though the distinction isn't always obvious. Just as the *National Enquirer* doesn't directly compete with the *New York Times*, the JPEG graphics format isn't a direct substitute for GIF. These two formats each have unique strengths and weaknesses. Similarly, PDF and PostScript are very similar in some ways, but shouldn't be used for the same purposes. Understanding these differences is important not only for the person creating these files, but for the person using them. Every format has inherent limitations, and it's helpful to understand those limits.

Each community has its favorite file formats as well. You may be surprised to find a lot of MIDI files on an Atari ST archive until you discover that the Atari's built-in MIDI port made it very popular with musicians. Similarly, a lot of early multimedia work was done on the Amiga; the Macintosh graphic interface still enjoys a loyal following among graphic designers; and MS-DOS is the mainstay of many business users.

Such history isn't as trivial as it sounds. When looking for a program to decode BinHex files on a Unix machine, I first looked in several Unix archives with no luck. BinHex is used primarily on the Macintosh; a popular Macintosh archive had a section for Unix programs that answered my need. Similarly, if you're looking for information about UUEncode, you might want to check a Unix archive, since UUEncode originated on Unix systems.

About Standards

Many arguments about the "best" file format for a particular purpose have been settled by the observation that one of the formats is a "standard." Unfortunately, this reasoning isn't always relevant.

The term "standard" sometimes simply refers to "accepted practice." Accepted practice can vary widely between groups of users, and is a difficult criterion to use in practice. The term "standard" is also used to refer to a formal standard produced by a national or international organization. Standards organizations attempt to define and promote common practices so that products manufactured by different companies can be used together. The theory is that these codified practices help both businesses and consumers. It's not surprising that some of the more sophisticated file formats in this book were created by standards organizations.[1]

Most standards organizations create standards through a consensus process that solicits input from many corporate and governmental bodies. Unfortunately, the politics involved in this process can go awry in a number of ways. One pitfall is that some participants may have their own agendas. As a result, some standards end up promoting a solution owned by a single company. For example, the V.42bis standard for modems relies on an algorithm patented by Unisys. Modem manufacturers who want to comply with this standard must pay royalties to Unisys.

Another danger for this process is when the standard appears too late or too early. Some standards have been produced that disagreed with existing widespread practice. Conversely, some standards have been produced before anyone had practical experience in the area, and were so complex and theoretical that compliance was almost impossible. Either situation can result in a formal standard that's generally ignored by the industry it was designed to help.

One of the major reasons that companies comply with formal standards is to allow their products to work with products from other companies. In markets with many small suppliers, this compatibility is very important. However, not all software markets are competitive enough for compatibility to be an important consideration. Frequently a few companies dominate a single market, so that their products become *de facto* standards. The popular GIF file format was never sanctioned by a standards organization, but it has become a widespread format simply because it was promoted by CompuServe, whose online service was a focal point for exchanging computer graphics.

All of the formats in this book are "standards" in some sense. A few are formal standards defined by some international body; the rest were created by

---

[1] The best known standards organizations are the American National Standards Institute (ANSI), International Organization for Standardization (ISO), and the International Telecommunications Union (ITU)—formerly the International Consultative Committee for Telephone and Telegraph (CCITT).

some company or individual to fill a particular need. All of them have become so widely used that you'll probably encounter most of them.

Researching File Formats

If you have a file in a format you don't understand and want to use it, what should you do? In this chapter, I'll discuss some resources that can help you track down the information you need.

Identifying the Format of a File

There are a number of tools you can use to identify the format of a file. The first is the name of the file. Filenames typically contain a period in them (sometimes several, depending on the system). The letters after the last period are the file *extension*. Traditionally, the extension is used to identify the type of the file. For example, in ocean.jpg, the extension is .jpg. If you look in the index, you'll quickly find that this is a short form for JPEG, the name of a popular graphics format used for photographic images. Sometimes, a file will have more than one extension. It's common for Unix users to see files such as library.tar.gz. Again, you can use the index to figure out that the .gz indicates this is a GZIP compressed file. After you uncompress it, you'll be left with library.tar, which is a TAR archive file.

But not all files have extensions, and even when they do, the extensions don't always reflect the type of data in the file. Some people use the extension for the date—such as report.817 for the August 17th version—or for the initials of the person creating the file—Joan Smith's report is named report.js while Greg Zambrana's is report.gz. If the file doesn't have a useful extension, you basically have to guess what the format is, although there are a few tricks you can use.

On some systems (especially Unix systems), there's a command named `file` that knows how to recognize many different types of files. For example, typing `file jeff` might reveal `jeff:  GIF picture - version 87a`. Again, the index will tell you that GIF files are CompuServe's *Graphics Interchange Format*, a popular picture format. The `file` program relies on a large table of *magic numbers*, special values that appear at certain locations in certain file formats. The quality of these tables varies dramatically; some programs only recognize a few file types while others recognize hundreds. Fortunately, the magic numbers are usually stored in a text file. You can add your own new entries to this list of magic numbers to make the `file` command more useful.

If you don't have a `file` command, it's time to look at the contents of the file. Before you try this, think carefully about what tools you have and what kind of file it might be. Files are generally divided into *text* files and *binary* files. Text files—often called ASCII files—only contain "safe" byte values, ones that correspond to letters, numbers, and punctuation marks. Binary files can contain any byte value. This division is a technical one that has little to do with the contents of the file; some graphics formats are text files that use letters, numbers, and punctuation marks to encode the picture data. Conversely, most word processor documents are binary files. The problem is that simply listing a binary file to your screen is rarely useful. Depending on the system, you can even lock up your computer or terminal (though you can't actually damage the computer this way).

Binary files frequently have some text near the beginning that identifies the type of the file. You can use a program such as the `dump` program I discuss on page 379, or the Unix `od` program. These programs read binary files, and output the numeric value or corresponding character for each byte. The `dump` program outputs both the numeric value and the character. (The `od` program can output many different formats.) The important point is that you can look at the contents of the file without having your screen go out of control. Usually, you'll send the output into `more` so you can skim through it a page at a time.[1]

---

[1] The Unix `strings` program can also be useful; it reads a file and outputs only the valid text characters in the file.

You can frequently read a binary file into a text editor. You should be very careful, however; *do not* save the file. Most text editors will slightly mangle binary files when they read them. If you save the file, you'll mangle the version on disk as well.

If it's a text format, of course, things are much simpler. You can simply list it to your screen or read it into a text editor to see what it looks like. Even if the bulk of it is unintelligible, the first line or two will frequently contain useful clues. For example, if the file begins with %PDF, then this is a PDF file (see page 109). If it contains xbtoa, then it's a BtoA file (see page 267).

Using the Files

Once you have some clues about the type of file, the next step is to figure out what you can do with it. Just knowing it's a graphics file isn't enough.

Of course, since you're already holding this book, the first thing you should do is see if the information you need is here. Each chapter ends with a *More Information* section that describes sources of suitable software, much of which is included on the accompanying CD-ROM. For some formats, especially graphics files, there are programs that handle many different formats. The *More Information* section in the *About Graphics* chapter (page 124) lists some sources of such software. That section also discusses other sources of information about graphics formats in general. The other *About . . .* chapters have similar information.

No book will have information on all of the formats you might encounter, and this one is no exception. If the information you want isn't here, there are a number of other resources available to you. Several of these resources are available on the Internet.

File Formats on the World Wide Web

The *World Wide Web* is a data access system that runs on the Internet. It allows people to access *pages* of information that can contain text, graphics and references to other pages of information. Graphical browser programs allow you to simply click on a reference to see the other related page. To get started, you need a *Universal Resource Locator (URL)*, which is much like a "telephone number" for a page on the World Wide Web (page 30 has more detailed information about URLs).

Several people have created Web pages to help people understand different file formats and locate associated software.

If you already have a World Wide Web browser, it probably has a button or menu entry that connects you to the home page of the people who produce the browser (such as Netscape, QuarterDeck, Spry, or NCSA). Those home pages usually have information about helper programs that work with their browser, as well as information on configuring the browser. Even if you're not specifically looking for assistance for your World Wide Web browser, most of these "helper" programs are generic view or play programs that can be easily used alone.

There are also a number of Web pages that people have created to help provide information about the various formats. Here are a few:

The Cross-Platform Page   Eric Bennett's index lists information about a variety of file formats, and tells you where to get software for a number of platforms. It's available at `http://www.mps.org/~ebennett`. Another copy is at `http://www.mcad.edu/guests/ericb/xplat.html`.

Common Internet File Formats   This Macintosh-oriented resource lists a number of different file formats and tells you where to get corresponding software. (`http://www.matisse.net/files/formats.html`)

The Ultimate Macintosh   This is a good guide to Macintosh resources on the World Wide Web. (`http://www.freepress.com/myee/umac.html`)

Multimedia File Formats on the Internet   Allison Zhang's highly-rated and nicely-decorated guide has general information and software pointers for PC users. (`http://ac.dal.ca/~dong/contents.html`)

WWW Viewer Test Page   This page helps you configure your Web browser, and has pointers to helper software for Macintosh, PC, and Unix systems. (`http://www-dsed.llnl.gov/documents/WWWtest.html`)

Name	Location
ftp://wuarchive.wustl.edu	St. Louis, Missouri, USA
ftp://ftp.cdrom.com	Walnut Creek, California, USA
ftp://ftp.digital.com	Palo Alto, California, USA
ftp://ftp.leo.org	Munich, Germany
ftp://archie.au	Melbourne, Australia

Table 2.1   Selected Large Archive Sites

Note: Many archives with names beginning in ftp also have corresponding World Wide Web access. Try replacing ftp://ftp with http://www, for example, http://www.leo.org.

Other File Format Resources

Even if you don't have access to the World Wide Web, you still can find many resources. Even the most basic Internet account typically allows you to access various databases using *FTP* (File Transfer Protocol) and *Gopher* (see Appendix D). FTP allows you to copy files from Internet databases down to your computer. There are a handful of *mail FTP* systems that accept FTP commands over electronic mail and return the results in the same fashion. The Gopher system is a system of linked menus that is similar to, but much older than, the World Wide Web. If you don't have any access to the Internet at all, you can frequently get CD-ROMs with the contents of one of these repositories.

I only have room to list a few of the many good resources on the Internet. To best take advantage of these resources, you should look on each site for a README file.[2] This file will tell you something about the archive and should also list *mirrors*, other archives that maintain exact copies of these archives. *Always find and use the mirror that's closest to you.* Using a nearby mirror makes it easier for you (international network links tend to be slow) and more pleasant for everyone else using the Internet. A sampling of large sites that mirror many different archives is shown in Table 2.1.

---

[2]Unfortunately, "read me" files have many slightly different names, including READ.ME, README.1ST, OOREADME, and readme.txt.

Keep in mind that none of these archives is devoted exclusively to a particular system. You'll frequently find MS-DOS software on OS/2 archives and Unix software on Macintosh archives.

MS-DOS　The SIMTEL collection contains a large amount of freeware and shareware for MS-DOS systems, including viewer programs for a variety of formats. It's a good place to start looking. Among the more accessible mirrors are `ftp.coast.net`, `oak.oakland.edu`, `wuarchive.wustl.edu`, and `ftp.cdrom.com`, all accessible by anonymous FTP.

The Finnish *Garbo* archive is located at `garbo.uwasa.fi`. It stores a variety of software for many systems, but is probably best known for its collection of MS-DOS software and information.

Windows　The Center for Innovative Computer Applications (CICA) at the University of Indiana hosts a sizable collection of software for all flavors of Microsoft Windows. The CICA archive is accessible from the World Wide Web (`http://winftp.cica.indiana.edu`), FTP (`ftp://winftp.cica.indiana.edu`), and Gopher (`gopher://winftp.cica.indiana.edu`).

Macintosh　The Info-Mac archives are substantial and widely mirrored. Because of the enormous load on `sumex-aim.stanford.edu` (the original site), you should probably avoid using it directly and instead use one of its many mirrors. Not surprisingly, Apple mirrors this and many other sites (`ftp://mirror.apple.com`). Another particularly interesting mirror is the *Hyper-Archive*, which provides a searchable World Wide Web interface to the archives (`http://hyperarchive.lcs.mit.edu/HyperArchive.html`).

The University of Michigan also maintains a sizable collection of Macintosh software (`http://www.umich.edu/~archive/mac`). You should start at `http://www.umich.edu/~archive` to find out information about the archive itself and how best to use it. This main page also accesses several other archives maintained at the same location.

The *Berkeley Macintosh User's Group* (BMUG) is the world's largest Macintosh user's group. They provide numerous services to their members, and maintain and distribute an enormous collection of freeware and shareware. You can find more information at `http://www.bmug.org`, or by writing to: BMUG, 1442A Walnut St. #62, Berkeley, CA, USA, 94709.

OS/2   The *Hobbes* archive at New Mexico State University collects many OS/2 programs. It's available at `ftp://ftp-os2.nmsu.edu`.

Unix   One of the greatest assets of any Unix system is the online *man pages*. Simply typing `man` `command` will give you documentation on the desired command. Many Unix users don't realize that the man pages also contain a wealth of information about file formats and other technical information. The man pages are divided into *sections*. For example, section 1 is used for user commands. Information on file formats is found in section 4 or 5 (depending on the system). For example, typing `man uuencode` will display information about the `uuencode` program. To see the file format used by UUEncode, you would type `man 5 uuencode` (on a BSD-derived system) or `man 4 uuencode` (on a SysV-derived system). There are many variations; consult `man man` for the details of using the `man` command on your particular system. If you don't have access to a Unix system, O'Reilly & Associates has published a five-volume set containing the complete man pages for 4.4BSD,[3] along with many other related documents. [USD94, URM94, PRM94, PSD94, SMM94].

The various `comp.sources` newsgroups are a source of new and interesting Unix software. These include `comp.sources.unix`, `comp.sources.x`, `comp.sources.sun`, and `comp.sources.3b1`. Many of these newsgroups are archived at `ftp.uu.net`. UUNet also archives many other newsgroups, and contains information and software for a variety of systems. Don't forget the GNU repository at `ftp://prep.ai.mit.edu`, which contains a lot of freely available software.

Amiga   *Aminet* is a large collection of Amiga software and information. The primary site at `ftp://ftp.wustl.edu` is extremely busy. It's mirrored at `ftp://ftp.cdrom.com` and `http://www.eunet.ch/~aminet`.

---

[3]The *Berkeley Standard Distribution* (BSD) is a collection of Unix software and operating system extensions contributed by people from around the world. The project has been coordinated by the Computer Science Research Group of the University of California at Berkeley since 1979. BSD has been very influential in Unix system development, and portions of it appear in many Unix-like systems, including SunOS, BSDI, and Linux. The free portions of 4.4BSD—available by anonymous FTP and on CD-ROM—are very nearly a complete replacement for Unix, and several groups have filled in the missing pieces to build free Unix-like systems from this base.

The Amiga Home Page at `http://www.omnipresence.com/amiga` has pointers to other archive sites and a variety of additional information.

General Research on the Internet

A number of resources exist for doing general research on the Internet. I'll discuss a few of the more important ones.

The following resources have a lot of overlap. The World Wide Web indexes include a lot of FTP and Gopher information, and Veronica (the Gopher index) also includes a lot of World Wide Web and FTP information. But each has a slightly different focus. Spend a little time familiarizing yourself with each of these resources and learning how to use them.

FAQ Archive *Frequently Asked Questions* (FAQ) files are lists of common questions and answers on specific topics. Many are regularly posted (usually about once per month) to different newsgroups. Answering common questions in this manner prevents the newsgroups from being constantly flooded with the same questions. If you know of a newsgroup that might have information you want, watch the newsgroup for several weeks and read the FAQ file before asking questions. Your question may be answered without you having to ask it. Collectively, the FAQ files are an enormously useful resource. Many of them have general overviews of a topic and bibliographies of books, articles, and other information about the topic.

Many FAQ files are available using anonymous FTP from the FAQ archive at `ftp://rtfm.mit.edu/pub/usenet`. Many FAQ files are also posted to the `news.answers` newsgroup.

Yahoo *Yahoo* (`http://www.yahoo.com`) is a searchable directory of the World Wide Web. It has a hierarchical directory you can browse, as well as a powerful search feature. Visiting this index is a good first step to find information on the World Wide Web.

Indexes that have search features are powerful tools, but you should use them carefully. Spend a few minutes thinking about the best terms to use. If you want QuickTime movies, for instance, search for `quicktime` and not for `movies`; the latter will produce a much longer list with a lot of things you don't want (like movie reviews and movie studios).

Spiders Yahoo is built primarily from contributions; people specifically ask for their Web pages to be added. The *Lycos* (`http://www.lycos.com`) and *WebCrawler* (`http://webcrawler.com`) databases are constructed in a different fashion. In addition to contributed references, Lycos and WebCrawler use "spider" or "robot" programs that follow links over the entire Web. These programs automatically find new World Wide Web pages and add them to a growing database. Lycos currently indexes over two million pages; WebCrawler has identified over 50,000 servers. One interesting aspect of both of these projects is the additional statistics they are collecting about the World Wide Web, currently the best statistics available.

Archie The *Archie* system is a collection of databases indexing files available by FTP. If you have a SLIP or PPP account, you can use Archie to locate a file. The only catch is that you need to know the name of the file first.

Veronica Just as Archie indexes FTP resources and Yahoo indexes World Wide Web resources, *Veronica* indexes Gopher pages. Like Lycos and WebCrawler, Veronica uses a mix of user submissions and automated searches to build its index. Veronica is referenced from many different Gopher servers. Its home is `gopher://veronica.scs.unr.edu:70/11/veronica`.

Part One
Text and Document Formats

About Text

Text files are the most common type of data found on the Internet and elsewhere. Although they seem very simple at first, there are two major complicating factors. The first complication is the enormous number of characters needed to support a variety of different languages. American programmers used to working with the 128 characters of the US ASCII character set need to keep in mind that well over 250 characters are needed just to deal with the two dozen or so European languages based on the Roman alphabet. Other alphabets—Cyrillic, Greek, Hebrew, Arabic, Devenagari, Sanskrit, and so on—add hundreds more characters, and the Chinese, Japanese, and Korean ideograms add tens of thousands more. While the Internet is still predominantly English-speaking, this is changing. Savvy software developers will want to take advantage of the opportunities for multilingual software. The next section describes the history of different character sets and provides some background for developing and using multinational software.

The other complicating factor is that text alone is increasingly inadequate. People want to augment their printed documents with graphics, charts, footnotes, headers, and font changes. Online documents may need to contain animation, links to networked databases, and audio annotations. Combining these different types of data results in *multimedia* documents. Text formats—because they are so basic—are the starting point for many multimedia document formats. Many of the formats in the next few chapters are not merely *text* formats, but are perhaps more accurately described as *document* formats, providing the overall framework in which text, graphics, and other forms of data can be combined.

Character Sets

If you take a critical look at various discussions of characters and character sets, you'll eventually realize that the idea of a "character" is hard to pin down. Because there are so many subtly different definitions already, I'm going to deliberately avoid using the word "character" or "character set" in any precise way. The terminology I'll use instead is taken from Dan Connolly's *"Character Set" Considered Harmful* [Con95].[1] Connolly's paper attempts to clarify the core ideas that appear in different standards by precisely defining certain terms. The title suggests that the term *character set* has been used in so many diverse ways as to become almost meaningless.

Most people would agree that *A* and A are the same character, even though they look different. Typographers use the word *glyph* to refer to the specific appearance of a particular character. Even though they represent the same character, A, *A*, A, **A**, *A*, **A**, 𝒜, A, and *A* are all different glyphs. More technically, a glyph is a *specific visual representation* of a character.

Of course, a single character or single glyph isn't all that useful. What you need is a selection of characters. For American English, a useful collection of characters consists of 52 uppercase and lowercase letters, ten digits, and a variety of punctuation marks. Such a collection is referred to as a character *repertoire*. A corresponding collection of glyphs, one for each character, is called a *font*.

There are many different character repertoires. One reason for this variety, of course, is language. An American English repertoire has little need for a ç character, which is essential in French. Another reason for a variety of repertoires is the special symbols that are required by certain people. For example, publishers use bullets (•), pilcrows (¶), and ligatures (ff, ffi); musicians need flats (♭) and sharps (♯); bridge players need card suits (♠, ♡); and mathematicians need a variety of special symbols (∞, ∀, ∮). Of course, having too many different repertoires is confusing, so there's a natural trend towards fewer distinct repertoires.

---

[1]Connolly's paper was published as an Internet Draft, a working document developed and distributed to solicit comments on new ideas. Although I've included a reference in the bibliography, Internet Drafts *are* temporary in nature, and the original document may be difficult to find.

Names and Numbers

We humans commonly refer to characters in two different ways. The first, of course, is to offer a representative glyph, such as &. Another is to give a name to the character, such as *ampersand*. Many of the file formats I'll describe in subsequent chapters use names for less common characters. For example, PostScript fonts use names such as `quotedblleft` for ", `ccedilla` for ç, and `Igrave` for Ì. The Hypertext Markup Language (HTML)[2] uses names such as `&amp;` for & and `&Igrave;` for Ì. (Note that the HTML names all begin with an ampersand and end with a semicolon.)

This approach is a bit circular, because these names are themselves expressed as sequences of characters. The PostScript name for the character I is simply I. For a computer, you have to represent at least some characters using the numbers that computers manipulate most naturally. Once you have enough characters represented in this way, you can use those characters to write names for the rest. There are two subtly different approaches: A *coded character set* simply assigns a particular character to each number, while a *character encoding* represents a sequence of characters as a sequence of byte values.

A coded character set thinks of each character as a single number. For example, in the ISO Latin 1 coded character set, the number 65 is used for A, 126 is used for ~, and 241 represents ñ. If you have a sequence of numbers, you can simply look up each number in a table to find out which character it represents.

Of course, different countries and languages need different collections of characters. The most convenient set of numbers to use for coded character sets has been the numbers from zero to 255 (the possible values of a single byte). Of course, with only 256 numbers, you can't give a unique code to every possible character, so people have developed different coded character sets. The ISO Latin 1 coded character set I mentioned earlier was developed by the International Organization for Standardization (ISO) to hold all of the characters needed for a certain group of languages (in this case, Western European languages using Roman letters). Other ISO coded character sets attempt to satisfy the needs of other groups, and most popular computer systems have their own peculiar coded character sets (such as IBM's "code pages" coded character sets used by MS-DOS and Windows).

---

[2]See page 29.

The simplest character encodings are based on a single coded character set with 256 or fewer codes. If you have a text file that uses such a character encoding, you can pick any byte from that file and tell what character it represents simply by looking up the byte value in a table. If you use several coded character sets in the same text file, life becomes more complex. In that case, you have special character codes that inform the program reading the file to switch to a different coded character set. Another international standard, ISO 2022, describes one way to switch among character encodings. Notice that you can't now simply look at a byte from the middle of the file and know what it means; you have to read the entire file from the beginning to see if any special escape sequences have changed the coding. Only then will you know which table to use.

Languages such as Chinese have far more than 256 characters to represent, so character encodings for these languages use multiple bytes for each character. These character encodings use a variety of different approaches. One approach switches among several different single-byte character encodings, each encoding a portion of the total character repertoire. Another approach uses more than one byte for each character. To save space, often some characters are encoded with one byte, and others with two or more. In practice, these approaches are usually combined, which makes reading text files using Chinese character encodings considerably more complex than the simple "one byte is one character" assumption familiar to so many Western computer programmers.

One attempt to consolidate this mess is the Unicode standard (also known as ISO 10646). Unicode is a coded character set that uses numbers from zero to 65,536 for character numbers. This larger range allows Unicode to number enough characters to satisfy the needs of most people on the planet. Many international standards are moving toward the use of Unicode to provide support for multiple languages. Future versions of HTML may be based on Unicode.

A Subtlety

One fine point that pops up in international standards bears some consideration. Many standards use special characters to mark commands or other special features in a file. For example, Rich Text Format (RTF) starts each command with a backslash (\) character. RTF files are usually written in US-ASCII, in which the backslash character is code 92. As a result, many RTF-reading programs simply skim the file looking for code 92. The problem is: What if RTF is written using a character encoding in which code 92 is not always a backslash? For example, encodings for Japanese often use two bytes per character, and the second character may be a 92. A program that simply looks for byte number 92 might interpret the second byte of a two-byte character as the backslash; worse, some international character encodings use code 92 for something completely different. The question arises: Is the start-of-command character in RTF a backslash or is it character 92?

Fortunately, this issue doesn't arise in RTF. RTF can only appear in a handful of character encodings, and the characters that have special importance in RTF are the same in all of those encodings. This point of confusion may become an issue for HTML, however. HTML may someday officially support character encodings other than ISO Latin 1[3], and this precise question is one of the stumbling blocks.

Why Bother?

Many Americans who have read this far are probably scratching their heads and wondering "Why should I care?" One answer is simply that the Internet *is* international. While the United States has dominated the Internet for many years, to the extent that American English is considered by many to be the unofficial "official" language of the Internet, this situation is changing. Even when text files are written in American English, it's increasingly common for them to appear in a character encoding other than simple ASCII.

Another reason that you should to be aware of these issues is that even within the United States, the character encodings used by popular computer systems do vary. Many Macintosh users have been perplexed by neatly formatted text such as:

```
/ffffffffffffø
≥   Hello   ≥
¿fffffffffffffŸ
```

---

[3]ISO Latin 1 is the current standard character encoding for HTML, although there is considerable pressure for HTML to support a larger repertoire.

when what was intended was:

```
r---------------1
|    Hello      |
L_____J
```

The original author could make sure that more people would appreciate this artistic touch by only using characters that are the same across most platforms:

```
+-------------+
|    Hello    |
+-------------+
```

While the effect is less impressive to other MS-DOS users, it is at least intelligible to people not using MS-DOS computers.

Because different computer systems use different coded character sets, this type of problem is rampant. It will be solved only when either everyone uses the same character encoding (which is unlikely to happen for a long time) or systems explicitly indicate which character encoding is being used by each text message, so that intelligent software can translate. Many new software standards are beginning to make this second option more of a reality.

Markup

Many text files are transferred as "plain" text. Unfortunately, plain text is exactly what it sounds like: plain. A plain text file doesn't have fonts, embedded graphics, headings, titles, footnotes, italics, or other features that would help to make the text more attractive and easier to understand. These additional features are called *markup*, and they can be vitally important. One simple form of markup is the inclusion of names for special characters, as I discussed in the previous section. Next I'll describe how other types of markup can be represented.

Logical vs. Physical Markup

The first point of which you should be aware is the distinction between *physical* and *logical* markup. Physical markup specifies the exact appearance of each piece of text, for example, "centered in 14pt Bold Oblique Futura Condensed." Logical markup specifies the logical significance of a piece of text, for example, "this is a chapter title."

These two types of markup are appropriate in different situations. Before you can print something on a printer, you clearly need to have physical markup. Decisions must be made about the size of margins, the format of footnotes, and the amount of indentation to use at the beginning of each paragraph. Early word processors used this type of markup exclusively, requiring you to specify the font, size, and style of each piece of text.

When exchanging information with other people, physical markup can be limiting. For example, standard paper sizes vary from country to country. Something that looks very nice on US letter-size paper can look quite awkward when printed on the slightly narrower and longer A4 paper used in Europe. The situation is even worse for purely electronic documents such as online help. Screen sizes and resolutions, fonts, and graphic support all vary widely among different systems, making it best if the document can be easily reformatted to fit the available display.

For these reasons, computer applications are increasingly moving to logical markup. Logical markup tags each part of the document with its logical significance. For example, a word might be tagged with "emphasis" rather than "italics." When the document is printed or displayed, this logical formatting will be converted into physical formatting that's appropriate for the situation. Emphasized words might be underlined on a system that doesn't support italics, or set in bold type in a country where bold is considered more appropriate.

Logical markup is very important in some situations. One is the exchange of electronic documents, such as World Wide Web pages. Another is in the development and publication of large works such as books. Many publishers store their books electronically using the Standard Generic Markup Language (SGML). This approach helps simplify the creation of books (there's no need to constantly remember the precise font and layout used in an earlier chapter) and it also simplifies the publication of books in different sizes and formats.

The conversion of logical markup into physical markup is controlled by a *style sheet*. A style sheet simply lists the visual appearance of each logical element. For example, this book uses a style sheet that specifies Adobe Garamond Italic for emphasized words. The details of this conversion are handled differently by different systems. In some cases, the logical markup is specified with text commands, and the entire document is processed to generate an output that contains physical markup. In others, the logical markup is stored in a binary word processor format, and the user edits the document with the full physical markup apparent.

Preserving Markup

When you want to transfer data between different computers, the easiest route is often to transfer plain text. When the markup is also important, you can use one of three general approaches.

The first way to preserve the markup is to include markup information in the text, for example: `the <bold> right <endbold> decision` might be "the **right** decision." The advantage of this approach is that the file *is* a text file (although admittedly rather funny-looking). As a text file, it's easier to transfer between different computers. If you have a program that understands the format, you can view it as the creator intended, but even if you don't have the right software, you may be able to understand it anyway. There are many different ways to represent the markup, including:

- HyperText Markup Language (HTML), used by the World Wide Web,

- TROFF, used for Unix manuals,

- TEX and LATEX, used by some academic publishers, and

- SGML (Standard Generalized Markup Language).

Each is discussed in more detail in later chapters.

The second way to preserve the markup is to transfer a picture of each page. Fax machines work this way; they take a picture of each page and then send that picture. One critically important aspect of this process is that the receiver of such an image gets *only* a picture of the page. In particular, before editing the contents, the receiver must retype the entire document. This restriction isn't always a bad thing: You don't always want the recipient to be able to easily alter what you send them. Two popular ways to share text files use exactly this approach. Fax modems make it possible to transfer documents directly from one computer to another. PostScript is a popular format for representing documents that, despite being a text format, can be very difficult to convert back into editable text without retyping.

The third way to preserve the markup is to develop a new kind of file specifically intended to contain both text and markup information. Most word processors and desktop publishing programs use this approach. The biggest problem is that almost every word processor and desktop publishing program uses a different format. While more expensive programs can often read files created by their competitors, this ability is not something you can assume. As a result, these specialized files are usually not a good choice for sharing documents.

HTML

The World Wide Web is built on three important standards. The first is the *Universal Resource Locator (URL)*, which provides a standard way to specify the location of any piece of accessible data on the global Internet. The second is the *HyperText Transfer Protocol (HTTP)*, which can directly access and transfer individual pieces of data located anywhere on the network. Finally, the *Hyper-Text Markup Language (HTML)* provides a way of enriching text documents with a variety of markup, including "links" specifying the URL of other pieces of data. Most often, these links specify other HTML documents, which can in turn be accessed with HTTP, providing users a global interconnected web of information.

HTML itself is widely misunderstood. Many HTML documents on the World Wide Web contain extensive, detailed formatting commands that allow the document to look very nice on a particular browser on a particular operating system and a particular size of screen. When viewed with a different browser, the document can be completely illegible. The author of the docu-

HTML at a Glance	
Name:	HTML, HyperText Markup Language
Extensions:	`.html`, `.htm`
Use For:	Electronic on-screen hyperlinked documents
Reference:	*The HTML Sourcebook* [Gra95]
On CD:	HTML editors for Macintosh, Windows

ment failed to realize a fundamental aspect of HTML: HTML does *not* allow you to control the appearance of a document. Rather, HTML allows you to *suggest* how the document should be displayed. Different browsers can (and should) interpret those suggestions in different ways. For example, HTML is designed to be easily converted into spoken text or braille for blind users; HTML is also intended to be easily displayed on graphical screens or text-only terminals. Authors that depend on the peculiarities of one browser should realize that they are limiting their audience.

Universal Resource Locators

Before you can fully appreciate HTML, you need a good understanding of URLs. URLs specify the *location* of a piece of data. They have a very specific format, which I'll explain in this section.

First, I'll discuss an analogy that may help explain one often-overlooked subtlety. Suppose you want to contact your old school friend Joan. One of the first questions you might ask is: "Should I call her or write?" If you decide to call, you'll need her phone number. If you want to write, you may need a variety of information: a ZIP code or postal code, country, state, city, street, mail stop, building, apartment number, and so on. *What* information you need depends on *how* you want to contact her.

The same is true of data on a network such as the Internet. First, you need to know *how* you're going to access the data. Then, depending on the method you choose, you may need a variety of additional information.

URLs specify first the method to use to access the data, and then a variety of additional information required to uniquely identify that data. Table 4.1 lists some sample URLs. As you can see, the precise information required varies depending on the access method. The following items will give you a more detailed explanation of each one of these access methods:

HTTP   The Hypertext Transfer Protocol was designed specifically for the World Wide Web. To use HTTP, you need to specify the machine name and additional information which that machine can use to find or create the needed data. This additional data often looks like a filename with directory information. Partly because the early work on the World Wide

URL	Description
`http://www.w3.org`	System home page
`ftp://ftp.coriolis.com/pub/index.txt`	Single file by FTP
`pgopher://info.itu.ch`	Top-level Gopher menu
`mailto:orders@coriolis.com`	Mail URL
`finger:kientzle@netcom.com`	Finger URL
`news:comp.newusers.announce`	Newsgroup
`news:3009951049270001@system3.com`	Single news article

Table 4.1 Sample URLs

Web was done on Unix, the slash character (/) is used to separate directory names and filenames when they appear in URLs.

FTP The File Transfer Protocol is an old access method that was designed to make it simple to transfer large quantities of data over the Internet. Because it is so old, it is widely available. To access a file or directory with FTP, you need to specify a machine name and the name of a file or directory on that machine.[1]

Gopher This method is similar to HTTP in some respects, but is more limited in the type of data it can support. Gopher is text-oriented, allowing you to browse menus and download files. The menus can contain references to files or other menus (possibly on other machines). To access data using Gopher, you need the name of the machine and the name of the file or menu.

Finger This system makes it easy for people to find out basic information about other network users, such as their account name and when they last logged in. A common extension allows you to create a file (usually called `.plan`) that will be returned to anyone who fingers you. This option exists so people can provide additional information such as a home phone number or mailing address, but a few people do publish HTML

[1]In normal FTP, a file name that includes a directory name uses the syntax of the host machine. For example, if you're retrieving a file from a VAX/VMS system, you may need to give a name like `[directory]filename.extension`. URLs, however, *always* use the Unix-style syntax of `directory/filename.extension`.

data in this way. Unfortunately, a bug in many Unix systems enabled people to break into computers that allowed finger access.[2] Although this particular problem has been fixed, many system administrators no longer allow finger access.

To access data using finger, you need the name of the machine and the account name of a user on that machine.

Mail Electronic mail is one of the oldest ways to relay data over the Internet. Unlike all of the methods listed above, mail is a *push* protocol; the sender actually initiates the movement of data from one computer to another. The other approaches are *pull* protocols; the data is made available somewhere and the recipient moves the data. Mail URLs use the term `mailto` to emphasize this distinction.

To mail data, you have to know the mail address of the receiver, which can be a user or program on another machine. If your system supports *domain addressing* (almost all systems do these days), the mail address will consist of a user name and machine name separated by an "at sign" (@). The mail address `joan@utopia.ny.pandora.com` refers to a user named `joan` on a computer named `utopia.ny.pandora.com`.

News News is a networked system that is divided into several thousand "groups." An article posted to a particular group is relayed to every other machine on the Internet that is interested in that group. Major Internet sites handle all several thousand groups; smaller sites may only handle a few hundred.

Identifying a specific news article is very different from the other transfer methods I've mentioned. Because news is relayed to machines all over the Internet, there's little point in specifying a particular machine. It's far more efficient for you to retrieve a specific article from your local machine or some nearby machine that carries that group. As a result, news URLs look quite different from other URLs. News URLs refer to an entire newsgroup by name or a single article by an article identifier (a

---

[2]The well-publicized "Morris Worm" was a program that exploited several bugs in popular Unix-like systems to copy itself to other computers. A few computers ended up with several hundred copies of this program running simultaneously, which blocked the use of those systems and disrupted the regular handling of mail and other network services. Fortunately, no serious damage was caused apart from this disruption.

horrendous-looking sequence created by the computer on which the article originated).

To limit the amount of disk space used by news, all systems *expire* news articles, deleting old articles to reclaim space for new ones. News URLs are even less permanent than other kinds of URLs. Many newsgroups are permanently archived, and their contents can be accessed by HTTP or FTP if you know the computer where those archives are kept.

A URL is like a phone number. If the data moves for any reason, the URL is no longer useful. A similar situation occurs when a person moves and gets a new phone number. However, as long as you know generally where the person lives, you can find the new phone number by calling directory assistance; no such facility currently exists for URLs. There is a project to develop a system of *Universal Resource Names* (URNs), which would assign unique names to pieces of data. You could then find the name in some widely available database (similar in concept to directory assistance) which would give you the URL for that data. Eventually, the World Wide Web will use such URNs instead of URLs; your browser program will automatically ask directory assistance for the correct URL for each URN, and then use the URL to access the data. Creating such a directory and figuring out how to maintain and access it is an enormous task, and it's unlikely to be available very soon.

About Domain Names

Many URLs depend on being able to specify a particular machine on the Internet. While there are many ways of naming a particular machine, the scheme currently in use on most of the Internet is called *domain naming*. In this scheme, you identify a machine by specifying successively more specific "domains." Contrary to what you might expect, the most general (largest) domain is placed on the right, and the names are separated by periods.

Consider the domain name utopia.ny.pandora.com. In this example, the least-specific (biggest) domain is com, which is used by commercial for-profit companies in the United States. The name pandora is the (fictitious) name of a single network[3], whose full name is pandora.com. The Pandora

---

[3]Remember that the name "Internet" refers to the idea that many individual networks are being connected.

Domain	Explanation
com	For-profit commercial
edu	Universities
gov	Government
mil	Military
net	Network services
org	Non-profit organizations
oz,au	Australia
ca	Canada
fi	Finland
de	Germany
ja	Japan
no	Norway
za	South Africa
es	Spain
ch	Switzerland
uk	United Kingdom
us	United States

Table 4.2   Selected Top-Level Domain Names

Corporation apparently has a New York office whose network is known as ny.pandora.com, with a machine named utopia.ny.pandora.com. The number of names that can appear in a machine address is not fixed; from two to five names is typical.

Table 4.2 lists a few of the "top-level" domains. The first six were inherited from the original ARPAnet, which preceded today's Internet. They are currently used primarily within the United States. As the Internet has grown into an international communications system, other domains have been based on geography, rather than an arbitrary categorization of users. Some countries have chosen to base their second-level domains on this original heirarchy, for example, edu.au for Australian universities.

The domain naming scheme allows a distributed form of routing. (*Routing* is the process of figuring out how to get an electronic message from one machine to another over a large network.) When your computer attempts to send data to `utopia.ny.pandora.com`, that data is first relayed (frequently by one of a few dozen major "backbone" computers) to the official representative of the `pandora.com` network, which knows how to reach the official representative of the `ny.pandora.com` network, which then sends it to the machine `utopia` on that network.[4]

For mail, the official representative systems sometimes know about actual end users. If Joan's full mail address is `joan@utopia.ny.pandora.com`, the machine that represents the `pandora.com` network may know how to get mail to Joan. The address `joan@pandora.com` may suffice to get the message all the way to `utopia` and into Joan's mailbox. Such fine points vary widely, though. This scheme also allows local networks to simulate non-existent machines. For example, many networks now pretend to have a machine name `www` for World Wide Web use.

While domain addressing is fairly widespread, some mail systems still use "UUCP-style" addressing.[5] This approach requires that you list each machine that needs to relay the data, separated by exclamation marks. The previous example might look like `netrelay!pandora1!nyhub!utopia!joan`. This address instructs your local computer to relay the mail to a computer named `netrelay`, which should send it to `pandora1`, then to `nyhub`, then to `utopia`, and finally to Joan's mailbox on `utopia`. This example assumes, of course, that your local system knows how to contact a machine named `netrelay`. You can see why domain addressing is preferred; UUCP-style addresses require you to know a lot about how different networked computers are connected. Domain addressing and UUCP-style addressing are occasionally mixed, but interpretation of mixed addresses is inconsistent at best.

About HTTP

Most of the URLs you use will be HTTP URLs. HTTP was designed specifically for use on the World Wide Web, and works essentially as follows:

1. The process starts when you request a particular URL, by typing one in, clicking on a link in a document, or submitting a form.

---

[4]This is, of course, a highly simplified description.

[5]*UUCP* is the *Unix to Unix Copy* system, a very early networking approach using modems. UUCP-style addressing is sometimes called "bang" addressing. "Bang" is one name for the exclamation point character used in these addresses.

2. Your browser dissects the URL to obtain several pieces of information: the name of the machine, the name of the document, and a possible modifier (see the next section).

3. Your browser sends an HTTP request to that machine for that document. (If a form is involved, your browser will also attach the contents of the form.) This request is received by an HTTP "server" program.

4. If the request requires a response (usually a document), the server program attempts to locate the requested data, which may be as simple as looking up a file with that name. If an imagemap or form is involved, the server may locate a program (usually a script of some sort) and run that program to create the document, or at least generate the URL of the document.[6]

5. The server program sends the requested document to your browser, which uses the MIME type (see page 273) to determine how to display it. If your browser discovers other documents are needed (such as embedded pictures), it will go through the entire request cycle again. Once all of the data is available, it can display the complete document for you. (Some of the more intelligent browsers display data as it becomes available, which allows you to read the text of a document before the pictures are available, or to begin reading a long text document before it's completely received.)

Sometimes, instead of returning a document, the server will return another URL that your browser should then request. This indirection is especially useful for search programs and indexes: Rather than returning the document pertaining to your request, the server can simply respond with the URL of the requested page. Your browser will then make a second request to obtain the actual document. (This approach may seem somewhat circuitous until you remember that the result of the search may be a document on another machine. This indirect approach means that the server won't have to request that document from another server just to pass it along to you.) Usually, this kind of multiple request is invisible to you.

An HTTP server is *stateless*. After it returns the document you requested, the HTTP server can simply forget about you. It doesn't need to remember

---

[6]One interesting point is that the HTTP server explicitly identifies the document type to the browser using MIME content type names (see page 273).

who you are or what you were doing, although more advanced servers will keep track of certain things about you for efficiency reasons. If you just requested a document with embedded images, you're likely to be requesting the actual images shortly, and the server can speed things up by locating those images in advance.

Contrast this stateless approach with a protocol such as FTP. In FTP, you first log in to the server. The server keeps track of who you are and what you're doing until you tell the server you're done. Because FTP was originally designed to require a password, the server needs to either remember who you are or require a password for every separate file you transfer. Also, because FTP is often used to retrieve many files at one time, the FTP server can simplify things by keeping track of what you're doing. However, the additional overhead required to keep track of what each user is doing makes FTP somewhat less efficient for the kind of sporadic access that is typical on the World Wide Web.

HTTP URL Modifiers

One point I omitted earlier is that HTTP URLs can use two special characters to indicate that a document should be retrieved in a particular fashion. For example, if you hand your browser the URL

```
http://utopia.ny.pandora.com/joan/useful#chapter2
```

it will dissect this lengthy URL into a request to use HTTP to connect to a machine called `utopia.ny.pandora.com` and request a document. This example uses the # character, which indicates a location within a larger document. With this particular URL, your browser would actually request a document called `joan/useful`, and then search the document for a location called `chapter2`. If it finds this location, it will display the document beginning at that location. Note that the `#chapter2` was not actually included in the document request.

In the previous paragraph, notice that I didn't say your browser would "request a *file* called `joan/useful`." In fact, there may not be such a file. The program that handles HTTP requests may use any of a variety of methods to obtain the document you request. It may use the document name as a filename; it may use the document name as an index into a large database; it may somehow create the document automatically. One common use of HTTP is to access large indexes. You request information from such an index by specifying a URL that includes a *search request*. A search request is indicated with a ? character. For example, consider the document name `joan/useful?http`. When you request this document, the server locates a database called `joan/useful` and searches for items that match `http`. It then creates a document containing those items and returns the resulting document to you. (Usually the server uses the name `joan/useful` to find a program, and runs that program to find or create a document corresponding to `http`.) Note the difference between the # and ? modifiers; the # modifier is handled by your browser, while the ? modifier is handled by the remote server.

This search mechanism has found two important uses. The first, obviously, is to add search capabilities to large World Wide Web servers. An *HTML form* allows you to fill in certain information in a document. When you finish, your browser requests a URL that includes a search term specifying the information you filled in, and the server responds with a constructed document that satisfies your search request. This method is used, for example,

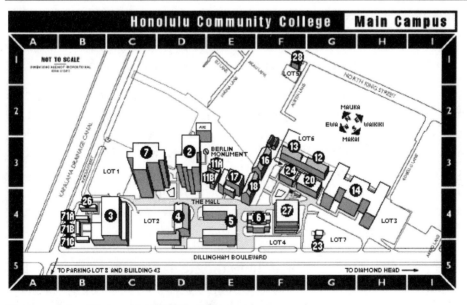

Figure 4.1   Example HTML Imagemap

by bookstores and libraries that allow you to search for particular books in their collections.[7]

The other use of the search modifier is with *HTML imagemaps*. An imagemap is a picture on which you can click. When you click on the picture, your browser requests a URL that contains a search request consisting of the coordinates where you clicked. For example, Figure 4.1 shows a map of the Honolulu Community College.[8] If you click on Building 6, your browser might generate a request for a URL ending in `hccmapd?309,242`. The server would then use the coordinates to decide which document to return. In this case, you would find out about the Administration and Student Services building.

It is possible—if you have either a fast connection or a lot of patience—to create graphical adventure games using imagemaps. The user clicks on each image, and receives a different image depending on where they click. In this way, they wander through an imaginary world.

An HTML Primer

The original HTML language was fairly simple, but a variety of pressures are causing HTML to rapidly become more complex. Companies marketing HTML browsers often distinguish their products by supporting extensions to the current HTML standard. The best of these proprietary extensions will be incorporated into the next version of the standard, along with other new features designed to satisfy the needs of new groups of users. This cycle of ongoing change is already well established, and will probably continue for many years. The current widespread standard is HTML 2. All currently available browsers should support that standard. HTML 3 is still being refined, but some of its features are already widely supported.

However, because HTML is based on the Standard Generalized Markup Language (SGML) (see page 77), the basics are quite stable.

---

[7]Forms are handled in two slightly different ways. One way is to include the form data as part of the URL; the other is to include the form data separately within the HTTP request. The difference is subtle, and completely transparent to the user.

[8]This map was copied from `http://www.hcc.hawaii.edu/hccmap/hccmap.html`.

Tags and Elements

HTML files are text files with embedded markup in the form of *tags*. A tag is surrounded by angle brackets <...>, has a name, and may have additional attributes. For example, the tag <A HREF="location"> has the name A, and the attribute HREF with the value "location". Most attributes have values.[9]

Some tags stand on their own. For example, the <P> tag indicates the start of a new paragraph. Most tags, however, come in matched pairs of a *start tag* and an *end tag*. End tags look just like start tags, except that the name has a / in front of it. For example, <H1> is a start tag; the corresponding end tag is </H1>.

Start and end tags surround some piece of text. To emphasize a section of text, you include <EM>emphasis</EM> to produce *emphasis*. This composition of a start tag, some text, and an end tag is referred to as an *element*. Elements can sometimes be nested; you can emphasize a single word in a heading with <H1>The <EM>Real</EM> McCoy</H1>.

Some people fall into the trap of thinking of <EM> as starting emphasis, and </EM> as ending emphasis. If you think of it that way, you might be tempted to try writing <B><EM>bold emphasis</B></EM> to get **bold emphasis**, on the logic that you're first turning on bold and emphasis and then turning off bold and emphasis. However, the browser tries to interpret this as one element nested within another. The correct way to write this request is <B><EM>bold emphasis</EM></B>, an emphasis element within a bold element.

One point bears repeating. Any markup within an HTML document is strictly a request. Some requests will be ignored by some browsers. For example, if you try to use the above example and the browser doesn't have a bold emphasized font, it may simply ignore the request and leave the text in the default font. Also, different browsers will interpret tags differently. For example, text-based browsers may simply omit embedded graphics, or replace them with the informative [picture]. It's the responsibility of HTML authors to make sure that their documents make sense with any reasonable interpretation of the tags.

---

[9]Technically, tags don't require a name. However, proper use of the empty tags <> and </> requires some care, and their use is generally discouraged.

```
<HTML>
    <HEAD>
            Head
    </HEAD>
    <BODY>
            Body
    </BODY>
</HTML>
```

Figure 4.2   Structure of an HTML Document

Structure of an HTML Document

An entire document is a single HTML element, which in turn contains HEAD and BODY elements. In simpler terms, every HTML document looks like Figure 4.2.

The head part of an HTML document contains information about the document that is *not displayed*. This information identifies the document, author, and other such information about the document. This information is important because it is used by many browsers. For example, the title of the window is typically set to the title of the document. This information is also used in the massive indexes of the entire Web being compiled by several groups (see page 15).

Unfortunately, the tags shown in Figure 4.2 are optional and often omitted in practice. As a result, the only reliable way to distinguish the head information from the body is to understand the kinds of tags that appear in each section.

HTML Head

The purpose of the head is to provide the browser and HTTP server with certain basic facts about the document.

The most common element used in this section is the TITLE element. The "title" of the document is used in a variety of ways: Many browsers display it in the title bar of the window when the document is displayed; users can often add it to a menu of favorite locations; and automatic indexing programs use the title to identify the page. These diverse uses make it somewhat difficult to select a good title. A good title is long enough to accurately identify that particular page in a menu or index, but short enough to fit into a menu or title bar. A title such as *Introduction* is not very useful in isolation; on the other hand, the following title from *Gulliver's Travels* [Swi26, Part III, Chapter VII] is clearly too long for most title bars:

> *The Author leaves Lagado, arrives at Maldonada. No ship ready. He takes a short voyage to Glubbdubdrib. His reception by the Governor.*

Three other tags frequently appear in the head. ISINDEX allows a simple type of database query. BASE tells the browser to pretend the document was pulled from a particular URL. LINK specifies other URLs that are related to this document.

The ISINDEX tag prompts the browser to request a string from the user and return it to the server. In essence, ISINDEX acts as a very simple fixed form. It is being displaced by the more flexible FORM element (see page 48).

It's easier to refer to related documents with abbreviated URLs that provide only the final name than to include the machine and full directory information in every link. These partial URLs require the browser to know the full URL of the current document; the browser can then substitute the partial information to build the full URL that it needs. This scheme breaks down if the base document is moved to another directory or another machine; the partial URLs will then be interpreted in the new context, rather than referring back to the original source. The BASE element specifies the base URL that the browser should use when interpreting partial URLs within that document.

One of the popular additions to HTML 3 is support for *style sheets*. Style sheets allow the document creator to suggest specific formatting (including fonts, colors, and alignment) for certain tags. Because the same style sheet is often shared by several documents, it's nice to store the style sheet separately. Specifying the URL of the associated style sheet is one use of the LINK element. Other uses have been suggested, but are not yet widely implemented.[10]

---

[10] Style sheets are quite different from the popular Netscape extensions. The Netscape extensions embed physical markup directly in the document. Style sheets are separate files which can be referenced by many HTML documents.

Element	Description
<H1>...</H1>	First-level heading; document title
<H2>...</H2>	Second-level heading
<H3>...</H3>	Third-level heading
<H4>...</H4>	Fourth-level heading
<H5>...</H5>	Fifth-level heading
<H6>...</H6>	Sixth-level heading

Table 4.3   HTML Heading Elements

Paragraphs

If you use electronic mail, you probably expect the text you type to appear exactly as you type it, line breaks and all. HTML normally ignores line breaks completely; the words are repackaged to fit onto lines however the HTML browser sees fit. Two common tags affect this process. The first tag is <P>, which marks the beginning of a paragraph. (There actually is a matching </P> tag to mark the end of a paragraph, but it is rarely used.)

The other important tag is <PRE>, which is used for *preformatted* text. Any text between <PRE> and </PRE> is displayed with line breaks and spacing exactly as you typed it. Usually, preformatted text is displayed in a typewriter font.

Headings

The title that occurs in the head is not displayed as part of the document. To display a title, you need to use one of the heading elements shown in Table 4.3. Headings in typical documents appear in *levels*. A first-level heading is usually larger or darker than a second-level heading. (If you look at this book, the phrase "Headings" above is a third-level heading; the corresponding second-level heading is "An HTML Primer" on page 39; the first-level heading is the chapter title "HTML" on page 29.)

Usually, HTML documents have a single first-level heading at the top of the document, then some number of second-level headings below that. It's unusual to see more than three levels of headings except in very long documents.

Tag	Description
`<EM>...</EM>`	*Emphasis*
`<STRONG>...</STRONG>`	***Strong emphasis***
`<CITE>...</CITE>`	*Reference to a book or other document*
`<CODE>...</CODE>`	`Short piece of computer code`
`<DFN>...</DFN>`	**Defining instance of a word**
`<KBD>...</KBD>`	`Literal keyboard input`
`<SAMP>...</SAMP>`	`Sample text`
`<VAR>...</VAR>`	*Variable name*
`<STRIKE>...</STRIKE>`	~~Removed Text~~

Table 4.4   Logical Text Styles

Text Styles

HTML supports both *logical* text styles, which specify the meaning of a block of text, and *physical* text styles, which specify the appearance of a block of text. Table 4.4 lists the most common logical text styles and suggests one way they might be displayed. Notice that these tags all have different meanings, even though in practice many of them have an identical appearance.

For comparison, Table 4.5 lists the physical text styles. You should use the logical styles whenever possible, to allow the target browser to choose the most appropriate appearance. Using logical styles also helps the reader. For example, a reader might search your document for the `<CITE>` tag in order to identify the citations. The physical styles are primarily for use by programs that convert from other formats to HTML, since it's impossible to automatically add logical formatting to a document.

Most browsers will honor nested requests, although the result can vary. A request for `<I><TT>Italic Typewriter</TT></I>` may yield *Italic Typewriter*, `Italic Typewriter`, *Italic Typewriter*, or even simply Italic Typewriter, depending on the browser.

Special Characters

Entities are a notation for special characters. Four characters have special meaning in HTML: < > " &. To include them explicitly in your document, you

Tag	Description
`<B>...</B>`	**Bold**
`<U>...</U>`	<u>Underline</u>
`<I>...</I>`	*Italics*
`<TT>...</TT>`	`Typewriter font`
`<S>...</S>`	~~Strike-through~~
`<SUB>...</SUB>`	Subscript
`<SUP>...</SUP>`	Superscript

Table 4.5   Physical Text Styles

have to refer to them by name. Although HTML currently uses the eight-bit ISO Latin 1 coded character set, not all text editors and other tools have direct support for that coded character set. As a result, HTML provides entity names for all of the ISO Latin 1 characters that aren't also in seven-bit ASCII. Table 4.6 is a complete list of the entity names supported by HTML 2. Note that all entity names begin with **&** and end with **;**.

HTML also allows you to identify characters by specifying the character code (HTML 2 uses the ISO Latin 1 coded character set). The entity names are easier to understand and preferred for most uses.

Links and Anchors

Of course, the point of HTML is to support the hyperlinked World Wide Web. HTML's *anchor tag* serves two purposes: It can define a button which, when selected, instructs the browser to retrieve another document, or it can mark a location within a document (see page 37). Put slightly differently, an anchor can serve either as the start or end of a link.

In everyday use, anchor tags take two forms. The most common form is `<A HREF="`*URL*`">This is an anchor.</A>`, which marks the text "This is an anchor." In many browsers, this text will be displayed in a different color, in a box, or with a small icon beside it. When selected, the browser will jump to the indicated URL.

The other form is `<A NAME="chapter2">Chapter 2</A>`. This kind of anchor creates a named location in an HTML document. (This anchor is

Symbol	Entity Name	Numerical Name	Symbol	Entity Name	Numerical Name
"	&quot;	&#34;	<	&lt;	&#60;
&	&amp;	&#38;	>	&gt;	&#62;
À	&Agrave;	&#192;	à	&agrave;	&#224;
Á	&Aacute;	&#193;	á	&aacute;	&#225;
Â	&Acirc;	&#194;	â	&acirc;	&#226;
Ã	&Atilde;	&#195;	ã	&atilde;	&#227;
Ä	&Auml;	&#196;	ä	&auml;	&#228;
Å	&Aring;	&#197;	å	&aring;	&#229;
Æ	&AElig;	&#198;	æ	&aelig;	&#230;
Ç	&Ccedil;	&#199;	ç	&ccedil;	&#231;
È	&Egrave;	&#200;	è	&egrave;	&#232;
É	&Eacute;	&#201;	é	&eacute;	&#233;
Ê	&Ecirc;	&#202;	ê	&ecirc;	&#234;
Ë	&Euml;	&#203;	ë	&euml;	&#235;
Ì	&Igrave;	&#204;	ì	&igrave;	&#236;
Í	&Iacute;	&#205;	í	&iacute;	&#237;
Î	&Icirc;	&#206;	î	&icirc;	&#238;
Ï	&Iuml;	&#207;	ï	&iuml;	&#239;
Ð	&ETH;	&#208;	ð	&eth;	&#240;
Ñ	&Ntilde;	&#209;	ñ	&ntilde;	&#241;
Ò	&Ograve;	&#210;	ò	&ograve;	&#242;
Ó	&Oacute;	&#211;	ó	&oacute;	&#243;
Ô	&Ocirc;	&#212;	ô	&ocirc;	&#244;
Õ	&Otilde;	&#213;	õ	&otilde;	&#245;
Ö	&Ouml;	&#214;	ö	&ouml;	&#246;
×		&#215;	÷		&#247;
Ø	&Oslash;	&#216;	ø	&oslash;	&#248;
Ù	&Ugrave;	&#217;	ù	&ugrave;	&#249;
Ú	&Uacute;	&#218;	ú	&uacute;	&#250;
Û	&Ucirc;	&#219;	û	&ucirc;	&#251;
Ü	&Uuml;	&#220;	ü	&uuml;	&#252;
Ý	&Yacute;	&#221;	ý	&yacute;	&#253;
Þ	&THORN;	&#222;	þ	&thorn;	&#254;
ß	&szlig;	&#223;	ÿ	&yuml;	&#255;

Table 4.6   Entity Names

Attribute	Description
HREF	Destination of this link
NAME	Create a named location
REL, REV	Relation between this document and the target document
URN	Destination of this link as a URN (not yet supported)
TITLE	Proposed title for target of link
METHOD	Proposed access methods
EFFECT	How to display new document
PRINT	Suggested format for printing new document
TYPE	Type of the new document

Table 4.7   Anchor Tag Attributes

called a *fragment* in the HTML standards.) Such a location can be referred to as part of a URL. Lengthy HTML files often have a "table of contents" at the beginning, with items such as `<A HREF="#chapter2">Chapter 2</A>`. Chapter 2's heading might look like `<H1><A NAME="chapter2">Chapter 2</A></H1>`. When a user selects the line in the table of contents, she'll be taken directly to the corresponding location in the text. A single anchor can have both a NAME and HREF attribute.

Because people access data in so many different contexts, anchor tags support a variety of attributes. HTML 2 added several new attributes, and HTML 3 is adding even more. As document structures become more complex, anchor tags will become even more sophisticated. Table 4.7 lists some of the attributes that have been proposed for anchor tags.

Graphics

One of the biggest selling points of the World Wide Web is that HTML supports graphics. Graphics are handled in two different ways. The first way is to treat the graphic as a document in its own right. This is possible because a link can refer to any type of data, including a separate picture. Especially for very large images, it's common to simply have a link to the actual picture.

The second way to handle graphics is to embed an image directly in the HTML document. The IMG tag embeds an image as if it were a single large character, allowing you to place images in the middle of a paragraph or have

Attribute	Description
SRC	URL to load the image from
ALT	Text alternative
ISMAP	Use this as an imagemap
ALIGN	How this aligns with nearby text

Table 4.8 IMG Tag Attributes

several images on a line. A typical use of the IMG tag is <IMG SRC="*URL* " ALT="*text* ">. The URL specifies the source of the image data, and the ALT keyword gives a text string that can substitute for the picture. This text string is used by text-only browsers. (For example, a company logo might use the company name here.)

IMG tags support many additional attributes. One attribute is ISMAP, which indicates that a graphic is actually an imagemap. This form of the IMG tag must be nested within an anchor tag; the anchor tag provides the URL for the final search and the IMG tag provides the image.

Forms

Unlike TEX and TROFF, HTML documents are intended to be used in a dynamic, interactive fashion. Forms are HTML documents with special *input fields*—areas that the reader of the document is able to change. After changing those elements, the reader can select a button embedded in the document to send the contents of the form back to the server. When the server receives the form, it usually looks up an appropriate program or script and hands the data to that program. Depending on the particular usage, this process can be either a one-way transaction where the contents of the form are silently accepted or a two-way transaction in which the server ultimately returns a new document as a result of the form.

Elements within a form are organized by *variables*. Each form element, whether it's a push button, scrolling list, or type-in field, has a variable name and value. When the form is submitted, the browser looks at each item, and tells the server the value of each variable. For example, Figure 4.3 shows a SELECT element, which the browser displays as a pop-up menu. The person reading this form can click on the menu and select any one of the three

```
I want to vote for:
<SELECT NAME="vote">
    <OPTION> Candidate 1
    <OPTION> Candidate 2
    <OPTION> Candidate 3
</SELECT>
```

Figure 4.3   Example of SELECT Tag

```
What flavors do you like?
<UL>
<LI> <INPUT TYPE="checkbox"
NAME="flavor" VALUE="Choc">
Chocolate
<LI> <INPUT TYPE="checkbox"
NAME="flavor" VALUE="Van">
Vanilla
<LI> <INPUT TYPE="checkbox"
NAME="flavor" VALUE="Straw">
Strawberry
<LI> <INPUT TYPE="checkbox"
NAME="flavor" VALUE="Ban">
Banana
</UL>
```

Figure 4.4   Example of INPUT Tag

options. If the user selects "Candidate 1," the server will be told (when the form is submitted) that the variable named *vote* has the value "Candidate 1."

One variable can have more than one value at a time. Figure 4.4 shows a form fragment with several checkboxes. If both Chocolate and Banana are checked, the returned form will specify both flavor=Choc and flavor=Ban.

Given the flexibility of forms, it's somewhat surprising how few tags are involved. Each form consists of a single FORM element containing various items. (Figures 4.3 and 4.4 are examples of items that can go within a FORM element.) The contents of the forms are specified by SELECT elements (pop-down menus and scrolling lists), TEXTAREA elements (multiline type-in fields), and INPUT

Tag	Description
SELECT	Pop-up menu of choices
SELECT MULTIPLE	Scrolling list allowing multiple selections
INPUT TYPE="checkbox"	
INPUT TYPE="radio"	Linked buttons; only one can be selected
INPUT TYPE="text"	Single-line text field
INPUT TYPE="reset"	Discard user changes
INPUT TYPE="submit"	Send form to server
INPUT TYPE="image"	Imagemap
TEXTAREA	Multi-line text field

Table 4.9   Tags Used in HTML Forms

elements (various types of buttons and single-line text fields). Table 4.9 lists some of the variations of these elements.

Tables

Tables are a new feature in HTML 3. The basic structure is very simple: A TABLE element contains a series of TR (row) elements, each of which in turn contains a series of items. Header items (TH elements) are used for column and row labels; data items (TD elements) are used for regular data. Figure 4.5 shows an example table, which was created by the HTML commands in Figure 4.6.[11] Note the use of nested tables to selectively include certain rules.

If you compare this table with the LaTeX example on page 72 and the TROFF example on page 88, you'll notice I made no attempt to force the text style and alignment to precisely match those examples. As with most aspects of HTML, it's important not to over-specify the appearance.

Mathematics

Mathematics support is another new feature in HTML 3. Within the MATH element, several new tags are available to produce subscripts (SUB), super-

---

[11] This table was adapted from an example in *UNIX in a Nutshell* [Gil92], and typeset with Netscape Navigator.

Horizontal Local Motions		
Function	**Effect in**	
	TROFF	**NROFF**
\h'n'	Move distance N	
\(space)	Unpaddable space-size space	
\0	Digit-size space	
\\|	1/6 em space	ignored
\^	1/12 em space	ignored

Figure 4.5   Example HTML Table[11]

scripts (SUP), fractions (BOX element and OVER tag), and other mathematical constructions. For example, the simple equation $\int_1^x \frac{dt}{t} = \ln x$ can be specified with:

```
<MATH> &int;<SUB>1</SUB><SUP>x</SUP>
<BOX>dt<OVER>t</BOX> = &ln; x </MATH>
```

This simple example illustrates several points about HTML's mathematics notation. Variables are normally set in italic type. Entity names are used both for special characters (such as ∫ for $\int$) and also for the names of special functions that are traditionally set in roman type (such as &ln; for ln). The construction <BOX> *numerator* <OVER> *denominator* </BOX> is used to build fractions. Note that HTML uses superscript and subscript constructions to place limits on integrals and summations.

Because the tag forms are a bit unwieldy, HTML 3 allows you to surround subscripts with _ characters and superscripts with ^ characters. Similarly, { and } can be used in place of <BOX> and </BOX>. When using these substitutions, HTML mathematics looks remarkably like TEX/LATEX mathematics (see page 74); HTML has even borrowed the names of many special symbols from TEX/LATEX. Table 4.10 gives some more examples. In the last example, note that you can't use the short form for nested subscripts.

```
<TABLE BORDER>
<TR><TH COLSPAN=3>Horizontal Local Motions
<TR><TH ROWSPAN=2>Function<TH COLSPAN=2>Effect in
<TR><TH>TROFF<TH>NROFF
<TR>
   <TD>  <TABLE>
         <TR><TD> \h'n'
         <TR><TD> \(space)
         <TR><TD> \0
         </TABLE>
   <TD COLSPAN=2>
         <TABLE NOWRAP>
         <TR><TD>Move distance N
         <TR><TD>Unpaddable space-size space
         <TR><TD>Digit-size space
         </TABLE>
<TR>
   <TD>  <TABLE>
         <TR><TD> \|
         <TR><TD> \^
         </TABLE>
   <TD>  <TABLE>
         <TR><TD>1/6 em space
         <TR><TD>1/12 em space
         </TABLE>
   <TD>  <TABLE>
         <TR><TD>ignored
         <TR><TD>ignored
         </TABLE>
</TABLE>
```

Figure 4.6   HTML Table Source

```
<MATH> e^x^= &sum;_i=0_^&inf;^
       {x^i^<OVER> i!} </MATH>
```

$$e^x = \sum_{i=0}^{\infty} \frac{x^i}{i!}$$

```
<MATH> &Psi; = {&pd;E <OVER> &pd;x} </MATH>
```

$$\Psi = \frac{\partial E}{\partial x}$$

```
<MATH> x<SUB>a<SUB>1</SUB></SUB>
       + x<SUB>a<SUB>2</SUB></SUB>
       + &cdots; = &pi;/4 </MATH>
```

$$x_{a_1} + x_{a_2} + \cdots = \pi/4$$

Table 4.10 Examples of HTML Mathematics

HTML Style Guidelines

Both creators and users of HTML should be aware of HTML style issues. There are good reasons why many HTML documents have a similar layout. Being aware of those reasons can help you make the best use of those pages.

HTML authors need to consider three general issues when they design their World Wide Web pages:

Maintenance An HTML document may be available on the Internet for months or even years. During that time, the document will need to be modified to correct errors, to add new information, and to keep up-to-date with changes on the system, on the Internet, and even in the HTML standard itself.

Accessibility Not everyone uses the same browser, and today's most popular browser may not be around tomorrow. For this reason, considerate designers avoid features that are available only in certain browsers. Remember that many people still use text-based browsers. In fact, many people prefer text-based browsers because they are so much faster, and they may use them even when graphical browsers are available.

Speed People have different Internet connections. Someone accessing through a 2400 baud modem may not appreciate waiting ten or fifteen minutes for a large picture to be received.

Many people blithely ignore these considerations, and create HTML documents that are intended to be read only by a few friends with high-speed connections, all using the same browser. However, many businesses hire professional designers who work very hard to create documents that are attractive and address these concerns. Here are a few specific ideas to consider:

Keep It Simple.   Professional designers spend years learning how different effects combine. They learn how to balance effects so that insignificant parts of the design (like a single emphasized word) don't overwhelm the rest of the document. Achieving this balance is made even harder by the fact that each browser handles things differently (for example, the alignment of images and text will vary between browsers). The most common mistake made by the creators of new World Wide Web documents is trying to use too many special effects.

Don't Use Deprecated Features.   Certain HTML tags (such as XMP, LISTING, or PLAINTEXT) are listed as *deprecated* in references. This label means that people who work with HTML extensively have decided these tags aren't a good idea. Newer browsers may not support these tags at all.

Use Interlaced Graphics.   The GIF graphics files used in most World Wide Web documents have an *interlaced* form in which every eighth line is transferred, then every fourth, and so on. On some browsers, the picture is incrementally displayed as it is transferred, allowing people to get a good idea what the picture is long before the whole thing is received.

Use Graphics Sparingly.   Graphics take much longer to transfer than text, and people with slow connections are unlikely to revisit a page that takes too long to display. With a little care, a few small images can provide the same impact as a more complex graphical image, but they will download and display much faster.

Use Stylized Graphics.   Graphics are transferred in a compressed form. The better the graphics compress, the faster they'll transfer. Graphics that have only a few colors compress much better. Stylized woodcut or art-deco images can look very modern while still compressing well. Graphics with smoothly varying colors, on the other hand, compress very poorly.

Defer Large Images.   Rather than placing a large image or imagemap in the middle of a page, considerate designers use a small version of the image as a link to the larger version. This way, people reading your page can decide whether or not they want to wait for the whole picture.

Use Repeated Graphics.   Most HTML browsers will recognize multiple uses of a single image and only download it once, even if it appears on many different pages. This approach allows more color on a page with little degradation in speed.

Choose Appropriate Sizes.   Different kinds of information fit on different page sizes. If you expect people to read it straight through, or to download it and read it later, put all the information on one page. If you expect people to read only small portions, break it into several pages so people can find and go directly to the part that interests them. Be wary of very large pages, which may be unusable by some people. (I've had browsers crash trying to read very large pages.)

Don't Use Browser-Specific Features.   If a particular feature is available in only a few browsers, be careful using that feature in your pages. The effect may look odd on other browsers. Also, keep in mind that other browsers may have deliberately chosen not to implement that feature. (What do they know that you don't?)

Be Cautious with Unusual Symbols.   The HTML standard currently specifies ISO Latin 1, but not all browsers have access to this character set. Be careful with non-ASCII characters. One common error that I've seen in HTML references is the claim that Microsoft Windows uses the ISO Latin 1 character set. This statement is not true; Microsoft Windows supports a number of characters that are missing from ISO Latin 1, including open and close quotes (" and "), en-dashes and em-dashes (– and —), and a few other such characters.

Use Rules.   Especially in larger pages, rules (horizontal lines that cross the page) are a simple and effective way to separate the major parts. Some HTML writers have attempted to substitute a long horizontal graphic. If you do so, be careful. Such images don't resize with the window; users who change the size of their browser window may be surprised.

Use Logical Markup.   While HTML does have tags to specify particular font effects (Bold, Italic, Underline), not all browsers support those specific effects. All browsers do support some form of emphasis, however.

Use Few Fonts.   One of the most common mistakes made by amateur graphics designers is to use too many fonts. Generally, plain text and emphasis are sufficient, with occasional use of tags such as `CODE` or `SAMP`.

Keep Links to Other Documents in One Place.   The worst maintenance headache encountered by HTML authors is making sure that all of the links to other people's documents are still valid. One way to simplify this task is to resist the temptation to scatter a lot of links throughout the pages. By gathering all external links on a single page entitled *Bibliography*, *More Information*, or *Other Cool Sites*, you only need to check one page to make sure all of the external links are still valid.

Use Relative Links.   Links between closely related pages don't need to use absolute URLs. By only giving the last part of the URL and letting the browser use the current URL to build the correct full address, the pages are better insulated against certain kinds of common changes.

Link to Your Own Home Page.   People periodically find themselves at an odd page, and want to find the corresponding home page. This situation can happen because someone else linked directly to a page, or because someone downloaded a page to review it more carefully. In either case, having a home page link on every page lets people find the home page.

Link to Other People's Home Pages.   People usually keep their home pages accessible, but often have few qualms about rearranging their other pages. When possible, link to other people's home pages rather than the specific page of interest. If you must link to the specific page, a nearby link to the corresponding home page helps ensure that people will be able to find the information even if the specific page has moved.

Sign Your Pages.   It has become traditional for every page to have a link labelled with the author's name or mail address. The target of this link is a page with information about the author, sometimes including a photograph, resume, or other information.

Proofread Your Pages.   One of the biggest things that distinguishes the few very good Internet resources from the huge clamor of poor ones is that the good ones are carefully reviewed and edited. Time spent proofreading, soliciting comments from friends, and conscientiously double-checking can impart that air of professionalism that will help your pages stand out. Such care takes time, which is exactly why so many people fail to do it.

More Information

If you have access to the World Wide Web, one good place to start is the home page of *W3*, which sponsors much of the development of World Wide Web standards. Point your browser to `http://www.w3.org` for more details. Even if you prefer to read a good book on the subject, this page is a good resource for up-to-date information. Because these standards are evolving so rapidly, any book will have some out-of-date information.

With the current rapid growth of interest in the World Wide Web, there are several good books devoted exclusively to the subject of HTML. Ian Graham's *HTML Sourcebook* [Gra95] is one good reference to HTML and HTTP.

HTML editors and other tools for the Macintosh can be found on the Info-Mac archives (see page 12) in the `text/_HTML` directory.

Yahoo (see page 14) has a well-organized listing of HTML tools for many platforms, including stand-alone editors and tools to convert many different word processor formats into HTML. From the main Yahoo index, select *Computers and Internet*, then *World Wide Web*, then *HTML Editors*.

T_EX and L^AT_EX

Donald Knuth, a computer science professor at Stanford University, developed the *T_EX* typesetting system (pronounced "tek") to simplify the production of books containing mathematics. He spent nearly ten years refining T_EX, and the resulting system has been ported to a variety of different computers. Free implementations of T_EX are available for most computers, and several commercial implementations are available for PC and Macintosh platforms.

T_EX has a powerful macro language that makes it relatively easy to add new capabilities. Several extensive macro packages have been created for T_EX. The most popular of these is L^AT_EX. Most T_EX systems today include L^AT_EX.

A T_EX system consists of a number of different programs. The most important one is `tex`, which reads a T_EX input file and interprets the text markup to produce a device-independent *DVI* output file. This DVI file

---

T_EX and L^AT_EX at a Glance

Names:	T_EX, L^AT_EX, TeX, LaTeX
Extensions:	`.tex, .ltx, .latex`
Use For:	Typesetting large documents, especially those with mathematics
References:	*L^AT_EX: A Document Preparation System* [Lam94]; *The T_EXbook* [Knu86a]
On CD:	*Alpha* editor for Macintosh; complete *Web2C* L^AT_EX system for Unix

specifies the font and position of each character on the page, and is designed
to be easily translated to generate output for any particular printer. The `tex`
program itself is completely printer-independent; it reads the input file and a
variety of other files that describe the available fonts and other information to
produce the correct output.

The TEX system (including the LATEX extensions) is quite popular, especially in universities. There are a number of reasons for this:

- TEX is free. Implementations for many different computers are available
  on the Internet. Commercial implementations offering greater speed
  and improved interfaces are also available for many systems.

- TEX is stable. Knuth has promised that TEX 3.0 (released in 1990) represents the last important change. This stability means that documents
  based on TEX will continue to be usable for the foreseeable future,
  which makes TEX a good choice for exchanging documents. Macro
  packages built on TEX have a solid, dependable base for developing
  new typesetting features.

- TEX has unparalleled support for mathematics typesetting. This support
  makes it very popular in academic settings, and explains why the American Mathematical Society (AMS) has adopted TEX for typesetting all of
  its journals. TEX's wide availability and mathematical capabilities allow
  the AMS to accept electronic submissions that require a minimum of
  editing before they are included directly in the final journal. The high
  quality of TEX's output makes the final result comparable in quality to
  more expensive approaches.

- TEX is flexible. TEX internally makes almost no assumptions about fonts
  or page layout. It can be adapted to generate a wide variety of output.[1]

TEX is used for publishing many academic journals, and has also found adher-
ents among textbook publishers and database publishers, who use sophisticated
programs to automatically produce a variety of listings from large databases
(parts of the *TV Guide* magazine are typeset with TEX).

---

[1] This flexibility also makes it possible for amateur designers to produce truly horrific
output, a problem TEX shares with many of the powerful publishing systems that are being
used today.

TEX input files are text with markup in the form of "macro commands." Commands typically begin with a \, and often accept arguments surrounded by { and }. For example, \uppercase{argument} produces ARGUMENT. The document can define new macros in terms of old ones and use these new macros to define new markup. TEX documents frequently begin with a long list of definitions of new macros that embody knowledge of particular typesetting issues and are then used in the rest of the document.

By isolating these macros, TEX provides support for logical markup (see page 24). A separate file of macro definitions can serve as a style sheet, defining how to translate logical macro names (such as \chapter{Introduction}) into specific low-level typesetting instructions (start a new page, typeset this text in a particular font, write it to the table-of-contents file, and enter it into a variable so it will appear in the running head). TEX's macro language provides a full-featured programming environment, and TEX macros exist to perform a number of routine formatting chores.

LATEX

LATEX uses separate files of macro definitions to add logical markup capabilities to TEX. LATEX is a collection of TEX macros that adds a great deal of functionality to the "Plain TEX" defined by Knuth. In addition to basic logical markup, LATEX supports a variety of page and document styles and provides automatic cross-referencing, table of contents, and footnotes.

LATEX files are usually typeset with a special version of the tex program called latex, which has the LATEX macros pre-loaded. LATEX files begin with a \documentclass or \documentstyle command.[2] The \documentstyle command is used by the older LATEX 2.09, which was widely used from 1987 until 1994, when an enhanced version of LATEX known as LATEX 2_ε became available. The newer LATEX 2_ε made major improvements to two specific areas: It improved the handling of fonts, and it added support for *packages*, collections of macros providing specific features. For example, packages can define new collections of fonts, redefine the page style, or add new types of tables, figures, bibliographies, or other structures.

---

[2]The \documentclass or \documentstyle command is not always the first line of the file. Several lines of comments may appear prior to that (comments in a LATEX file begin with %), and a handful of LATEX commands can precede the \documentclass command.

Other TEX Variants

LATEX is not the only extended macro collection created for TEX. Other variants include:

eplain   This macro package is an enhanced version of Knuth's original Plain TEX macros. It provides some of the cross-referencing and other capabilities of LATEX.

$\mathcal{A}_{\mathcal{M}}\mathcal{S}$-TEX   This variant was developed for the American Mathematical Society. It includes a large collection of mathematical symbol fonts and macros for specialized mathematics typesetting.

LA$\mathcal{M}$S-TEX and $\mathcal{A}_{\mathcal{M}}\mathcal{S}$-LATEX   These collections are two early attempts to combine the document structuring features of LATEX with the mathematical typesetting capabilities of $\mathcal{A}_{\mathcal{M}}\mathcal{S}$-TEX. (Both have been supplanted by LATEX 2_{ε}'s amstex package.)

texinfo   This format is a fairly limited one, designed to be processed by tex into typeset documentation, or converted by the texinfo program into a hyperlinked online document. This format is used by the Free Software Foundation to document their software tools.

fontinst   This specialized TEX dialect does no typesetting. Rather, it is used to generate *virtual font* descriptions, which interface TEX's native font system to other font technologies, especially PostScript.

Many other variants have been created to provide special typesetting capabilities for particular environments. Many of these formats are being converted into LATEX packages, to make it possible to combine various typesetting capabilities in a single document.

Recognizing TEX and LATEX Files

As with any loosely-structured text format, it's not always easy to identify a TEX or LATEX document. If you know the actual file name, you can often use the file extension. Unfortunately, the most popular extension for TEX and LATEX documents is .tex, which is also used by many people for plain text documents. If you don't know the file extension, here are a few clues you can use:

- The most obvious clue is the `\documentclass` or `\documentstyle` command that must appear in every LATEX document. Usually, this command will be at the beginning of the document.

- TEX and LATEX files use a percent sign (%) to indicate the beginning of a comment. Several lines of comments often appear near the beginning of a file. Of course, many text formats (including PostScript) use the percent sign as a comment indicator.

- The third useful clue is the appearance of the embedded commands. TEX and LATEX commands begin with a backslash (\), and sometimes have arguments surrounded by {...} or [...].

Of course, not all TEX and LATEX files are documents. Here are some other file extensions you may see:

`.latex`, `.ltx` A few people consistently use these extensions for LATEX files instead of the more confusing `.tex` extension.

`.sty`, `.cls`, `.clo` These files describe LATEX packages and document classes. Often, they will accompany a LATEX document file.

`.fd`, `.def`, `.tfm`, `.pl` These files describe fonts to TEX or LATEX. To process a document, TEX does not need to know what the fonts actually look like; it only needs to know the size of each character and a few other basic facts about the font. In particular, although these files may be sufficient to *typeset* the document, they are not sufficient to *print* the document.

`.pk` Most TEX systems use "bitmapped" fonts that were built for a specific printer resolution. The result looks very good as long as the correct resolution fonts are used. (Bitmap fonts do not scale well.) The `.pk` format is the most widely used format for storing these fonts.

`.mf` *METAFONT* files are programs in a special language that describes fonts using a combination of outline and stroke techniques. The `mf` program is required to convert these descriptions into a bitmap form suitable for printing.

.vf, .vpl Virtual font files are used by various programs to convert DVI output for a particular printer. These files specify how to to match characters used by TEX with those available on a particular printer.

.afm, .pfa, .pfb Improved font support is a major feature of LATEX 2_{ε}. In particular, it became much easier to use PostScript fonts. These files are discussed in more detail beginning on page 95.

Using TEX and LATEX Files

You're likely to encounter TEX and LATEX files in three different formats. The first format you may see is TEX or LATEX source files, which are text files. How you handle those files depends on whether or not you have a TEX or LATEX system available.

The second format you may see is TEX's DVI output format. DVI is a very dense binary format that describes the position and font of each character, and needs to be translated into a form suitable for your screen or printer. If you don't have a suitable translation program available (and the several megabytes of associated fonts and other programs that may be required), you can use dvi2tty (or crudetype) to convert the DVI file into a very rough text approximation. The output of dvi2tty has many problems (in particular, dvi2tty doesn't know about all the different fonts, so sometimes substitutes the wrong character), but the output is generally sufficient for reading the contents.

The final format you may encounter is PostScript that has been generated by one of the DVI-to-PostScript conversion programs, such as dvips. While dvips generates high-quality PostScript output that should easily print on any PostScript printer, you should be aware of two limitations. Most TEX installations use bitmap fonts by default. The dvips program selects bitmap fonts whose resolution matches the device that dvips thinks will be used for the final printing. Usually, 300 dpi fonts will be used. The problem is that the file will look best only on a device with the correct resolution. In particular, it may look poor if you use a PostScript previewer to display the result on the screen. The other potential limitation is that if the creator of the file used PostScript outline fonts other than the standard Times Roman, Helvetica, and Courier, she probably did not include those fonts in the PostScript file, and you may have difficulty printing the file. This problem is inherent to PostScript; see pages 104–105 for more details.

If you receive a TEX or LATEX source file and you have access to the `tex` or `latex` programs, you should be able to simply type `tex filename` or `latex filename` to generate a DVI output file. How you print that file will depend on the particular system. On Unix, you may be able to print the DVI files directly using the system `lp` or `lpr` command; on other systems you may need to use a program (whose name typically begins with `dvi`) to convert the DVI file into a more appropriate format, and then print the result of that conversion.

You may encounter a few problems when you try to process a TEX or LATEX source file:

- Older versions of the TEX program were often compiled with fairly limited capacity. Some newer documents may require more capacity, requiring you to replace or reconfigure the `tex` program.

- Some dialects require specialized fonts. These fonts are typically available in METAFONT format, which is the font-building program developed by Knuth to accompany TEX. If your TEX system either doesn't use METAFONT (a few use PostScript or TrueType fonts instead) or doesn't include METAFONT (many include pre-built versions of the most common fonts instead of the METAFONT program), you may have to obtain the fonts in a form suitable for your system.

- LATEX documents may require a variety of different packages. If you don't have those packages, you may need to obtain them. They should be available from the same source as the original document. If you have Internet access, they may be available from one of the CTAN (Comprehensive TEX Archive Network) sites (see page 75). Some packages aren't really necessary to process the document; they only have a cosmetic effect. In that case, you can comment out the corresponding \usepackage command by placing a % at the beginning of the line.

- Some substantial changes were made between the older LATEX 2.09 and the current LATEX 2ε. While most older documents should be correctly handled by the new system, a few (especially those that tried to manipulate fonts) will not be correctly processed. Documents designed for

```
\documentclass{...}
        Preamble
\begin{document}
        Body
\end{document}
```

Figure 5.1   The Structure of a LATEX File

the newer version are unlikely to be correctly processed by the older version. Again, if you are using an older version of LATEX, you should be able to obtain the necessary updates from the CTAN archives.

A LATEX Primer

If you see a LATEX document and you don't have the `latex` program available, you should simply print it (LATEX files are plain text files) and try to read it. While it won't look as pretty as originally intended, it should be fairly intelligible. This section will help you to understand the embedded commands.

Plain TEX imposes almost no structure on a document file, which can make documents written for Plain TEX quite difficult to understand. LATEX, on the other hand, does impose a certain structure on documents. The most general structure is shown in Figure 5.1. As you can see, LATEX files are divided into a *preamble*, which tells LATEX how to format the file, and a *body*, which contains the actual text of the document.

Preamble

As a logical markup system, LATEX attempts to separate the *meaning* of a document element (for example, `\chapter{Introduction}`) from the *appearance* of that element (the specific font and positioning). Generally, commands in the preamble (preceding `\begin{document}`) define the appearance of the document, while commands in the body define the meaning of various parts of the document. For example, if a document contains "keywords," it may define a `\keyword` command. The body of the text will use that command as in

`\keyword{floogleblatz}`. The command may be defined in the preamble to typeset keywords in italics (*floogleblatz*) or bold (**floogleblatz**) or even in a different font (floogleblatz). If you're reading the raw file, you may see `Now let's discuss a \keyword{floogleblatz}`.

General information about a document and its appearance goes into the preamble. Usually, if you're reading the raw file, you'll simply skip the entire preamble. If you're using a text editor, search for the `\begin{document}` command.

If you get confused, you can quickly skim the preamble for the following commands, which may help you to understand what the author intended:

`\documentclass` This command appears at the beginning of the file to set the basic format, for example, `\documentclass{article}` or `\documentclass{book}`. The `book` class creates a separate title page; the `article` class places the title at the top of the first page. The older LaTeX 2.09 used the similar `\documentstyle` command instead.

`\setlength` This command adjusts a variety of typesetting parameters, from the page margins to the paragraph indentation.

`\newcommand` This command is used to define new commands such as `\keyword`. Commands can be defined to accept arguments surrounded by { and } or optional arguments surrounded by [and]. For example, the `\documentclass` command can accept options that affect the general layout of the document; `\documentclass[11pt]{article}` selects a default font size of 11 points. Commands can also make general changes to the appearance of subsequent text. For example, the `\ttfamily` command selects a `typewriter style` font. The effect of such commands can be restricted by surrounding a part of your document with { and } characters, as in `{\ttfamily typewriter style}`.

`\newenvironment` Commands are sometimes awkward, so LaTeX also has *environments*, which begin with `\begin{`*environment-name*`}` and end with a matching `\end{`*environment-name*`}`. An environment alters the way text within it is formatted. For example, the `raggedright` environment produces an effect like this paragraph.

`\usepackage` The `\usepackage` command reads in a package, which may define a collection of new commands and environments (the `amstex` package defines a large number of macros for mathematical typesetting), alter the way some standard LATEX operations work (the `fancyheadings` package changes the way headers and footers are defined), or otherwise affect how the document appears (the `makeidx` package causes an index to be generated).

Paragraphs

As with many text-based document formats, LATEX ignores the line breaks you type. Instead, LATEX considers a blank line as a paragraph break. All of the words in a paragraph are strung together, and LATEX then determines the best way to arrange them into a paragraph. The underlying TEX engine is very particular about breaking paragraphs into lines. If it can't find a solution that meets its stringent standards, it usually will leave one line obviously too long, and complain about an *overfull hbox* (an "hbox" is just a horizontal line of text).

Likewise, TEX doesn't care how much space you put between words or at the beginning of a paragraph. One or more spaces or tabs simply serve to separate words; TEX will explicitly decide how much space to use. This approach differs from many popular word processors, where additional spaces in the input will result in additional space in the output. By default, TEX adds a small amount of additional space after certain punctuation marks to help separate major phrases and sentences.[3]

> There are several environments that produce special kinds of paragraphs. For example, `\begin{quote}`...`\end{quote}` is used to present quoted material, which is usually typeset like this paragraph. The `raggedright` environment produces ragged-right paragraphs, the `center` environment centers whatever appears

---

[3]One interesting variation in typesetting fashion over the years has been the amount of space placed between sentences. Hand-set type traditionally placed extra space between sentences, partly because it is easier to justify a line by placing additional space at one point than to carefully distribute small slivers of metal. This practice was adopted by typists who developed the practice of putting a double space after full stops. On the other hand, early computerized typesetting couldn't easily handle such distinctions, which led to the current preference for even spacing everywhere. It will be interesting to see whether improved computer software will prompt a return to the varying spaces of hand-set type.

Command	Description
\part{...}	Broad division, often unnumbered
\chapter{...}	Main division of a book or report
\section{...}	Main division of an article
\subsection{...}	Minor division
\subsubsection{...}	Minor division
\paragraph{...}	Minor division
\subparagraph{...}	Smallest division

Table 5.1   LATEX Heading Commands

inside of it, and a variety of other environments produce lists, typeset poetry, and perform many other tasks.

Headings

LATEX provides a number of commands to specify different divisions of the document, as shown in Table 5.1. Depending on various settings (which can be adjusted in the preamble) these commands can also contribute information to the table of contents or automatically number the headings. Each command takes the title of the chapter or section as an argument. Frequently, this title is also used in the table of contents and running headers or footers.[4]

Text Styles

The most common text style command is the \emph{...} command, which *emphasizes* its argument. The \text... commands provide more direct control. These commands typeset their argument in typewriter (\texttt), sans serif (\textsf), *italic* (\textit), or **bold** (\textbf) font. These commands can be combined to produce effects such as ***bold italic*** characters (\textbf{\textit{bold italic}}). However, the precise combinations

---

[4]"Running" headers or footers are the information that's repeated at the top or bottom of each page of a book. Contrast these with "subheads," which indicate major divisions within the text.

Char	Command	Char	Command	Char	Command
Å	\AA	Ø	\O	$	\$
å	\aa	ø	\o	#	\#
Æ	\AE	ß	\ss	&	\&
æ	\ae	Þ	\TH	_	_
Đ	\DH	þ	\th	{	\{
ð	\dh	†	\dag	}	\}
Ł	\L	§	\S	%	\%
ł	\l	¶	\P	\	$\backslash$
Œ	\OE	©	\copyright	^	\^{ }
œ	\oe	£	\pounds	~	\~{ }

Table 5.2   L^AT_EX Special Character Commands

available depend on the available fonts. For example, the default Computer Modern fonts lack a bold typewriter variant.

These commands are new with LaTeX 2ε. The previous version of LaTeX used two-letter commands that did not accept an argument and could not be combined; for example, {\bf bold} for **bold**, or {\em emphasis} for *emphasis*; but {\bf\em bold emphasis} is only *bold emphasis*. The braces limit the effect of the font change.

Special Characters

The accented characters used in many European languages are produced with a variety of short commands. These commands add an accent to the character that follows: ò (\`{o}), ó (\'{o}), ô (\^{o}), ö (\"{o}), ñ (\~{n}), ç (\c{c}). Other special characters can be accessed as shown in Table 5.2. The entries in the last column of Table 5.2 are needed to access characters that otherwise have special meanings to LaTeX.[5]

---

[5] The last three entries in the last column deserve some explanation. Because the simple commands \\, \~, and \^ have other definitions in LaTeX, some additional tinkering is required to generate these characters. The \ character can be generated as a math symbol, and the other two can be generated by placing an appropriate accent over nothing. They are fortunately very rare in normal text.

Char	Command	Char	Command	Char	Command
fi	fi	"	` `	¿	?`
fl	fl	"	' '	¡	!`
ff	ff	–	-- (en-dash)		
ffi	ffi	—	--- (em-dash)		
ffl	ffl				

Table 5.3   LaTeX Ligatures

The TeX typesetting engine makes extensive use of *ligatures,* single glyphs that combine more than one character. For example, when it sees an **f** followed by an **i**, it automatically substitutes a single **fi** glyph. This process is controlled by parameters in the font; a typewriter font usually lacks an fi ligature, so this replacement isn't done. The ligature mechanism is also used to make several common characters easy to type. Table 5.3 lists several of these characters.

Graphics and Figures

LaTeX has only minimal direct support for graphics and figures. A `picture` environment allows simple figures to be created using lines, dots, and a handful of other shapes from a special graphics font. Several packages extend this approach to build fairly complex diagrams for specific uses in mathematics, physics, and chemistry.

More elaborate graphics are generally handled with \special commands that are not interpreted directly by LaTeX or TeX, but are instead stored verbatim in the DVI file to be interpreted by the program that converts the DVI file for the printer.

There are two popular ways to exploit this mechanism. One is based on TROFF's *PIC* language. A program called `tpic` can be used to process picture descriptions in the PIC language and output a file containing the corresponding \special commands. Macro packages that can generate these \special commands from within TeX and LaTeX are also available. In either case, the program that converts the DVI file for the printer must recognize the PIC codes.

Horizontal Local Motions		
Function	Effect in	
	TROFF	NROFF
\h'n'	Move distance N	
\(space)	Unpaddable space-size space	
\0	Digit-size space	
|	1/6 em space	ignored
\^	1/12 em space	ignored

Figure 5.2   Example LATEX Table[6]

This approach is also used to embed raw PostScript commands. Most of the DVI-to-PostScript converter programs support this mechanism, which allows LATEX files to exploit the graphical capabilities of PostScript, either by including Encapsulated PostScript (EPSF) graphics files (see page 100) or by including literal PostScript commands. A PostScript printer must be available to print the result, unlike the `picture` environment, which can be used on any LATEX system, or the PIC approach, which can be used with a variety of different printers.

Tables

The `tabular` environment defines tables in LATEX. Each row is terminated with \\, and items on a row are separated by & characters. Figure 5.2 shows a table example, which was created by the LATEX commands shown in Figure 5.3.[6]

Don't confuse the `tabular` environment with the similarly-named `table` environment. The `table` (and `figure`) environments allow their contents to "float" to an appropriate place in the text (usually the top or bottom of a following page), and optionally create an entry in a table of figures or table of tables. The most significant difference between the two is how they word the caption.

---

[6]This table was adapted from an example in *UNIX in a Nutshell* [Gil92], and typeset with LATEX 2ε.

```
\newcommand{\BS}{\texttt{\symbol{92}}} % Access special symbols
\newcommand{\VERT}{\texttt{\symbol{124}}}
\newcommand{\CARET}{\texttt{\symbol{94}}}
\begin{tabular}{|c|l|l|}
\hline
        \multicolumn{3}{|c|}{\textbf{Horizontal Local Motions}}\\
\hline
        \raisebox{-1.5ex}[0pt][0pt]{\textit{Function}}
        & \multicolumn{2}{c|}{\textit{Effect in}} \\
\cline{2-3}
        & \multicolumn{1}{c|}{\textit{TROFF}}
        & \multicolumn{1}{c|}{\textit{NROFF}} \\
\hline
        \BS h'n'
        & \multicolumn{2}{l|}{Move distance N} \\
        \BS (space)
        & \multicolumn{2}{l|}{Unpaddable space-size space}\\
        \BS 0
        & \multicolumn{2}{l|}{Digit-size space} \\
\hline
        \BS\VERT
        & 1/6 em space
        & ignored \\
        \BS\CARET
        & 1/12 em space
        & ignored \\
\hline
\end{tabular}
```

Figure 5.3   Example LATEX Table Source

Mathematics

TEX and LATEX have a separate "mathematics mode" in which certain characters have special meanings. A large number of additional symbols are available in mathematics mode. This mode is used within certain LATEX environments (such as the `equation` environment) or surrounded by special markers. For example, to obtain the simple equation $\int_1^x \frac{dt}{t} = \ln x$, you type:

```
$\int_1^x {dt \over t} = \ln x$
```

The $ characters mark this as a mathematical equation. Several different markers are used in different situations. The $...$ or \(...\) markers are used for equations in text, where a somewhat more compact form is appropriate. The alternative is a *displayed* equation, which is set off from the text like this:

$$e^x = \sum_{i=0}^{\infty} \frac{x^i}{i!}$$

Displayed equations use larger symbols and more generous spacing than equations in the text, and can be marked with $$...$$ or \[...\]. The above display might be written:

```
$$e^x=\sum_{i=0}^{\infty}\frac{x^i}{i!}$$
```

This example also shows how the ^ (superscript) and _ (subscript) characters are used both for normal superscripts and subscripts and for the limits above and below large operators. The lower limit of the summation required {...} to indicate that the entire i=0 should be treated as a subscript.

Of course, mathematics support requires a variety of special symbols. Greek letters and many other symbols can be generated with special commands. The equation $\Psi = \frac{\partial E}{\partial x}$ can be written:

```
\(\Psi =\frac{\partial E}{\partial x}\)
```

Finally, here's a displayed equation with multiple subscripts:

$$x_{a_1} + x_{a_2} + \cdots = \pi/4$$

This example requires {...} to group the subscripts:

```
\[x_{a_1} + x_{a_2} + \cdots = \pi/4\]
```

Using centered dots ($\cdots$) rather than lowered dots (...) and setting the fraction as $\pi/4$ rather than $\frac{\pi}{4}$ are fine touches that are best learned by experience. Good mathematical typesetting requires judgment and experience as well as flexible tools.

More Information

More files on the Internet are in LaTeX format than any of the other TeX dialects. If you want to understand what's in those files, a good place to start is with Leslie Lamport's book *LaTeX: A Document Preparation System* [Lam94]. Serious users of LaTeX will want to have a more comprehensive reference, such as *The LaTeX Companion* [GMS94].

The core TeX system has been thoroughly documented by its creator, Donald Knuth, in *The TeXbook* [Knu86a]. *The TeXbook* is the first in a series of books written by Knuth about computerized typesetting. The other volumes present Knuth's METAFONT font-description language [Knu86c], his Computer Modern collection of fonts [Knu86e], and the complete, annotated source code for the TeX and METAFONT programs [Knu86b, Knu86d].

If you're interested in using TeX and LaTeX, two excellent Internet resources are the `comp.text.tex` newsgroup and the Comprehensive TeX Archive Network (CTAN). CTAN is a collection of FTP sites that lives up to its name. The three primary sites are `ftp.shsu.edu` in the US, `ftp.tex.ac.uk` in Great Britain, and `ftp.dante.de` in Germany. Here you can find free TeX and LaTeX systems for many popular computer systems, as well as a large quantity of associated information.

The American Mathematical Society also has an index of TeX-related information on its World Wide Web site (`http://e-math.ams.org`).

For the Macintosh, Andrew Trevorrow's *OzTeX* system is an easy way to get started. It's complete, free, and easy to use. It's available using anonymous FTP to `midway.uchicago.edu` in the `pub/OzTeX` directory. The *Alpha* text editor, available from the same location, is a nice tool for editing TeX and LaTeX source code.

Web2C TeX system is the standard Unix TeX system, named after the tools used to compile the suite of programs. This distribution consists of several large archives, containing all of the core TeX programs, a number of macro and font packages, including LaTeX, and some documentation. It compiles easily on most Unix-like systems. The only omission is that the Web2C distribution does not include any DVI translators. Most people use `xdvi` to preview DVI files under X, `dvips` to convert DVI files into high-quality PostScript, and `dvilj` to convert DVI files for the popular Hewlett-Packard LaserJet printers. All of these are available in *k* versions which use Karl Berry's path search library to allow easy configuration of the directory layout for the hundreds of different files used by large TEX installations.

The CTAN archives also contain several complete TEX systems for MS-DOS. These work fine with Windows with the addition of a DVI previewer. Several Windows previewers are available from the same source. Many of these programs are also available from SIMTEL in the `msdos/tex` and `win3/tex` directories.

SGML

The idea I've referred to as *logical markup* (see page 24) isn't new. It goes back to the late 1960s under the name *generic coding*. At that time, a number of people began to realize the distinction between the *content* of a document and its *presentation*. This observation led to work at IBM and other places on systems that would explicitly mark the content of a document ("this is a chapter title") separately from the presentation ("this is in 24pt Helvetica Oblique, starts a new right-hand page, with one-half inch of space below").

This distinction may seem somewhat academic if you're used to creating one-page documents that are printed and promptly deleted. But imagine you're in charge of the documentation for a new battleship design for the military. Not only are there hundreds of thousands of pages of documents, you have to make sure those documents will still be usable for as long as that battleship exists, which might be fifty years or more. A word processor format isn't sufficient; you can't even be sure that word processor will still exist in fifty years, and you can't afford to convert all of your documents every few years to keep track of changes and updates to that word processor. You may also

SGML at a Glance	
Name:	SGML, Standard Generalized Markup Language
Extension:	`.sgml`
Use For:	Managing large collections of documents
References:	ISO Standard 8879; *Practical SGML* [vH94]

have requirements for different kinds of printed and online versions of the documentation, which means that the same documents have to be formatted differently to fit different screen types and manual sizes. Worse, those requirements may change periodically, forcing you to reformat all of those documents to match the new guidelines.

A similar problem is faced by many book publishers. Book styles change from year to year, and book publishers who need to reprint five- or ten-year-old books want those books to look as current as possible, without having to manually reformat the entire book.

The solution is to carefully define three separate pieces, so that you can conveniently change any one whenever you want. You need to:

- Explicitly define what markup you're using in these documents.

- Have documents using that markup.

- Have some way to translate that markup into a visual appearance.

An International Standard Markup Language

The system IBM developed to support this division was called the *Generalized Markup Language* (GML). This system was later extended and became an international standard in 1986, the *Standard Generalized Markup Language* (SGML).

SGML actually only deals with the first two items I described above. SGML provides a way to define what markup is being used in a document. In fact, HTML is defined using SGML.[1] Translating that markup into a particular visual format requires additional software that understands the markup you're using. In practice, this translation may involve converting your SGML

---

[1] *Entities* and *elements* are standard SGML terms, and many of the tags used in HTML are taken directly from the SGML *reference concrete syntax*, a "sample markup language" that is given in the ISO standard.

markup into TROFF or TEX, and then using those tools to actually create printable output.[2]

If you have to translate the result into some other format to print it, why not just use that other format directly? The first reason deals with the three distinct pieces I described earlier. Recall that SGML asks you to explicitly define what markup you're using, and encourages you to avoid shortcuts:

> "I'll just put this one word in italics; I'm in a hurry and don't want to bother to create a new character style just for this."

Over the lifetime of a document (measured in decades), such shortcuts slowly pile up into a mess that makes it difficult to change the appearance of the document. By explicitly defining your markup system, you can limit such shortcuts, or at least document them so they'll be easier to find and update in the future.

Another reason for preferring SGML relates to maintenance. SGML was designed for industrial settings where documents need to be available for a long time. In ten or twenty years, the system you used may not be available or may have changed enough to require substantial updating of your software. Having an explicit definition of the markup in your documents makes it much easier to create new software, if necessary, to handle that particular markup. For a large project, the documentation may be far larger than the software used to process the documentation. As a result, it may be cheaper to completely replace the software than to convert the documentation into a new format.

SGML's approach to generic markup has several advantages when used to manage large amounts of data. One advantage is that it allows many properties of documents to be automatically verified. For example, it's possible to scan hundreds of megabytes of technical documentation to make sure that each manual contains a summary (which isn't too long), table of contents, bibliography, and index. This kind of automatic verification is possible with SGML because each of these components is specified as a separate element. In fact, you can treat a large collection of SGML documents as a database where you can extract only the summaries for all the documents, or merge the indexes to do rapid searches through a group of documents.

---

[2]A more technical explanation is that SGML is used to define the *syntax* (what the markup looks like), but not the *semantics* (what the markup means). If you're a programmer, here's a useful analogy: SGML is to HTML as YACC is to C.

More Information

Joan Smith's *SGML and Related Standards* [Smi92] is a good survey that will help you understand the purpose of the various ISO document standards.

Eric van Herwijnen's *Practical SGML* [vH94] may be more appropriate if you want to understand how SGML is used in practice.

TROFF

The original Unix manuals were developed with a simple text formatter designed for the line printers available at the time. Because Unix was being used in universities and other large companies and the formatter program was part of Unix, it was easy to include the electronic source of the manuals with the system software so that the company or university using Unix could print as many copies of the manuals as needed.

With a formatter that generated output suitable for line printers and the manual source available online, it was a small step to create a program that formatted any requested part of the manual and printed it to a computer screen. Thus, the Unix man command was born. It's now taken for granted by Unix users that man *command* will produce a description of any Unix command. The *man pages*, as this electronic resource is now called, also include information for programmers and descriptions of many system resource files. Although printed versions of this information are available, they're rarely used.

TROFF at a Glance	
Names:	TROFF, NROFF, DITROFF, GROFF, etc.
Extensions:	.man, .ms, .me, .1 – .9
Used For:	Unix online manuals, program documentation
References:	*4.4BSD User's Supplementary Documents* [USD94]; *Unix in a Nutshell* [Gil92]
On CD:	GROFF system for MS-DOS

The original Unix formatter was named *ROFF*, which was an abbreviation for "run off," as in "would you please run off four copies of this memo?" It has since been superceded by *NROFF* (New Roff, used to format text for screens and line printers) and *TROFF* (Typesetting Roff, which formats for high-resolution printers and typesetters), and many other programs with similar names and capabilities. These programs were heavily used for typesetting reports and memorandums at AT&T Bell Labs and elsewhere for many years. Although less widely used today, these programs are still important because they can produce either high-quality typeset output or output suitable for simple text terminals and printers. Either form of output can be produced from the same original source.

Because TROFF and NROFF accept identical input (with a very few exceptions), I'll refer to TROFF throughout. You should remember that NROFF functions identically, just with different-looking output.

Using TROFF Files

Formatting a file with TROFF requires that you know two things:

- Which macro package this file expects.

- Which preprocessors should be used.

Like TEX/LATEX, TROFF allows you to define "macros" to encapsulate common chores. For example, a simple macro might leave a blank line and indent for a new paragraph. Several *macro packages* are fairly standard and available on most systems. The three most common are man, ms, and me. As you can guess, man is used to format Unix manual pages. The ms and me packages are used for more general formatting of reports and articles.

These macro packages augment the built-in capabilities of TROFF. Another approach is to use a *preprocessor*, a separate program that understands certain complex commands and converts them into TROFF commands. The common preprocessors all work in essentially the same way:

PIC   PIC recognizes certain special TROFF macros as the start and end of a picture description. PIC interprets the picture description and replaces it with a series of rather cryptic TROFF commands. When processed by TROFF, these commands create the requested figure.

TBL   TBL functions similarly to PIC, but recognizes a language used to describe tables.

EQN   EQN recognizes mathematical equations and converts them into TROFF commands.

REFER   REFER recognizes specially marked bibliographic references in the text, looks them up in a separate database, and replaces them with an accurate bibliographic citation, which can include full information in a footnote or endnote. It can also be used to build a traditional bibliography.

SOELIM   One problem with the above preprocessors is that they don't recognize any TROFF commands except for their own special additions. In particular, they don't recognize the `.so` command to read in a separate file. SOELIM eliminates `.so` commands by replacing each one with the contents of the corresponding file. This allows you to place PIC or TBL instructions in separate files.

Processing a TROFF file requires first invoking the appropriate preprocessors, then feeding the result to TROFF—with the correct macro package loaded—to generate the final output. On Unix, this process is usually handled with a *pipeline*, which lets the output of one program feed into the input of another. A typical TROFF command on Unix will look something like:

```
pic filename | tbl | eqn | troff -ms -t >output_file
```

This tells Unix to run the `pic` command on the file, feed the output of `pic` into `tbl`, feed the output of `tbl` into `eqn`, and feed the output of `eqn` into TROFF. The > sign instructs Unix to put the final output (of TROFF) into some output file. This example uses the `ms` macro package. To use another macro package, substitute the appropriate name. I've also instructed TROFF to send its output to the standard output path (`-t`). Additional options depend on the particular implementation of TROFF you're using. For GNU GROFF, you may want to use the `-Tps` option to generate PostScript output.

The standard preprocessors leave unaltered anything that isn't marked specifically for that preprocessor, so you can almost always use a particular preprocessor even if it's not needed. If you're unsure what preprocessors are required, you can usually just use them all, as in the example above.

NROFF is used identically to TROFF, except that you must use `neqn` instead of `eqn` to process equations for NROFF. Note that generally, though, trying to process equations with NROFF is not a good idea, except for very hasty proofreading.

A TROFF Primer

TROFF reads a plain text file with embedded markup and generates an output file that can be displayed or printed with the appropriate software. The particular output format will depend on the version of TROFF you use. Many versions generate output for the extinct C/A/T phototypesetter, and provide postprocessor programs to convert it into something more useful. Others produce PostScript, TEX DVI format, DITROFF format output (a device-independent text format similar in concept to DVI), or another comparable format. The output of NROFF can also be tailored to a variety of line printers and terminals.

The markup appears in two forms: *Dot commands* are indicated by a period at the beginning of a line, while *escapes* are preceded by a backslash (\) character and can occur anywhere on a line. Dot commands are usually two characters and take the rest of the line as arguments to the command. For example, the line

```
.ft I
```

starts with the command to select a font; the argument I selects the italic font. In NROFF, this font request produces underlined text if the display supports it. (Most terminals and line printers can support both underlined and bold text.)

Many escapes also accept arguments. Most escapes are a single letter, possibly followed by an argument. The argument is either a single character, or two characters preceded by a (. For example, the \f escape selects a new font; the following character determines the font selected: I for italic, B for bold, P for the previously selected font. Thus, \fI selects the italic font. Some versions of TROFF have fonts with two-character names. These fonts are selected by \f(, which takes the next two characters as an argument, such as \f(CW for a constant-width typewriter font. When one or two characters isn't enough, as with escapes that require a distance argument, the arguments are surrounded by single quotes ('), as in \h'1in' to move horizontally by one inch.

The dot commands always begin at the start of a line, while escapes can appear anywhere within a line. Typically, dot commands are used for structural commands, such as paragraphs and headings, while escapes are used for special symbols. This rule isn't hard and fast; many tasks can be done either way. Also note that all dot commands and escapes are case sensitive: \L and \l are quite different.

Paragraphs

TROFF is normally in *fill mode*, where it combines consecutive lines and uses them to "fill" paragraphs. A new paragraph can be indicated with a blank line or an indented line. Usually, however, the macro package will define a special macro that should be used to begin a new paragraph. For example, the ms macros use .PP or .LP to start a paragraph, and the me macros use .pp or .lp. (The .PP or .pp macros start an indented paragraph; .LP or .lp start a non-indented paragraph.) For example, the start of this paragraph appears like this using the ms macros:

```
.LP
TROFF is normally in \fIfill mode\fP, where it
combines consecutive lines and uses them
```

The \fI escape switches to italics; the \fP escape switches back to the previous font.

Each macro package defines a variety of macros to start different types of paragraphs, including bulleted paragraphs for building lists and indented paragraphs for displaying quoted material.

Text Styles

While most modern versions of TROFF do support a variety of fonts, the original program was designed for a particular phototypesetter that only had four fonts: Roman, *Italic*, **Bold**, and a symbol font. As a result, using fonts other than these four is heavily site-specific. Some old systems still use over-printing to simulate ***bold italic*** (by printing the words twice at a slight offset) and other styles. These special styles can be tricky to use correctly; the original documentation for the me macros contains a warning about misuse of the *bolbolditalic* feature.

Char	Escape	Char	Escape	Char	Escape
•	\(bu	®	\(rg	fi	\(fi
□	\(sq	©	\(co	fl	\(fl
†	\(dg	¼	\(14	ff	\(ff
¢	\(ct	½	\(12	ffi	\(Fi
°	\(de	¾	\(34	ffl	\(Fl
—	\(em				

Table 7.1   TROFF Escapes for Special Characters in the Standard
Fonts

However, even this early phototypesetter supported a wide range of symbols, including standard publishing and mathematics symbols. Tables 7.1 and 7.2 show some of the characters that are standard in most TROFF implementations. Most of these characters are not available in NROFF, although some NROFF systems can simulate them by overstriking (for example, ∑ for Σ).

Headings

TROFF's basic ability to select various font sizes and styles allows heading macros to be defined in much the same way LaTeX document classes (see page 67) define different macros to handle headings.

The ms macros use .NH and .SH to begin a numbered or unnumbered heading, respectively. An optional trailing number gives the level of the heading, as in:

```
.SH 1
A TROFF Primer
⋮
.SH 2
Headings
```

The me macros use .sh for numbered sections, and .uh for unnumbered sections.

Char	Escape	Char	Escape	Char	Escape
§	\(sc	α	\(*a	A	\(*A
‡	\(dd	β	\(*b	B	\(*B
○	\(ci	γ	\(*g	Γ	\(*G
´	\(aa	δ	\(*d	Δ	\(*D
`	\(ga	ε	\(*e	E	\(*E
→	\(->	ζ	\(*z	Z	\(*Z
←	\(<-	η	\(*y	H	\(*Y
↑	\(ua	θ	\(*h	Θ	\(*H
↓	\(da	ι	\(*i	I	\(*I
+	\(pl	κ	\(*k	K	\(*K
-	\(mi	λ	\(*l	L	\(*L
*	\(**	μ	\(*m	M	\(*M
×	\(mu	ν	\(*n	N	\(*N
÷	\(di	ξ	\(*c	Ξ	\(*C
=	\(eq	o	\(*o	O	\(*O
≥	\(>=	π	\(*p	Π	\(*P
≤	\(<=	ρ	\(*r	P	\(*R
≠	\(!=	σ	\(*s	Σ	\(*S
±	\(+-	ς	\(ts		
		τ	\(*t	T	\(*T
		υ	\(*u	Y	\(*U
		ϕ	\(*f	Φ	\(*F
		χ	\(*x	X	\(*X
		ψ	\(*q	Ψ	\(*Q
		ω	\(*w	Ω	\(*W

Table 7.2   TROFF Escapes for Special Characters in the Symbol Font

Horizontal Local Motions		
Function	*Effect in*	
	TROFF	*NROFF*
\h'n' \(space) \0	Move distance N Unpaddable space-size space Digit-size space	
| \^	1/6 em space 1/12 em space	ignored ignored

Figure 7.1   Example TBL Table[1]

Graphics and Figures

Besides the ability to place any character at any point, many versions of TROFF support special drawing commands. These commands allow TROFF to draw lines, circles, and other simple graphic elements. Using the special drawing escapes directly is fairly cumbersome, however, so these facilities are usually exploited indirectly. The PIC preprocessor recognizes lines beginning with .PS and .PE commands, translating text between them into suitable TROFF commands.

Tables

Tables are usually handled by the TBL program, which reads table descriptions between .TS and .TE macros, and replaces them with the lower-level TROFF commands to produce the table. Figure 7.1 shows the results generated by the GNU version of TBL and TROFF with the input in Figure 7.2.[1]

A table consists of several sections, each of which contains *declarations* describing general properties of the table, *templates* with formatting information for each column, and *data* to be formatted into those columns. The table shown in Figure 7.2 has three sections, separated by .T& macros. The first

---

[1]This table was adapted from an example in *UNIX in a Nutshell* [Gil92], and generated by GNU GROFF.

```
.TS
center box linesize(6) tab(@);
cb s s.
Horizontal Local Motions
_
.T&
ci | ci s
ci | ci s
ci | ci | ci
c  | l s.
Function@Effect in
\^@_
\^@TROFF@NROFF

_
\eh'n'@Move distance N
\e(space)@Unpaddable space-size space
\e0@Digit-size space

_
.T&
c | l | l.
\e|@1/6 em space@ignored
\e^@1/12 em space@ignored
.TE
```

Figure 7.2   TBL Table Source

section has one line of declarations (terminated by a semicolon), which specifies that the @ character will be used to separate items in different columns. The second section contains four lines of templates (the last one ends in a period), followed by eight lines of data. The template `ci |ci s` applies to the data `Function@Effect in`. This template specifies that the first column is centered in an italic font, a vertical rule separates the first two columns, the second column is also centered and in italics, and the third column is part of the second column (the entry "spans" the second and third columns). Special commands in the data are used to indicate vertical spanning (\^) and horizontal rules (_). The \e escape is a standard TROFF command to generate the current escape character (generally \).

Mathematics

EQN looks for lines beginning with .EQ and .EN, and interprets text between those lines as mathematical equations in a special language. EQN translates these mathematical equations into low-level TROFF commands that, after being processed by TROFF, produce the final equation. For example, the lines

```
.EQ
int from 1 to x {dt} over t = ln x
.EN
```

produce the formula:

$$\int_1^x \frac{dt}{t} = \ln x$$

One of the appealing aspects of EQN is that the equations read fairly naturally. EQN recognizes many special words in the input (such as `ln` in the above example) and chooses special ways to typeset them.

EQN leaves the .EQ and .EN macros in the converted output. Various TROFF macro packages define these macros in various ways, for example to set the formula as a displayed equation:

$$e^x = \sum_{i=0}^{\infty} \frac{x^i}{i!}$$

This formula can be generated with the EQN input:

```
.EQ
e sup x = sum from i=0 to inf {x sup i} over {i!}
.EN
```

EQN differs from LaTeX and HTML in that it doesn't use superscript and subscript constructions to handle limits on large operators. The `from` and `to` commands handle limits.

Of course, not all equations are set as displays. To get an equation in the text, such as $\Psi = \frac{\partial E}{\partial x}$, you need to mark the equation in a different way. One of the special EQN commands allows you to define special characters to delimit equations in the text:

```
.EQ
delim $$
.EN
⋮
To get an equation in the text,
such as $Psi = {partial E} over {partial x}$, you need
to mark the equation in a different way.
```

Not all of EQN's special commands are words. It also recognizes several other symbols, including `->` for $\rightarrow$ and `+-` for $\pm$. EQN supports multiple subscripts fairly simply, for example:

$$x_{a_1} + x_{a_2} + \cdots = \pi/4$$

can be generated with:

```
x sub a sub 1 + x sub a sub 2 + ... = pi / 4
```

More Information

TROFF and its friends were heavily used at AT&T Bell Labs for text processing by everyone from computer researchers to secretaries, and the documentation written there is remarkably clear.

If you want to know more about TROFF, a good starting place is Brian Kernighan's *A TROFF Tutorial* [Ker79]. Joseph Ossanna's *NROFF/TROFF*

User's Manual [Oss79] gives more complete information. These documents are reproduced in the *4.4BSD User's Supplementary Documents* [USD94], along with several other papers discussing the various macro packages and preprocessors.

Most Unix systems already include NROFF. A few fail to include TROFF, however. You can get the GNU GROFF system from any repository of GNU software (see page 13). GROFF includes implementations of all the programs mentioned in this chapter. It also includes the useful `groff` program that provides a simpler way to run the various preprocessors and postprocessors.

The GROFF system is also available for MS-DOS from the *Garbo* archive, in the `pc/unix` directory.

One somewhat extreme way to get TROFF and NROFF for a PC is to install a complete Unix-like system. There are three complete, freely available Unix-like systems for PCs: Linux, FreeBSD, and NetBSD. All three include GROFF and a host of related utilities.

PostScript

PostScript is a complete programming language that has a powerful set of graphics and font-manipulating operations. It is widely used in printers and high-end graphics systems, and has become the *lingua franca* of most of today's publishing industry.

PostScript was created by Adobe Systems in 1984, and was quickly adopted by Apple Computer for use in its LaserWriter printers. From there, it was adopted by many other printer manufacturers, and is now standard in mid-range laser printers through to high-end imagesetters. PostScript's graphics engine—in the form of a programming system called *Display PostScript*—has also been adopted by NeXT and the X windowing system for on-screen display.

Some people write PostScript programs by hand, but the bulk of all PostScript is generated by machine. Typically, word processors or desktop

PostScript at a Glance	
Names:	PostScript, Encapsulated PostScript, Type 1 Font, Type 3 Font
Extensions:	`.ps`, `.eps`, `.epsf`, `.pfa`, `.pfb`, `.afm`, `.pfm`
Use For:	Printing, storing fonts; can be used to exchange formatted documents if you are careful about font usage
References:	*PostScript Language Reference Manual* [Ado90b]; *Adobe Type 1 Font Format* [Ado90a]
On CD:	PostScript previewers for Windows, Macintosh

publishing programs translate their internal formats into a PostScript program that is relayed to a printer. The printer interprets the PostScript on-the-fly to generate a graphical image of one or more pages.

PostScript's biggest strength is that it uses a *device-independent rendering model*. In plain English, that means that a PostScript file describes what a page should look like without assuming anything about the printer or screen that will display it. The same PostScript file can be displayed on a 72 dpi (dot-per-inch) screen or a 2400 dpi imagesetter, and the result in either case will be the best ouput possible from that device. Publishers can be assured that the PostScript file they previewed on their 300 dpi laser printer will take full advantage of the 2400 dpi imagesetter used to print the final book.

One drawback of PostScript's flexibility is that understanding an arbitrary PostScript file is quite difficult. PostScript interpreters are complex, and very few applications can justify the additional expense of a full PostScript interpreter. So, several kinds of PostScript files use only a small subset of PostScript's capabilities. The most common PostScript files are font files in Adobe Type 1 format. These files contain a handful of definitions of font properties and an encoded set of outlines describing the font appearance. This very restricted format makes it possible to write programs that read and understand Type 1 font files without understanding the entire PostScript language. Another approach to handling PostScript's complexity is to combine a PostScript description with another, simpler format. "Encapsulated PostScript Files" (EPSF) often contain a low-resolution bitmapped preview that can be easily and quickly extracted.

Recognizing PostScript Files

PostScript is a programming language, and generally, recognizing a source file for a programming language is difficult. Because PostScript files are usually created and consumed by machine, Adobe defined a convention for rapidly determining if a file is a PostScript file.

The % character is a comment indicator in PostScript. The first line of any PostScript file is a comment line beginning with the two characters %!. Usually, the rest of the line will identify the type of the file. Table 8.1 shows some different first lines and what they mean.

First Line	Extension	File Format
`%!`	`.ps`	PostScript file
`%!PS-Adobe-3.0`	`.ps`	Structured PostScript file
`%!PS-Adobe-3.0 EPSF-3.0`	`.eps, .epsf`	Encapsulated PostScript file
`%!PS-AdobeFont-1.0`	`.pfa, .pfb`	Type 1 Font file
`%!FontType1-1.0`	`.pfa, .pfb`	Type 1 Font file

Table 8.1   Identifying a PostScript File by the First Line

There are two cases in which data will appear before the initial `%!` line. One case is Type 1 font files in binary format. The other case is Encapsulated PostScript files containing a machine-specific preview. I'll discuss each of these in later sections.

PostScript Font Files

PostScript's font machinery is very general. It thinks of a font as a collection of PostScript procedures. Whenever a character from that font needs to be drawn, the corresponding PostScript procedure is executed. A PostScript font file provides a variety of information about the font, a procedure for every "glyph," a default mapping of character codes to glyph names,[1] and a transformation to be applied to each character as it is drawn.

PostScript font files are PostScript programs that define a fairly complex data structure. The first part of the definition is always in plain text, and gives such information as the name of the font, copyright information, and the "encoding"[2] used by the font. The remainder of the definition provides procedures for drawing each individual character.

---

[1]A *glyph* is a pattern on a screen or paper. For example, "a" and "*a*" are different glyphs. See page 20 for more details. In general, a *font* consists of a collection of glyphs together with an *encoding*, which specifies how to select glyphs (see page 20).

[2]The *encoding* determines the glyph that should be used for each character code. For example, Adobe's `StandardEncoding` selects the glyph named "dagger" (†) to print character 178.

Type 3 Fonts

PostScript identifies different *types* of fonts. *Type 3* fonts are the most general. PostScript Type 3 fonts define each glyph with a PostScript procedure. Type 3 fonts are capable of spectacular effects, including multicolored characters or characters that change their appearance each time they're drawn.

The drawback is that Type 3 fonts require a complete PostScript interpreter, since the process of drawing a character may require almost any PostScript operator. Because of this limitation, Type 3 fonts are fairly unusual. Instead, most fonts are in a more restrictive format that can be interpreted by a program much simpler than a full PostScript implementation.

Type 1 Fonts

Type 1 fonts are the most common PostScript fonts. Type 1 fonts describe each character with an outline. In normal use, the outline is filled to create a solid character, but a variety of PostScript operators can be used to take advantage of this outline in other ways. (For example, Figure 8.1 was created by drawing the outline of each character first with a thick black line, then with a narrow white line.) Despite being somewhat more restricted than Type 3, Type 1 fonts have several advantages over Type 3 fonts. The biggest advantage is that Type 1 fonts contain *hints* that indicate the significance of certain font features. This additional information allows the PostScript interpreter to adjust the font outlines slightly for the best possible appearance at small sizes or low resolutions.[3]

The actual outline information in a Type 1 font file is encoded in a dense binary format and then encrypted. The full details of the encoding and encryption are available in *Adobe Type 1 Font Format* [Ado90a].

Type 1 fonts come in two slightly different flavors. *PFB* (PostScript Font–Binary) files store the encrypted outline data in a raw binary form. This more compact format is somewhat more troublesome to handle. *PFA* (PostScript Font–ASCII) files encode the outline data in hexadecimal, which is easier

---

[3]The presence of high-quality hints is the biggest difference between professionally-designed fonts and the cheap imitations that have become so common recently. Hints are critically important at the low resolution used by computer monitors, and the effect of hinting is noticeable on 300 dpi and 600 dpi printers.

Figure 8.1   Character Outline

Bytes	Description
1	Flag byte: 128
1	Format of following data
4	Length of following data, from LSB to MSB

Table 8.2   Data Format Markers for PFB Files

to handle but somewhat larger. Both file formats carry precisely the same information, and freely available utilities can convert between the two.

To simplify programs that want to understand Type 1 fonts, PFB files contain binary markers that can be used to rapidly identify parts of the file data. These markers are six bytes long, as indicated in Table 8.2. The format byte is 1 for ASCII data, 2 for binary data that can be converted into ASCII hexadecimal, and 3 for end-of-file. These markers simplify downloading fonts to a printer, because a PFB file can be rapidly converted into a PFA file, which is more appropriate for many printers.

Other Font Types

Other font types are used to indicate other font formats. *Type 4* and *Type 5* formats are used for the built-in fonts in certain PostScript printers.

Type 42 is used to print TrueType fonts on some PostScript printers. True-Type fonts are similar in concept to Type 1 fonts. They were originally developed by Apple as an alternative to Type 1, and were later adopted by Microsoft for its popular Windows operating system.

Other Font-Related Files

While the PFA or PFB file contains all the information needed to use a font, these files are overkill for many situations. Word processors and desktop publishing programs don't need to know exactly what the font looks like; they'll use a low-resolution screen font to display the text on the screen. But, to get accurate results on the printer, they need to know the exact *metrics* of the actual PostScript characters. For PostScript fonts, this metric information—in addition to being contained in the PFA or PFB file—is available in a *PFM* (PostScript Font Metrics) or *AFM* (Adobe Font Metrics) file.

PFM and AFM files contain slightly different information in very different formats. PFM files are stored in binary, and are used by Windows. AFM files are in a text format, and are used by most Unix software. (The Macintosh uses its own special format for metric information.) Because they are in a text format, it is generally easier to work with AFM files. Utilities are available to convert between PFM and AFM format. When you purchase PostScript fonts, you usually receive a PFA or PFB file and both PFM and AFM files for each font.

Adobe also distributes *PPD* (PostScript Printer Description) files for a variety of printers. These files are used by print manager systems to describe the capabilities of a particular printer.

Structured PostScript Files

PostScript files are often assembled from several pieces. Most applications build a PostScript file first by copying a standard "prologue" file, then copying one or more font files, then spitting out PostScript commands to draw the pages for the document. Along the way, the application may copy other PostScript files containing commands to draw special images.

Ideally, applications shouldn't have to copy special prologues or fonts into every PostScript file they create, since this extra data bloats the generated PostScript. Many printers allow special prologues and fonts to be stored permanently in the printer, which removes the need for these files to be copied into every file that uses them. The problem is that the application may not know what special resources are stored on the printer.

On many systems, an individual application doesn't deal directly with the printer (this is especially true when the printer is located elsewhere on a large network). To allow the program that's managing the printer to selectively remove PostScript commands that are already resident in the printer, or to selectively add fonts or prologues that aren't already available, PostScript files need a structure that can be easily understood. This structure also allows PostScript files to be easily manipulated, for example, to select or rearrange pages.

Adobe has defined the *PostScript Document Structuring Conventions* (DSC), which consists of special *structured comments*, beginning with %%, that indicate certain aspects of the document. The full list of these comments is available in Adobe's *PostScript Language Reference Manual* [Ado90b]. PostScript documents that follow these conventions are informally referred to as "structured PostScript files."

Adherence to Adobe's DSC allows printer management software to select the best printer for a particular job and optimize printing in a variety of ways. For example, the printer management software can automatically add required fonts to a document prior to printing, which removes the need to copy font files over the network and consolidates font storage. The software can detect often-used fonts and download them directly to the printer, further speeding the printing of documents. Pages can be automatically rearranged for face-up or two-sided printing.

While sophisticated document management is primarily useful to large organizations with a battalion of networked printers, structured PostScript does have benefits for less sophisticated environments. Many people use simple utilities to select and rearrange pages or produce "thumbnails" of a large document. This is especially useful when you're only interested in a few pages of a large PostScript document. In particular, the popular GhostView previewer uses the structured comments to identify pages within a document. Unfortunately, many PostScript-generating programs don't properly generate these structured comments, which makes it difficult to manipulate the documents in PostScript form.

Keep in mind that these structured comments are almost always ignored by a PostScript printer. They're purely for the use of an intermediate program that might want to use or alter the PostScript file before it is printed. If you are writing an application that outputs or manipulates DSC files, you should study Adobe's documentation carefully.

Encapsulated PostScript

Because so many programs know how to generate PostScript output, you may need to include a PostScript file in another document. Such inclusion is fairly simple if the PostScript program to be included is well-behaved. PostScript is a complete programming language, so an included file can easily alter the printing environment and prevent the rest of the document from printing correctly.

To help avoid this problem, Adobe has defined the *Encapsulated PostScript File* (EPSF) format. An EPSF file is a PostScript file that adheres to the DSC (so the application that reads it can make sense of it) and is careful not to do anything anti-social. The restrictions are quite reasonable, and many PostScript files can be converted into Encapsulated PostScript files with two minor changes. The first line has to look like %!PS-Adobe-3.0 EPSF-3.0, and a %%BoundingBox comment must be near the beginning of the file.[4]

The %%BoundingBox comment tells the application that uses the EPSF file the size of the graphic image defined by the EPSF file. The two corners are specified using *PostScript points*, which are exactly 1/72 of an inch. For example, an image one inch high and two inches wide might have these bounding box coordinates: 0 0 144 72. If printed alone, this image would sit at the lower left corner of the page, and extend two inches to the right and one inch up.

```
%%BoundingBox:    <lower left corner> <upper right corner>
```

Encapsulated PostScript Previews

Because displaying EPSF files requires a full PostScript interpreter, many EPSF files also contain a bitmap that can be used by application programs to display the contents of the file. This dual approach allows interactive applications to quickly display the contents of the file using the bitmapped preview information, while preserving the more accurate PostScript version for printing. Four different types of previews are in common use.

---

[4]The version numbers refer to the current version of the Document Structuring conventions and the EPSF standard, respectively. Some older applications require specific version numbers other than 3.0.

EPSI Previews

PostScript files are often carried from one computer to another, so it's convenient to have a preview format that can be easily decoded on almost any platform. The *Encapsulated PostScript Interchange* (EPSI) format stores the preview as a simple, uncompressed bitmap contained in a series of comments at the beginning of the PostScript file.

Macintosh Previews

The Macintosh operating system stores a file in two *forks*. The "data fork" contains the file data, while the "resource fork" contains a database of additional information. Macintosh EPSF files typically store a standard Macintosh PICT preview in the resource fork.

TIFF and Windows Metafile Previews

Other systems lack the flexibility of Macintosh's separate resource fork, so the preview data must be stored with the EPSF data. The preview can be stored as an EPSI preview, as described above, or as a TIFF or Windows Metafile image. In this latter approach, a short directory is attached to the beginning of the file indicating where the PostScript, TIFF, and Metafile data is stored in the file. Table 8.3 details the format of this header. Note that the "magic number" is the ASCII representation of EPSF, with the high bit of each byte set.

PostScript Dialects

The original PostScript language supported the needs of black and white printers reasonably well. Over time, Adobe and other vendors have added a variety of extensions to PostScript to support color printers and on-screen display, provide better access to the features of high-end printers, and provide more sophisticated graphics functionality. As a result, PostScript now has three major dialects.

The original PostScript language is now known as *PostScript Level 1*. It is still supported by many printers, and forms the core of the newer dialects. Level 1's primary drawback is its lack of color support.

Bytes	Contents
4	Magic number: hex C5 D0 D3 C6
4	File offset of start of PS data
4	Size of PS data
4	File offset of start of Metafile data
4	Size of Metafile data
4	File offset of start of TIFF data
4	Size of TIFF data
2	Checksum of previous bytes

Table 8.3 Preview Directory

Adobe developed *Display PostScript* (DPS) to provide a more sophisticated way for programs to draw on the screen. DPS is part of the NeXT graphical interface and many commercial versions of the X window system for Unix. DPS adds color and multitasking support to the original PostScript Level 1, as well as an interface that allows programs written in a variety of languages to execute fragments of PostScript code and recover the results.

The current PostScript language used in most newer printers is *PostScript Level 2*. PostScript Level 2 adds a variety of new features, including sophisticated color support, a standard way to access the features of high-end printers, and new operators to simplify many kinds of PostScript programs.

Most applications now generate PostScript output that checks whether the printer supports Level 1 or Level 2. If the printer supports Level 2, the program will take advantage of those features. If not, the program will attempt to simulate the effect of such features. Because of this simulation, PostScript files will often print slightly faster and with slightly better quality on true Level 2 printers than on comparable Level 1 printers.

A few relatively minor compatibility problems exist. The first problem is that many PostScript files are not written to work with generic Level 1 printers, but rather with the Apple LaserWriter, which included a handful of specific extensions to the Level 1 standard. Fortunately, better Level 1 printers do emulate these LaserWriter extensions. Another occasional problem is that Level 2 is not precisely an extension of Level 1. A few (relatively minor) details of PostScript are not compatible, which is why many Level 2 printers also support a separate Level 1 emulation. This is a minor concern simply because Level 2 has been available for long enough that few applications rely on those details.

Hints for Handling PostScript

PostScript files are usually text files, and as such, can be read into a text editor and altered if necessary. One of the most common alterations you might want to make is to convert a normal PostScript file into an Encapsulated PostScript file so you can insert it into another document. You need to edit the first line, and make sure there's an accurate bounding box comment at the beginning of the file. If not, you'll need to add one. The easiest way is to print the file and use a ruler to draw a rectangle enclosing the image. Then measure the position of the lower left corner and upper right corner of the rectangle. If you measure in inches, multiply each dimension by 72 and use those in the %%BoundingBox comment (see page 100).[5] Frequently, this alteration will be sufficient to include the PostScript file in another document.

The %%Pages comment indicates the number of pages in the document. You can consult this value when deciding whether to print a file you've received or view it using a PostScript viewer such as GhostView.

Each page of a structured PostScript file begins with a %%Page comment that provides a *label* (usually the label is the number printed on the page) and an ordinal page number (which always starts at 1). Generally, pages can be removed or rearranged with impunity. Just be careful to keep everything that defines a single page together.

If you're going to use a PostScript file repeatedly, you may want to trim it to conserve disk space. Often, stripping out comments and removing extraneous spaces can reduce a PostScript file by 20 percent or more. Spaces are not necessary before or after certain punctuation (including {, }, [, and]) and can usually be removed before /, <, and (, and after > and). You do need to be careful not to alter anything in a string; strings in PostScript are enclosed in (and).

Removing the binary preview will also reduce the size of a PostScript file considerably. The PostScript file proper begins with %! and ends with an

---

[5]In PostScript, a point is precisely 1/72 of an inch. This occasionally causes problems because the standard point used by printers for over a century is slightly smaller. You sometimes see people refer to PostScript points as *DTP points*, as opposed to *printer's points*.

%%EOF comment. Anything outside of that can be safely removed without affecting how the PostScript file will print. Frequently, this step alone reduces the total size of the file by 50 percent or more.

PostScript files are usually completely ASCII, so you can edit them easily with a standard text editor. A few PostScript files have binary data embedded in them, however, so it's best if you use a text editor that doesn't have arbitrary line-length limitations that damage binary data. (I often use GNU Emacs for this kind of work.) As always, you should edit a copy of the file and make sure the altered version prints identically before you delete the original.

Legal Issues

PostScript files often have to include other data. The most common example is the use of non-standard fonts. To print the file, you must either have that font in your printer or include the font as part of the PostScript file. If you want to give the PostScript file to someone else, you usually have to include the required font; you can't always assume that they have the font you used.

The problem is that fonts are usually copyrighted; you probably don't have the right to give the other person a copy of the font. If you include the font in the PostScript file, you've given the person a copy of the font, since they can easily pull the PostScript file into a plain text editor and separate the font information. As a result, you usually can't legally include the font in the PostScript file.

The current status of fonts with regard to US copyright law is a bit confusing. Under current US copyright law, the *visual appearance* of a font can't be copyrighted. Under most circumstances, you can make visual copies (for example, on a photocopier or printing press) of a font without violating any copyright. However, PostScript fonts (and other similar font formats, such as TrueType, Sun F3, and Speedo fonts) are considered *programs*, and programs can be copyrighted. Because of this dichotomy, it's often impossible to legally distribute the PostScript file of a document you create (because it contains copyrighted fonts), even though you can legally print and give away photocopies of the same document.[6]

---

[6]I'm simplifying this issue enormously. For example, only parts of a font file are subject to copyright protection. The distinction between *visual appearance* and *program* that I've

The easiest way around this problem is to stick to the handful of fonts that are present in every PostScript-compatible printer, namely Times Roman, Helvetica, and Courier.[7] If you use only those fonts, you can distribute your PostScript document easily because you won't have to include any font files.

Conventional wisdom says that because the visual appearance of a font cannot be copyrighted, neither can the bitmapped version of a font. As a result, converting Type 1 fonts into fixed-resolution bitmap fonts and including those in your document probably suffices to get around this restriction.[8] Font foundries currently claim that the copyrights on their PostScript font descriptions also apply to any font description converted from their PostScript fonts. It's unclear whether this applies to bitmaps created from those descriptions, or just to translations of those descriptions into other comparable formats (a TrueType conversion of a copyrighted Type 1 font is still copyrighted). To my knowledge, this ambiguity hasn't been tested in court, and until it is, it's hard to say whether or not the distribution of bitmaps derived from PostScript outline fonts is legal.

Strengths and Weaknesses

One way to summarize the previous section is to say that PostScript, while an excellent format for document *description*, is a poor choice for document *interchange*. This weakness is one of the reasons for the development of file formats specifically targeted for document interchange, such as Adobe's *Portable Document Format* (also known as *Acrobat*), which I discuss in the next chapter.

PostScript's other major weakness is that is complex. As a full-fledged programming language, it's not possible for a program to be able to understand an arbitrary PostScript file well enough to effectively alter it if necessary. As a

given here is a convenient way to think about this problem, but the actual legal issues are considerably more subtle.

[7]Although the appearance of a font can't be protected, the names can be. The names *Times Roman* and *Helvetica* are trademarks of Linotype-Hell, which explains why many "look alikes" have slightly different names. Courier was originally designed for IBM; the name appears to never have been trademarked. As a result, many different fonts have the name "Courier."

[8]Bitmapped fonts can be stored as PostScript Type 3 fonts. Such fonts can be used at any resolution, but tend to look rather poor at resolutions other than the resolution for which they were created.

result, few applications even attempt to read and utilize data from PostScript files.

It's relatively easy to build PostScript files that make no assumptions about the resolution, color support, or other capabilities of the final output device. However, PostScript does support bitmapped images, color printing, and other features to take advantage of such capabilities when they are available. A large market exists for professional-quality fonts and clip art in PostScript formats, and much of the printing and publishing industry relies heavily on PostScript.

PostScript files are usually text files, which makes it simple to store, manipulate, and transport files. PostScript printers are designed to accept any common end-of-line termination, making them compatible with PC, Macintosh, and Unix systems.

More Information

Adobe has thoroughly documented most aspects of PostScript in a series of books. The principal ones have become known as the "color" books, because they were originally published with solid-colored covers that made them quite distinctive. Adobe's *PostScript Language Tutorial and Cookbook* [Ado85] (the "blue book"), *PostScript Language Program Design* [Ado88] (the "green book"), and *PostScript Language Reference Manual* [Ado90b] (the "red book") are worth investigating if you want to use and understand the PostScript language. The *Adobe Type 1 Font Format* [Ado90a] (the "black book") describes the storage and concepts behind Type 1 font files in considerable detail.

On the Internet, you can find active discussion of PostScript in the newsgroups `comp.lang.postscript` and `comp.fonts`.

Norman Walsh's *The comp.fonts Home Page* (`http://jasper.ora.com`) has information about PostScript fonts as well as pointers to other PostScript-related resources. This same site has information on many other related topics, including TEX/LATEX and SGML. Aaron Wigley's *Internet PostScript Resources* is also useful (`http://yoyo.cc.monash.edu.au/~wigs/postscript`).

GhostScript is a full-blown PostScript interpreter that can print PostScript files on a variety of non-PostScript printers and display PostScript files to the screen on most systems. Versions of GhostScript for Windows, MS-DOS and Unix are available from `ftp://ftp.cs.wisc.edu/pub/ghost`.

The *GhostView* program simplifies displaying displaying PostScript files on the screen with GhostScript. Versions for Windows and OS/2 are available in `ftp://oak.oakland.edu/simtel/win3/printer/gsview12.zip`. A Unix version is available from `ftp://prep.ai.mit.edu/pub/gnu`.

The *ViewPS* program displays PostScript files on the Macintosh. It's available from `ftp://ftp.shsu.edu/tex-archive/systems/mac/cmactex`.

PDF (Acrobat)

The general method that PostScript uses to describe a document is quite applicable to electronically distributed documents (see Chapter 8). Electronically distributed documents have to look good at any resolution, from screen to imagesetter, and PostScript excels at this.

However, PostScript *per se* isn't particularly well-suited to electronic distribution. One problem is that copyrights prevent embedding fonts in a PostScript file, which makes it difficult to distribute PostScript files that use anything other than the most common PostScript fonts. Another problem is that finding a particular page in a PostScript file requires scanning through the entire document from the beginning.

Adobe's *Portable Document Format* (PDF), also known as *Acrobat*, addresses these limitations. PDF uses the same general approach to page description as PostScript. Also like PostScript, PDF is a text format, which simplifies the

---

PDF at a Glance

Names:	PDF, Portable Document Format, Acrobat
Extension:	`.pdf`
Use For:	Exchanging formatted documents
Reference:	*Portable Document Format Reference Manual* [Ado93]
On CD:	*Acrobat* PDF viewers for Macintosh, Windows, MS-DOS; *Common Ground* viewers for Macintosh, Windows; *Envoy* viewers for Macintosh, MS-DOS

exchange of PDF documents. However, PDF is better suited for electronic distribution. PDF stores just enough information about a font to allow the viewer to substitute a similar font, removing the need to include the actual font outlines in the PDF file.[1] PDF's hierarchical structure includes a directory at the end of the file, allowing any page to be rapidly located. Finally, PDF's structure is simpler and more restricted than PostScript, which makes PDF files much easier to read and understand.

Using PDF

Many desktop publishing programs can now create PDF files. Free PDF viewers are available from `ftp://ftp.adobe.com`. Adobe also sells its *Acrobat Distiller*, which can translate any PostScript file into an equivalent PDF file. On certain systems, this product allows any program to create PDF files by simply printing through the PostScript printer driver and converting the resulting file with Acrobat Distiller.

How PDF Works

A PDF file is a text file.[2] The first line of the file contains `%PDF-1.0`, where the number 1.0 refers to the current version of the PDF standard. The rest of the file is a sequence of numbered *objects*. At the end of a file is a cross-reference table that allows an application to locate any specific object in the file. The cross-reference table specifies the byte offset in the file of each numbered object. A reading application starts at the end of the PDF file, where a trailer specifies the location of the cross-reference table and object number of the "root" object. Each object reference is an object number, which can be looked up in the cross-reference table. By following object references from the root

---

[1]PDF stores the font *metrics*—the width and height of each character—which can be used to scale another font to fit. This information is insufficient for special symbol fonts. In that case, PDF stores outlines for only those characters necessary to display the document.

[2]Curiously, despite being a purely text format, PDF files should always be transferred as binary data. The damage caused by text transfer can be easily repaired by savvy PDF-reading applications, but binary transfer helps avoid even minor problems.

object, every object in the document (including individual pages, thumbnails, and an optional outline) can be quickly accessed.

This structure allows an application to rapidly find any particular item in the file, without keeping the entire file in memory or scanning the entire file from the beginning. Another advantage of this indirection is that objects can be updated by appending a revised copy of the object to the end of the file and extending the cross-reference table. PDF allows the cross-reference table to be in several pieces, with later pieces superseding earlier ones. A PDF file can be incrementally modified (for example, to add annotations) without changing any of the original data.

Larger objects are compressed, to save size, and encoded so that PDF files can be easily transferred through mail or other text-oriented mechanisms. After being decoded and decompressed, the lowest-level objects contain graphics instructions similar to those used in PostScript.

Strengths and Weaknesses

PDF is a *physical markup system* (see page 24). Like a fax, you can't easily reformat a PDF document, although you can usually copy text and graphics from the PDF file into another document. PDF is a good choice when the precise formatting must be preserved. Some publishing houses are considering various forms of "on-demand" publishing, in which books or leaflets are printed only when needed, rather than the current scheme of printing tens of thousands of copies to be kept in a warehouse. Many large companies want to make formatted manuals available online so they can be printed out whenever needed. PDF is well-suited to this type of distribution.

Adobe has proposed PDF as a format for publishing on the World Wide Web. However, as a physical markup system, it's not particularly well-suited for this type of work. PDF files are rigid, and can't easily be reformatted to suit the requirements of various output devices. Having to scroll the document from side-to-side on a low-resolution screen is awkward at best; it's far more appropriate to use a *logical markup system* (see page 24) which allows the text to be reformatted to suit the output device.

Of course, it's much easier to convert existing documents into PDF than to insert the logical markup necessary to convert them into a less rigid format. This makes PDF a good choice for publishing pre-existing documents on the World Wide Web. Many of these documents are in PostScript or word-processor formats.

PDF vs. PostScript

PDF includes all of the basic graphics and drawing capabilities of PostScript, which allows you to do very sophisticated graphics in PDF. Indeed, any PostScript page description can be converted into a PDF file. Conversely, any PDF file can be converted into a PostScript file for printing.

Despite this fundamental similarity, PDF and PostScript are intended for different uses. PDF's hierarchical structure makes it easy to find particular pieces in a file on disk, but difficult to display a file as it becomes available. Conversely, PostScript is designed to be displayed as it is read. This distinction makes PDF ideal for online display and browsing, but makes PostScript better for printing. PDF and PostScript should be looked at as a complementary pair of formats: one for electronic distribution, the other for printing.

Alternatives to PDF

PDF is not the only file format designed to fill this niche. Common Ground Software's *DigitalPaper* (which uses extension .dp) and Novell's *Envoy* (which uses extension .evy) are formats that provide similar functionality.

More Information

Adobe has thoroughly documented the PDF format in its *Portable Document Format Reference Manual* [Ado93]. Adobe also distributes free viewer programs that allow users of Macintosh, Windows, MS-DOS, and Sun Solaris to read PDF files. Some information is also available on Adobe's World Wide Web site at http://www.adobe.com.

The newest version of GhostScript (see page 106) supports PDF files.

Envoy information is available from http://www.novell.com. Digital-Paper information is available from http://www.commonground.com.

Word Processors 10

The "text" formats people deal with most frequently are the common word processor formats. If two people use the same word processor or desktop publisher program, it makes perfect sense for them to exchange word processor files. Be careful, though, because there are some hidden traps.

One thing that deserves some inspection is whether the word processor has an alternate text-based format. Framemaker's *MIF* (Maker Interchange Format) and Microsoft's *RTF* (Rich Text Format) are text versions of their standard binary word processor formats. Although these text versions don't always store the same information, they are often easier to transfer between different computers. Such formats are also more likely to be supported by other software. RTF, in particular, has been documented by Microsoft and is supported by several non-Microsoft word processors.

While many people regularly exchange word processor files with no problems at all, many people do run into obstacles:

- Many programs claim to read and write competing formats. Such support varies widely. Your document can lose most of the formatting (fonts, alignment) when you use this method.

- Different versions of the same program can't always trade files easily. Going from a newer version to an older version is especially problematic.

- It's not always easy to exchange files between the same program on different systems. Macintosh and Windows versions of a word processor don't necessarily read and write the same files.

- Worse, even with the same word processor on the same system, files don't always transfer correctly. For example, people who exchange files between Western and Eastern Europe have discovered that popular word processors don't always mark the font encoding used. The different font encodings used in these countries cause the file to appear as gibberish when opened in a different national version of the same program and operating system.

Before deciding what format to use to send a file to someone else, try to figure out what they'll do with the file.

- If the recipient is just going to print it, you can send PostScript (if a PostScript printer is available) or PDF. (You may even be able to include a copy of the freely available PDF viewer.) Fax machines also work well in this case.

- Many publishers and magazines that have to accept files from a variety of people end up purchasing "one of each" so that they can read many word processor formats. Frequently, they read the file into the word processor, export it as plain ASCII, import the ASCII into a publishing system, and then manually reformat the document. In this case, you should just send a plain ASCII file. If the formatting is critical, send a printout as well.

The best approach is to make sure you know what software they have before you try to send them a file. If you're going to publish something on the Internet or World Wide Web, you don't know what software the recipients might have. You may want to try to offer the file in several different formats: a word processor format, a printer format (such as PostScript), and a plain ASCII format.

More Information

Günter Born's *File Formats Handbook* [Bor95] covers many proprietary word processor formats in detail.

Part Two
Graphics Formats

About Graphics   *11*

The computers on display in your local computer store aren't running demonstrations of word processors and spreadsheets. They're showing graphics, ranging from simple slide shows to animated games to full-motion recorded video. Similarly, on most electronic services, the most popular items to download are graphics. For many years, the Internet has been used as a repository for images, ranging from astronomical and medical images to photographs of a proud parent's new baby. One could even make a case that the current enormous popularity of the World Wide Web is in large part due to the fact that it's one of the first widely available Internet services supporting integrated graphics.

There are an enormous number of different file formats used for graphics, including some of the formats I discussed in Part One (such as PostScript and PDF). One reason for this variety is that many program authors create simple formats of their own rather than adopting more complex "standard" formats. Another reason is that steady improvements in computer hardware have altered expectations. In the early 1980s, CompuServe's online service had a standard graphics format that supported black and white pictures up to 256 by 192 pixels. When a large number of computers had better graphics support, they replaced that format with one that supported much larger images with up to 256 colors. CompuServe is now adopting the new PNG format (see page 139) to support even higher-quality images. As graphics hardware, storage capacity, and modem speeds continue to improve, there is also increasing interest in formats such as TIFF that once were used almost exclusively by professional graphics designers.

Color and Resolution

Another reason for the variety of graphics formats is that different kinds of pictures lend themselves naturally to different kinds of storage. The most obvious two properties of an image are its *color depth* and *resolution*. Briefly, color depth refers to the number of different colors that can be in a picture. Resolution refers to the number of pixels in the picture.

Images from a fax machine or the most common printers are *bilevel* images; they only have two colors, usually black and white. The next step up is *grayscale*. Grayscale images are typically characterized by the number of bits used for each pixel. For example, a four bit per pixel (bpp) image can have sixteen (2^4) different shades of gray, including pure black and pure white. A sixteen bpp image can have over 65,000 (2^{16}) shades of gray.

Color images are often preferred to bilevel or grayscale. The simplest way to store a color image is to store the precise color of each separate pixel. This method is usually referred to as *direct color* or *true color*. Typically, a single color requires either 24 or 32 bits per pixel, which is a lot of memory. A 1024 by 768 pixel screen that uses 32 bits per pixel requires three megabytes of memory. A 1600 by 1200 screen, commonly used by professional graphics designers, requires over seven megabytes of memory if you store the color directly. Such a large amount of data creates many problems. Not only does the data require a lot of video memory, it requires a lot of disk storage for the images, and it creates design problems for the video card, monitor, and even the video cable. That 1600 by 1200 screen requires the video card to transfer over 500 megabytes of picture data from video memory to the monitor every second!

To reduce memory requirements and simplify the design of video cards, many systems use a *color look-up table* (CLUT). In this approach, only eight bits are stored for each pixel, allowing 256 colors. The video circuitry stores a table that converts each of these numbers into a different color. As long as you don't need more than 256 colors at one time, you get the same results as a direct color approach, but with only one-third of the memory requirement. The CLUT method even has an interesting advantage. Because the color table can be quickly reprogrammed, you can do a simple form of animation by altering the colors. This type of animation is very simple and fast, since the actual picture data is never altered.

As you can see, there is a trade-off between color depth (the number of bits per pixel) and resolution. Greater color depth requires more memory, which typically restricts the resolution you can use, and vice versa. Fortunately, this trade-off also appears in the human visual system. With clever programming, grayscale screens appear to have higher resolution by using shades of gray to smooth out the jagged edges. Conversely, high resolution screens can use "dithering" or "halftoning" techniques to increase the apparent color depth, effectively blending two or more colors.

Kinds of Colors

There is a theory that the human retina has three different kinds of color receptors, one sensitive to red light, one to green light, and one to blue light. This theory is the origin of the popular *RGB* (Red-Green-Blue) system of specifying colors. Color computer monitors use three electron beams to elicit light from three different colors of phosphors. By varying the intensity of the electron beams, you can generate different intensities of red, green, and blue light. Most computer video hardware uses this approach directly; a color is specified to the video hardware by setting levels for each of these three color channels.[1]

The RGB system is simple, but it doesn't work for all devices. Ink on paper, for example, reflects light instead of producing it. Color printers must instead use the "opposite" colors: cyan, magenta, and yellow (*CMY*). In theory, these three inks, printed on bright white paper, can produce the same range of colors as an RGB monitor. In practice, you can't produce a really dark black this way, so printers usually add black ink (*K*), which gives the familiar *CMYK* four-color system used in most color printing. Even with this addition, CMYK printing can't reproduce every color. Very high-quality printing will often augment CMYK with other ink colors to reproduce specific colors accurately. If you tear open the flaps on the bottom of your cereal box, you'll find test patterns that show the ink colors used to print that box.

---

[1]Conventional wisdom says that eight bits is sufficient for each color channel. As a result, 24 bits per pixel has become the standard for high-end color graphics. Computer researchers and some graphics professionals do use 48 bits per pixel or more, although such "deep-pixel" images are usually converted to 24 bits per pixel before they are displayed.

A problem that both RGB and CMYK share is that, although they do seem to match how the human eye works, they don't really match how we think about color. When we see a color, we don't see a mixture of three or four colors, but rather a single *hue*, with a certain *saturation* and *value*. Saturation is how "strong" the color is; a red sports car is very saturated while a pale pink rose is very unsaturated. Totally unsaturated colors are shades of gray. Value is how "light" or "dark" the color is; a cherry soda has a high value; a red wine has a low value. A zero value is black. Artists and graphics designers often want to deal directly with these *HSV* (Hue-Saturation-Value) colors, rather than the less-intuitive RGB or CMYK systems.

Unfortunately, none of the above color systems is perfectly standardized; an RGB color of (51,27,31) will give slightly different colors on different monitors. Two systems that are totally standard are the *CIE XYZ* color system and the *Pantone* system. The CIE XYZ color system is defined in terms of specific wavelengths of light, so a particular set of numbers always define the exact same color. Pantone is a commercial system of numbered colors; printed samples can be purchased that are guaranteed by the manufacturer to be exactly the same color as all other samples with that name.

Converting between these various systems is difficult in practice. Although simple formulas can be used to get approximate conversions, these formulas are frustrated by many issues. The most obvious problem is that not all color-producing devices behave identically. For example, different computer monitors use phosphors that have slightly different colors. Even a pure red on two different monitors may look distinctly different. The situation is worse when you try to convert between different types of devices. RGB Monitors can produce colors that CMYK printers cannot. Correct translation from RGB to CMYK sometimes requires significant care to maintain the overall appearance of a picture, even if the technical accuracy of the color conversion is sacrificed. Finally, no color device, including the human eye, is completely linear. Doubling the intensity of an electron beam doesn't produce precisely twice as much light from the monitor. Even if it did, you wouldn't perceive precisely "twice as much color." The exact relations are complex and not completely understood.

Most popular graphics formats use the RGB system to specify colors. Because RGB is not standardized, the formats used by graphics professionals try to do more. Sometimes these formats use a different color system; PostScript can accept CIE XYZ colors. Sometimes these formats include extra information so that the recipient can decipher the RGB numbers; TIFF images can specify the original RGB phosphor colors in terms of another CIE color system.

Besides the color itself, another piece of information that can be useful is the *transparency* or *alpha*. Images are almost always stored as rectangles. If you overlay a picture of a rose on top of the image of a table, you don't want a black rectangle surrounding the rose. Many graphics formats allow you to specify parts of the picture as transparent, typically with a special "color" in the picture.[2] Sometimes, you need to specify that parts of the picture will blend with what is underneath; this way you can see part of the lunch counter through the cherry soda. The alpha of a pixel indicates the opacity of that spot. A completely opaque pixel obscures what is behind it; a completely transparent one is invisible. An intermediate value blends with the background, such as the cherry soda that makes the counter behind it look pinkish.

Kinds of Images

One reason there are so many ways to describe color is that there are many different kinds of pictures. Charlie Brown's striped shirt does not need to be exactly the same shade of red in every newspaper's Sunday comics. On the other hand, a movie poster that displays a sexy starlet with a slight greenish tint to her skin could seriously impact the box-office earnings.

The kind of picture has many other effects as well. People who work with graphics generally distinguish three kinds of pictures. *Bilevel* (black and white) images generally contain text and other solid lines and simple patterns. *Line art* or *synthetic* images are like cartoons; they usually have only a few colors with lines and simple patterns, and are often stored using a color look-up table. Finally, *continuous tone* or *photographic* images have smoothly varying shades. Note that continuous tone images can be either grayscale or color.

Different kinds of images can be handled in different ways. For example, line art often can be reduced to a set of drawing commands specifying lines

---

[2]This approach is similar to the "blue screen" used in television and motion picture production. A particular shade of blue is interpreted by some television equipment as "transparent." Your TV weather forecaster is actually walking in front of a blue curtain that tells the television equipment to let the weather map "show through." This technique can produce amusing effects if her clothes happen to be the same color as the curtain.

and colors of areas. Continuous tone images usually cannot be reduced to a set of simple drawing commands. Also, color accuracy is usually more important for continuous tone photographs than synthetic images.

Compression

Even a single picture can require significant amounts of storage. But one picture rarely stands alone; a product catalog on the World Wide Web might have thousands of images of different products. To reduce these storage requirements, an enormous amount of work has gone into finding ways to *compress* images.

One Size Doesn't Fit All

Like many other aspects of image handling, different types of compression are suitable for different types of pictures. For bilevel images, two general compression approaches are used. The first approach is *run-length encoding*. Because bilevel images typically contain areas of a solid color, they can often be described as repetitions, or *runs*, of a single color. Instead of listing the black and white pixels on a line, you might instead say "27 white, 3 black, 48 white, 23 black, … " This idea is used by the common Group 3 fax compression. Another approach is to consider the *context* of each pixel. If you look at several nearby pixels, you'll find that you can often predict the color of the next pixel. This idea is used by the new JBIG compression method.[3]

Run-length encoding can also be effective on simple color images. Generally, however, other methods work better. Most compression methods for images with 256 or fewer colors use standard compression techniques as a starting point, and augment them with a few simple tricks. One trick is to remember that images are, in fact, two-dimensional, while standard compression techniques deal only with a one-dimensional list of pixels. These compression methods fail to take advantage of the vertical redundancy in most images. To exploit this redundancy, you could list the pixels on the first line of the image,

---

[3]JBIG stands for the Joint BIlevel Experts Group, the name of a group formed specifically to develop an effective compression method for bilevel images.

then list the numerical differences between successive rows of the image. Vertical similarities will show up as zero values in the differences, and these zero values compress very well. This type of preprocessing is often referred to as a *predictor*. A predictor is a simple function that tries to guess the next pixel value.

A successful predictor can greatly improve compression. Intuitively, anything the predictor can successfully predict doesn't need to be stored, since the decompressor can use the same predictor to guess those pixels correctly. Only pixels the predictor gets wrong need be stored. In practice, a predictor such as "each pixel is the same as the previous pixel" can work remarkably well. Simple images have blocks of solid colors, and this predictor will always be right within such blocks. Essentially, only the edges of solid color blocks will need to be stored. (This predictor is essentially just doing run-length encoding.)

The combination of predictors and standard compression methods can also work well on continuous tone images. Of course, the predictors are more sophisticated; one popular predictor averages several nearby pixels. Many continuous tone images come from photographs, however, and any physical process (such as a camera, scanner, or camcorder) will introduce *noise*. Technically, noise is random variations. Usually, this noise doesn't impact the image—in fact, it's very often completely invisible to the eye—but it does make the image more difficult to compress.

Lossy Compression

One way to address the noise problem is to use *lossy compression*. Lossy compression deliberately throws out some data in order to obtain better compression. The challenge is to remove data that does not impact the appearance of the image but does help improve the compressibility.

There's another way to think about lossy compression. The way a computer screen draws a picture, by specifying the color of each pixel, does not match how the human visual system works. The human retina has several layers of neurons that, in essence, preprocess the image seen by the eye, altering the image data into a form that's easier for the brain to understand. In the process, some visual data is lost. Because this data will be removed by your eye before you "see" the image, you don't need to store that data on your hard disk.

JPEG (see page 157) is one of the best-known lossy compression methods. It is based on the fact that the human eye is more sensitive to changes in brightness than in color, and more sensitive to gradations of color than to rapid variations within that gradation. JPEG maintains most of the brightness information while dropping some color information, and retains gradual changes of color while throwing out some more rapid variations in color. As a result, JPEG is very effective at compressing continuous tone images, but introduces noticeable distortion around the sharp edges of many synthetic images (where rapid variations in color are important). While JPEG's compression is impressive, it is not a substitute for the many "lossless" compression techniques developed for other types of images.

More Information

There are several excellent books on graphics storage and file formats. James D. Murray and William vanRyper's *Encyclopedia of Graphics File Formats* [Mv94] has comprehensive coverage of a variety of different graphics formats. It covers over one hundred graphics formats, and the accompanying CD-ROM includes official specifications, source code, sample images, and viewers for a variety of platforms.

Mark Nelson's *The Data Compression Book* [Nel92] is an excellent introduction to the principles of data compression.

If you're interested in programming for these formats, you may want to examine Jef Poskanzer's *PBM* (Portable BitMap) collection. This collection includes a programming library of generic bitmap manipulation routines and a suite of programs that can convert between a huge variety of different formats. See page 179 for more information.

Graphics viewer programs are plentiful, and most major archive sites have several from which to choose. The SIMTEL archives have MS-DOS viewers and utilities under `msdos/graphics`. Viewers for Unix machines running X are available from `ftp.x.org` in the various `contrib` directories. Graphics utilities are also available from `ftp.uu.net`; look especially in the `graphics` and `usenet/comp.sources.x` directories. Macintosh graphics utilities are on the Info-Mac archives in the `_Graphic_&_Sound_Tool/_Graphic` directory.

ASCII Graphics

In the excitement of new technology, many people forget that the Internet is primarily a communications tool. Fancy formats and sophisticated compression are useless if the person receiving your file can't make sense of it.

The one format that is almost universally understood is seven-bit ASCII text, and you can use the variety of different punctuation and letter shapes to draw simple diagrams and figures. With a little creativity, you can create very interesting designs in this way. A good place to look for creative uses of this type of graphics is in the "signatures" that many people routinely append to their news and mail postings.

How to Use ASCII Graphics

The simplest forms of ASCII graphics are rectangular diagrams using |, -, and _ for vertical and horizontal lines, and + for intersections of lines. This approach is often used to draw simple maps, boxes, and tables. For example, Figure 12.1 shows one way to create the table from page 72 using ASCII graphics.[1] Notice the use of all capital letters for the table heading. Capital letters in plain text are used for emphasis.

ASCII graphics have even found their way into formal standards. One of the goals of HTML (HyperText Markup Language) is to support text-only terminals, which requires tables and mathematics to be displayed using ASCII

---

[1]This table was adapted from an example in *UNIX in a Nutshell* [Gil92].

```
+--------------------------------------------+
|              HORIZONTAL LOCAL MOTIONS       |
+----------+---------------------------------+
|          |             Effects in          |
| Function +---------------+-------------+
|          |     TROFF     |    NROFF    |
+----------+---------------+-------------+
| \h'n'    | Move distance N             |
| \(space) | Unpaddable space-size space |
| \0       | Digit-size space            |
+----------+---------------+-------------+
| \|       | 1/6 em space  | ignored     |
| \^       | 1/12 em space | ignore      |
+----------+---------------+-------------+
```

Figure 12.1   Example Table Using ASCII Graphics[1]

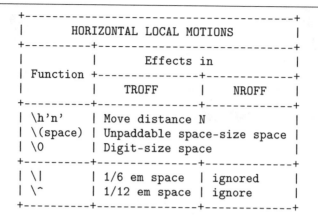

Figure 12.2   Mathematics Using ASCII Graphics

graphics. Figure 12.1 shows how a table might be displayed on a text terminal. On page 53, I gave several examples of HTML mathematics and showed how they might look when typeset. On a text terminal, they could be displayed as shown in Figure 12.2.

With a little practice, it's relatively easy to create this type of image. By expanding your repertoire to include angled lines (/ and \), various arrows (<^>v), and the creative use of other punctuation, you can create maps and other types of line graphics, as shown in Figure 12.3.

More abstract graphics are also possible. Many people now decorate their mail messages with graphical "signatures," similar to Figure 12.4. Elaborate images of animals, cars, planes, and even stylized self-portraits have been condensed into five or six lines of ASCII graphics.

```
Highway 25     |
======================================
               |
               |Green Road
Left Turn --> _____
                      \ <-- Right Turn
         River        |
         ~~~~~~~~~)|(~~~~~~~~~~~~
                  ^ | Bridge
About 2.5 miles | |
                | | +
MY HOUSE! >---------->*   v | O Church
7234 Red Road        ---------|
Phone: 555-1234          ^    |
                         |    |
                    Red Road  |
```

Figure 12.3   A Map Drawn with ASCII Graphics

Figure 12.4   A Signature

One of the earliest examples of computer graphics was a scheme for producing graphics on old line printers. By overstriking characters, it's possible to produce black blocks (for example, ▓ was created by overstriking *O/\=WM); different combinations of overstruck characters produce different darknesses of block. By combining such blocks, you can create remarkably high-quality grayscale images on wide printers. Many old computer rooms were decorated with images of the Statue of Liberty or Albert Einstein produced in this way. Figure 12.5 should give you the general idea. (It helps if you hold this picture at arms length and squint.)

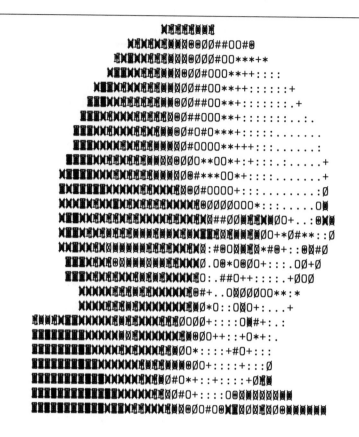

Figure 12.5   An Example of "Line Printer Art"

More Information

Jan Wolter's cursive program can automatically generate script text similar to that shown in Figure 12.4. It's available in C source form from Volume 2 of the comp.sources.games archives. These archives are available on ftp://ftp.digital.com.

---

[2]Image copied from a signature seen on Usenet.

GIF

13

CompuServe's *Graphics Interchange Format* (GIF) is one of the most widely used graphics file formats. It is currently in use on nearly every platform, and is the standard image format used on the World Wide Web. Designed in 1987, GIF overshadowed formats such as MacPaint or PCX for several reasons. First, GIF was designed to be used on many platforms. It explicitly includes all of the information needed to display the image and omits features that would only be useful on a handful of systems. Second, GIF uses a powerful compression algorithm (LZW) with a freely-available implementation (the Unix compress program). Finally, CompuServe successfully encouraged the development of GIF viewers and translators for many systems.

CompuServe introduced GIF to fill a very specific need. CompuServe's *Special Interest Groups* (SIGs) attracted users of a huge variety of different computer systems. They needed a format for storing color graphics that would be usable on all of these different systems. CompuServe also wanted a compact format that could be downloaded quickly and displayed during download.

GIF at a Glance

Name:	GIF, Graphics Interchange Format
Extension:	.gif
Use For:	Exchanging eight-bit graphics
Reference:	CompuServe's definitions of the GIF format
On CD:	Various graphics viewers, converters, GIF specifications

No existing format really filled this requirement. Popular graphics formats on many systems assumed resolutions or color depth (such as 320x200 with 16 colors) appropriate for a specific computer system. Similarly, many graphics formats either used no compression at all, or used simple run-length encoding techniques that only offered modest compression.

In contrast, GIF supports any resolution up to 65,536 by 65,536 and any color depth from 1 to 8 bits per pixel. It uses the 12-bit LZW compression algorithm (see page 185), which offers good compression and requires less than 16 kilobytes of memory for compression or decompression, making it useful on all but the smallest microcomputers. GIF makes some concessions to simplify implementations. It uses a color table (or palette) for every picture. Also, it only stores information that is useful on nearly every system, omitting such things as an alpha channel or animation information.

Although designed primarily for viewing online graphics, GIF support was quickly added to a variety of applications. Today, GIF is probably the single most widely supported graphics format.

When to Use GIF

GIF is generally a good choice for exchanging pictures between systems. BBS systems and Internet sites frequently contain archives of GIF images. GIF is widely supported by many graphical applications, including all graphical World Wide Web browsers.

However, GIF does have an important limitation: It does not support more than eight bits per pixel. Generally, eight bits per pixel is fine for synthetic images such as cartoons and drawings, which tend to use fewer colors, or for small images, where it's easier for an application to select 256 colors that can accurately represent the image. For large photographic images, however, the JPEG or TIFF formats may be better (see pages 157 and 149, respectively).

While the LZW compression algorithm used by GIF is one of the better general-purpose compression algorithms, it wasn't designed specifically for graphics. It doesn't work very well for bilevel (black and white) or true color images. For bilevel images, fax-style Group 3 or Group 4 compression (supported by TIFF) or JBIG compression generally work better. Similarly, JPEG is often better for continuous tone photographic images.

Recognizing GIF Files

The first six bytes of a GIF file are the version identifier, either GIF87a or GIF89a.

How to Use GIF

The GIF format has two variants. The first official version of GIF was *GIF87a*, named after the year when the official description was published. The format was later updated to provide a handful of additional features; the new version is called *GIF89a*. By now, most programs that read GIF files support GIF89a, although a handful of older programs don't handle the newer extensions.

The features added by GIF89a are not particularly exciting. GIF89a adds the ability to include text (either text overlays or text comments) with the file, overlay multiple images from a single file, specify a "transparent" color, or include additional application-specific information. When none of these features is needed, a good GIF writing program will create a GIF87a file (which is identical to a GIF89a file except for the version and the lack of GIF89a extension blocks), which helps simplify portability. As a result, even programs that only understand GIF87a can comfortably handle most of the images found on the Internet and elsewhere.

GIF allows the graphics data to be stored in two different orders. The normal order stores the lines of data consecutively from top to bottom. The other order, known as *interlaced*, stores every eighth row, then every fourth, and so on. When displaying interlaced GIF images, you have a rough preview with only one-eighth of the data available. This is especially useful for applications where pictures are displayed as they are received, such as with World Wide Web browsers. When you have an option, store GIF files in the interlaced form.

GIF's LZW compression is very similar to the compression used by popular archiving programs. As a result, it's rarely useful to attempt to further compress a GIF file.[1]

---

[1]If you attempt to compress something twice with the same method, you rarely obtain any significant additional compression. See page 250 for a lengthier discussion of this phenomenon.

Block ID	Block Name		
hex 2C	Image (comma)		
hex 3B	End-of-file (semicolon)		
hex 21	Extension (!)		
	SubID	**Description**	
	hex 01	Plain text	
	hex F9	Graphic control	
	hex FE	Comment extension	
	hex FF	Application extension	

Table 13.1   GIF Block Types

Legal Issues

When CompuServe designed GIF, they apparently were unaware that the LZW compression algorithm they chose was patented. For many years, this patent was of little concern, but in 1994, Unisys (who currently owns one of the patents on LZW) reached an agreement with CompuServe about licensing the LZW compression algorithm for use with GIF. This agreement affects everyone who has written software to read or write GIF files.

This change in the legal landscape has created a flurry of interest in replacing GIF with a newer format that does not use a patented compression algorithm. PNG (the Portable Network Graphics format, discussed in the next chapter) is one proposed alternative. Replacing GIF will be difficult, however. Not only is GIF widely available, it is thoroughly understood by developers, and is fairly simple to read and write.

How GIF Works

A GIF file is organized as a header followed by a series of blocks. The header holds general information about the pictures, including a color table that applies to all images in the file. Each block begins with one or two bytes that identify the type of block. Table 13.1 lists the block types currently supported by GIF.

Size	Description
3	GIF
3	Version, currently either 87a or 89a
2	Width of screen
2	Height of screen
1	Screen and color information

	Bits	Description
	0–2	Size of global palette
	3	1 if palette is sorted
	4–6	Color resolution (number of bits minus 1)
	7	1 if there is a global palette

Size	Description
1	Background color
1	Aspect ratio
3×n	Global palette

Table 13.2 GIF Header

GIF Header

GIF's header, detailed in Table 13.2, is divided into three sections. The *signature* is used to identify GIF files. The *Logical Screen Descriptor* describes the screen assumed by the file. The third section contains the default color palette.

The signature is six bytes. The first three bytes are always GIF and the next three bytes are the version. Currently, the version is either 87a or 89a.

One idea underlying a multi-image GIF file is that a particular file is intended for display on a certain kind of screen. The header describes that "ideal" screen, including the resolution (no picture in the file is larger than this size), color depth, aspect ratio, background color, and default color palette. Each successive picture from the file will be displayed on the same screen.

One interesting optimization is that the palette size and color resolution are stored in a very compact manner. Since palettes are typically a power of two in size, GIF stores one less than the power. For a screen with two colors, GIF stores a zero for the color resolution ($2 = 2^{0+1}$). For a screen with 256 colors, GIF stores a seven for the color resolution ($256 = 2^{7+1}$). This method allows GIF to store the palette size and color resolution in only three bits.[2]

---

[2]Of course, many pictures won't require a palette that's precisely a power of two in size, so GIF's scheme wastes several bytes storing additional palette entries just so it can save a few

Size	Description
1	Block type: hex 2C
2	X position of image on screen
2	Y position of image on screen
2	Width of image
2	Height of image
1	Image information

Bits	Description
0	1 if there is a local palette
1	1 if image is interlaced
2	1 if palette is sorted
3–4	Reserved: always zero
5–7	Size of local palette

Size	Description
3×n	Local palette (optional)
	Sub-blocks containing compressed image data

Table 13.3   GIF Image

GIF Terminator

The last block in any GIF file consists of a single semicolon (hex 3B).

GIF Image

An image block, detailed in Table 13.3, contains three sections. The first section describes the image and how it is stored in the file. The second (optional) section is a color palette that applies to only this image. The third section is the actual picture data.

Each image in a GIF file is displayed on the screen indicated in the header. However, each image does not necessarily contain the same color palette, nor is each image necessarily the same size. A single GIF file can hold a "slide show" in which successive images overlay different parts of the full picture. Note that this type of partial overlay requires the use of a global palette, because few systems can use different palettes for different parts of the screen.

---

bits on the palette size. Ultimately, though, any wastage or savings in this part of the file will be dwarfed by the size of the graphics data, so it's not an important issue in any case.

The actual image data is contained in a series of *sub-blocks*. Each sub-block contains a one-byte count, followed by the indicated number of bytes. A sub-block with a count of zero marks the end of the compressed image data. The sub-block boundaries have no relation to the graphics data; conceptually, the data from all of the sub-blocks is strung together and decompressed into a series of pixels. Those pixels are then divided into separate scan lines and placed on the screen. In practice, of course, these operations are frequently interwoven so that data can be decompressed and placed onto the screen as quickly as it is available.

GIF Extension Blocks

All GIF extension blocks have the same general format. This format makes it easy to simply skip any extension block that a reader doesn't recognize. A GIF extension block starts with hex 21 (an exclamation mark), which is followed by a one byte extension type (see Table 13.1) and a series of sub-blocks. Just as with an image block, the end of the extension block is indicated by a sub-block with a count of zero. For most extension types, the first sub-block is somewhat special, containing specific information about this extension block.

Comment Extension

The simplest extension block is the *comment extension block*. The sub-blocks simply contain ASCII text. These comments are not intended to be displayed as part of the image. A GIF-savvy reader will usually show these comments in a separate window or screen only when the user asks to see them.

Text Extension

A multi-image GIF file can be looked upon as either a slide show or a set of images that must be combined to produce a single picture. A *text extension block* allows text to form an image of its own, or serve as an overlay of another graphic image. Storing text explicitly requires less space than the graphic equivalent, and allows programs to search GIF files for specific text strings. Also, the quality is usually much higher; the decoder may have to make compromises to effectively display the graphic image, but it can always display text characters using the highest quality supported by the hardware. In particular,

Size	Description
2	X position of start of text area
2	Y position of start of text area
2	Width of text area in pixels
2	Height of text area in pixels
1	Character width in pixels
1	Character height in pixels
1	Palette number of text foreground color
1	Palette number of text background color

Table 13.4   GIF Text Extension Data

decoders may use dithering or halftoning to simulate unavailable colors when decoding the graphics data. Dithering often renders text completely illegible. By specifying the text separately, the decoder can dither the graphic image, but draw the text in a solid color to improve legibility.

For consistent results, you must make sure the text is displayed in the same position and at approximately the same size by all decoders. The first sub-block of the text extension block specifies the size and position of the text. It contains the data described in Table 13.4. Remaining sub-blocks contain the actual text data, using the US ASCII character encoding.

Graphics Control Extension

Multi-image files were not very widely used with GIF87a, partly because it was never clear what to do with multiple images. GIF89a resolves this problem by allowing any image (or text extension block) to be immediately preceded by a *graphics control extension block*. This block essentially informs the decoder how the following image interacts with the rest of the images. It specifies what the decoder should do after the following image or text is displayed:

- The image may be erased to the background color.
- The previous image may be restored.
- The decoder might wait for user input before proceeding.
- The decoder might wait for a period of time before proceeding.

Size	Description
1	What to do when graphic is finished

Bits	Description
0	1 if there is a transparent color
1	1 if decoder should wait for user
2	1 to leave graphic on screen when done
3	1 to erase graphic to background color
4	1 to restore previous image
5–7	Reserved: always zero

Size	Description
2	Delay after this image (100ths of seconds)
1	Treat this palette color as transparent

Table 13.5   GIF Graphics Control Extension Data

A graphics control extension block contains a single sub-block of four bytes. Its contents are described in Table 13.5.

Application Extension

Because so many people use GIF for so many different purposes, GIF89a includes *application extension blocks* to allow individual applications to store any information they want within the GIF file. This extension block may be used to specify a variety of application or system specific data. The first sub-block is always eleven bytes. It specifies two codes, an eight-byte ASCII code and a three-byte binary code that an application can use to identify extensions that it understands.

More Information

CompuServe's detailed GIF specifications [GIF87, Gra90] are available from `ftp://x2ftp.oulu.fi/pub/msdos/programming/formats`.

PNG

14

While CompuServe's Graphics Interchange Format (GIF) is probably the most widely used graphics format in existence (see page 129), it has developed a few leaks. The increasing availability of 24-bit graphics boards makes GIF's limit of eight bits per pixel look a bit miserly. Worse, the LZW compression algorithm used by GIF is patented. For many years, this patent was not a problem, but in 1994 Unisys (who owns the patent on LZW) began to collect royalties from developers who use GIF.

A large group of software developers have designed the *Portable Network Graphics* (PNG) format as a successor to GIF. Like GIF, PNG (pronounced "ping") is usable on a wide variety of platforms, omitting features that are usable on only a few systems. Unlike GIF, PNG is unencumbered by patents, and it supports up to 64 bits per pixel. PNG also adds a handful of new features, such as transparency information (alpha), improved compression, and other options that will make PNG viable for many years.

This chapter is based on an article first published in *PC Techniques*, June/July 1995.

PNG at a Glance	
Name:	PNG, Portable Network Graphics
Extension:	`.png`
Use For:	Eight-bit and 24-bit graphics
Reference:	`http://sunsite.unc.edu/boutell`
On CD:	Various graphics viewers, converters

When to Use PNG

PNG is a good candidate to replace GIF. It does almost everything that GIF does (PNG doesn't support multiple images), and a few things that GIF doesn't but arguably should (PNG supports 24 bit per pixel direct color images). Like GIF, PNG files can be read and displayed incrementally. PNG files have an "interlaced" mode similar in concept to GIF's (see page 131), which makes them a good candidate for the World Wide Web and other systems where incremental display is important. Royalty-free source code to read and write PNG files is freely available, so it should be easy for developers to add PNG support to their applications. Finally, PNG is not subject to any patents, which makes it an attractive alternative to GIF in the eyes of many developers.

Before I look at the details of the PNG format, I'll discuss some of the things that PNG does *not* try to do. First, PNG does not support multiple images. The PNG designers decided that multiple image files were not common enough to justify the additional complexity. To reduce complexity further, PNG does not support any data except bitmapped graphics and text comments. Finally, PNG does not support "lossy" compression (see page 123). The PNG designers felt that JPEG was already an effective standard for lossy image compression.

How PNG Works

A PNG file consists of an eight-byte *signature* followed by a series of *chunks*. The signature is a fixed sequence of bytes that is specifically designed to let the reader detect common types of file corruption early. Each chunk contains a different piece of information about the picture, and within certain broad limits, the chunks can appear in any order. The name of the chunk uses a simple trick to help file readers intelligently deal with chunks they don't understand. Every chunk includes a 32-bit CRC to guard against corruption.

The use of individually labelled chunks for storing information was chosen for several reasons. First of all, no successful file format is static; extensions and changes are inevitable. But you don't want changes to the format to break existing programs. The easiest way to avoid this problem is to identify each piece of information. Programs can then simply ignore data they don't understand. This approach also allows the creation of simple utilities that, for

Decimal	137	80	78	71	13	10	26	10
Hexadecimal	89	50	4e	47	0d	0a	1a	0a
C notation	\211	P	N	G	\r	\n	\032	\n

Figure 14.1   PNG Signature

example, find and print out any text comments in the file. Such utilities need only know how to identify a chunk and how to deal with a few particular types of chunks. They don't need to understand many variants of the file format with different version numbers.

PNG Signature

PNG's file signature includes a number of tricks that other file format designers would do well to imitate. By design, the signature should be damaged if any part of the file is damaged; this property allows a PNG reader to immediately detect if the file has been corrupted. The most common types of corruption occur when transferring files: A PNG file might be transferred over a seven-bit connection, or it might be transferred as text, with automatic end-of-line translation. PNG's signature, shown in Figure 14.1, detects both types of damage. The inclusion of an eight-bit value, and two different kinds of end-of-line markers helps ensure that the signature will be damaged in the cases described above.

The signature also contains the name of the format in ASCII characters and a Control-Z byte, which is an end-of-file indicator on MS-DOS. This character will stop the file from being listed to the screen or printer on such a system.[1] Finally, the first two bytes of the signature differ from any other file format, so a PNG file can be detected based on just these two bytes.

PNG Chunks

Similar care was taken with the chunk design shown in Figure 14.2. A chunk consists of a four-byte length, a four-byte name, some data, and a four-byte

---

[1]On the two most common IBM PC code pages, code 137 is ë. As a result, an attempt to TYPE a PNG file to the screen under MS-DOS displays ëPNG.

CRC check. The length (like all numbers in a PNG file) is stored starting with the most significant byte. The name indicates the type of data in the chunk. The CRC is computed over both the name and data to detect corruption of the data.

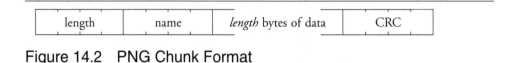

Figure 14.2   PNG Chunk Format

The PNG format can easily be extended by adding new chunks. There's no need to change the meaning of existing chunks. This approach allows old software to handle new files reasonably well. A problem occurs if the new chunks are actually critical to the meaning of the data. PNG uses the case of the four letters in the chunk name to indicate certain basic facts about the chunk. If the first letter is uppercase, the picture cannot be understood without understanding this chunk (an IDAT chunk contains the actual image data). If the first letter is lowercase, it's possible to get a useful image even if this chunk is not understood (a tEXt chunk contains a text comment). The case of the last letter indicates if an unrecognized chunk can be copied to a different file without modification. For example, a tEXt chunk can be copied to a different file; a tIME chunk with the last modification time of the file cannot be meaningfully copied. The second and third letters are always uppercase for the standard chunks. A lowercase second letter indicates a private or experimental chunk. These conventions allow programs to do simple surgery on PNG files without having to understand the complete format. They also allow programs to intelligently handle unrecognized chunks.

The four required chunk types (chunks with the first letter capitalized) are: IHDR, PLTE, IDAT, and IEND. The PNG signature is always followed immediately by the IHDR (Image Header) chunk. Following the IHDR are the PLTE (palette information) and a collection of optional chunks that carry a variety of information about the picture. The actual compressed picture data is held in one or more IDAT (Image Data) chunks, and an IEND (Image End) chunk marks the end of the file.

Image Header Chunk

Table 14.1 describes the information in the IHDR chunk. The bit depth indicates the number of bits in each picture sample. Unlike GIF, PNG only allows certain values. Color palette images may only contain 1, 2, 4, or 8 bits per pixel. Grayscale images without an alpha channel may contain 1, 2, 4, 8, or 16 bits per pixel. Other picture formats may only use 8 or 16 bits. The color type code indicates the type of picture, using three bits to indicate the presence of a palette, color, and alpha information. At one extreme, color type 0 with a bit depth of 1 is a plain black and white image. At the other extreme, color type 6 (color image with alpha channel and no palette) with a bit depth of 16 is a true color image with a total of 64 bits per pixel (16 bits each for red, green, blue, and alpha). A GIF-style palette image with 16 colors is color type 3 (color image with palette and no alpha) with a bit depth of 4. I'll discuss the filtering and interlacing later.

Picture Information Chunks

A number of chunks can be used to convey additional information about the picture. These chunks must all precede any IDAT image data chunks. The PLTE chunk is required for a palette image.

PLTE   This chunk carries a GIF-style color palette. The palette is simply a list of three-byte RGB colors.

sBIT   To speed decoding, PNG restricts the number of bits used to store each pixel to one of a handful of values. Some pictures use different color depths, however. While the actual color depth of the original picture isn't important for most decoders, some decoders can utilize this information. This chunk allows the encoder to specify the actual number of bits in the original color data.

pHYs   One common problem is that not all graphics devices have the same *aspect ratio*. The aspect ratio is the ratio of height to width. Currently, most

Size	Description
4	Picture width, in pixels
4	Picture height
1	Bit depth
1	Color type

Bit	Description
0	1 if palette is used
1	1 if image is color
2	1 if alpha channel included
3–7	Reserved

Size	Description
1	Compression. The only value defined in the first version of PNG is 0, indicating the image data is compressed in Ziplib format.
1	Type of filtering applied to the image before compression. In the first version of PNG, this must be 0, indicating a per-line adaptive scheme.
1	How the image is interlaced. No interlacing is indicated by 0; a value of 1 indicates an interlaced image.

Table 14.1   IHDR Chunk Information

monitors have square pixels and a 4:3 ratio of width-to-height overall. However, many printers and scanners have different horizontal and vertical resolutions. The pHYs chunk allows the encoder to specify the actual physical size and aspect ratio of the picture, so that the decoder can display the picture without it looking unnaturally tall or wide.

tRNS   One of PNG's features is that it allows for full transparency, which is necessary for correctly overlaying different types of graphics. However, specifying the precise transparency of each individual pixel is usually not necessary. The tRNS chunk allows for a simpler type of transparency. For palette images, the tRNS chunk specifies the transparency of each color in the palette. For grayscale and direct-color images, it specifies a single color that should be considered transparent.

bKGD   The bKGD chunk specifies the background color against which the image should be displayed.

hIST   If the decoder is not physically capable of displaying all of the colors in the image, it will have to somehow choose which colors to display. Most color-selection algorithms need to know how often each color appears in the picture. The problem is that this requirement prevents the decoder from displaying the picture as it arrives; it must first have the entire picture available before it can analyze the colors to decide how to display it. The only way to prevent this delay is for the encoder to provide this statistical information in advance. The hIST chunk allows the encoder to record the relative frequency of each color in the image, so that the decoder can decide how to display the image before it begins to receive and decode the image data.

gAMA   The gAMA chunk indicates the "gamma response" used by the picture. Few systems have truly linear color response; this number allows high-end graphics systems to correct for non-linearity in the picture data.

cHRM   The cHRM chunk specifies the exact color of the red, green, and blue primaries, and the white point, using CIE XYZ coordinates. This chunk allows high-end graphics systems to correct for differences in the phosphor color between different monitors.

Image Data

Image data is carried in one or more IDAT chunks. Conceptually, to recover the image, you combine the data from all of the IDAT chunks, decompress the data, and then undo the filtering. Chunk boundaries have no significance at all. The PNG encoder is free to place the entire compressed image in a single IDAT chunk, or place each separate byte in its own chunk.

To avoid patent problems, PNG uses the Deflation compression algorithm (see page 219). This algorithm is used in many "zip" programs, including PKZIP and GNU GZIP, and is widely believed to be free of patents. Freely-usable implementations are available on the Internet.

Like most general-purpose compression algorithms, Deflation is not ideal for image compression, because it doesn't exploit the two-dimensional nature of the picture. PNG uses *filtering* to help improve the compression. Before compressing the data, the encoder applies a set of simple functions to the image data. For example, one function simply subtracts each pixel from the one to its right. This step converts large areas of nearly the same color to large areas with very small values. Other functions do slightly more sophisticated transformations, but the general idea is the same. Deflation, like many other compression algorithms, works much better when the data to be compressed has a lot of very small values. The encoder indicates, for each scan line, which filter function was used on that scan line. After decompressing the raw data, the decoder can undo the filtering to recover the original image.

PNG supports an *interlaced* format similar in concept to GIF's interlaced format, but somewhat more ambitious. GIF's method allows a viewable image with only one-eighth of the image data, and requires four passes to transfer the entire image. PNG starts by transferring every eighth pixel of every eighth scan line, allowing a viewable image with only 1/64 of the image data. The remaining seven passes are carefully arranged so that each pass can be compressed and encoded as if it were a complete rectangular image in its own right.

Optional Chunks

Several optional chunks can either follow or precede IDAT chunks, but cannot appear between IDAT chunks. The tEXt and zTXt chunks allow textual information to be attached to the file. Each chunk contains a keyword (such as "Author"), a null byte to mark the end of the keyword, and text. The zTXt chunk stores the text in a compressed form (but the keyword is *not* compressed). These text chunks are comments; they are not displayed as part of the image. (PNG does not have an analogue of GIF's text extension blocks.) The tIME chunk carries the time that the image was last modified.

End-of-Data Chunk

The IEND chunk marks the end of the PNG file. Any data after the IEND chunk is simply ignored. An explicit end-of-file marker is important for any file format that might be lengthened in the process of being transferred from system to system. Common file transfer protocols, particularly XModem, add garbage bytes to the end of each file transferred. Having a definite marker within the file prevents the decoder from becoming confused.

More Information

At this time, the complete description of PNG is available on the World Wide Web at `http://sunsite.unc.edu/boutell`. Information on the Deflation compression algorithm and the Ziplib compressed data format is available from `ftp://quest.jpl.nasa.gov/beta/ziplib`. Information is also available in the `comp.graphics` and `comp.compression` newsgroups.

Lee Daniel Crocker's *PNG: The Portable Network Graphic Format* [Cro95] in *Dr. Dobb's Journal* provides some additional information and the C source code for a complete PNG-to-TIFF conversion utility.

Support for PNG is rapidly being added to many graphics utilities. You can ask the manufacturer of your favorite graphics software if they support PNG.

TIFF

The *Tagged Image File Format* (TIFF) was originally developed by Aldus Corporation to store high-resolution grayscale images from scanners. It was later adopted by many professional graphics packages, and has been extended several times to support better compression, several types of color images, and a variety of additional picture information. TIFF's major strengths are that it is flexible and it stores images in a piecemeal format that allows applications to rapidly access parts of a large image.

When to Use TIFF

TIFF's primary strengths are its support for very large images, multi-image files, and a variety of different compression methods. These features make TIFF well-suited to professional graphics work (which deals with large images)

TIFF at a Glance	
Name:	TIFF, Tagged Image File Format
Extensions:	`.tiff`, `.tif`
Use For:	Working with large, high-resolution images
Reference:	*TIFF Revision 6.0 Specification* [TIF92]
On CD:	Various graphics viewers, converters, sample images, specifications

and fax (which needs multi-page images and support for fax-specific compression methods).

TIFF supports a color image format that is similar to GIF (see page 129), making TIFF viable for exchanging most types of graphics. TIFF's one major disadvantage compared to GIF is that TIFF files cannot generally be displayed as they are read. GIF and PNG are better choices for situations where you want to be able to see a partial image as it is downloaded.

Strengths and Weaknesses

TIFF is well-suited to handling large graphic images. Graphics professionals need formats that allow fast access to any part of the picture. They also need lossless compression so that the picture will not degrade with repeated manipulation. As a result, TIFF is a popular format for clip art and photographic images intended for use by graphics designers and publishers.

The TIFF standard is large, and includes many optional extensions. As a result, there have been TIFF applications that understood distinct subsets of the standard, and had problems exchanging TIFF files. The TIFF standards have taken two different approaches to minimize this problem. The TIFF 5.0 specification defined several different subsets of TIFF, called *classes*. Table 15.1 lists the different classes. Each application was free to choose one or more of these four classes to support. Enough overlap exists among four classes that any reader supporting one class will be able to at least recognize the other classes. The TIFF 6.0 specification took a slightly different approach. TIFF 6.0 defines *Baseline TIFF*, which all TIFF readers should support. Baseline TIFF includes minimal support for all four classes. TIFF 6.0 then defines a large number of optional features. Apparently, the intention is to provide a way for the standard to evolve: Experimental features developed by various people will be added to the standard as optional extensions and, if they receive widespread support, will become part of the baseline.

Although TIFF 6.0 has been available as a standard for some time now, a huge number of images were created with TIFF 5.0-compatible software. Better software should support both TIFF 5.0 and TIFF 6.0. Fortunately, TIFF 6.0 is primarily a superset of TIFF 5.0; a program that supports TIFF 6.0 well should be able to handle all TIFF 5.0 images.

Class	Description
B	Bilevel images
G	Grayscale images
P	Palette-color images
R	Full color images

Table 15.1   TIFF 5.0 Classes

The LZW patent that has plagued GIF (see page 132) is also a concern for TIFF. Due to this patent conflict, LZW compression, which was a popular part of TIFF 5.0, is not a part of Baseline TIFF 6.0. Some new TIFF programs do not support this (now optional) extension. This omission may cause problems reading older TIFF 5.0 files, many of which were stored with LZW compression.

TIFF stores data in a file very differently from other graphics formats. TIFF does not store the data in the file in any particular order. Instead, a program must follow references within the file to find various pieces of data. This makes it easy for well-written applications to access any part of the image quickly. It also makes it more difficult to write a good TIFF application. There have been TIFF viewers that could only read files created by certain programs, because the viewer expected the data to be in a certain order in the file.

Fortunately, several good programming libraries can read and write TIFF files. As software developers increasingly depend on these libraries, there should be better conformance between different TIFF-using applications. Serious incompatibilities should be much less common than before, although transferring files from high-end software that relies on TIFF's more esoteric extensions to older software that doesn't understand these extensions will always cause some problems.

How TIFF Works

TIFF is a random-access file format. Structures within the file use file offsets to indicate the position of other data in the file. The result is a tree structure, which begins with the TIFF header. The header contains the file position of the first image in the file. Each image contains the file position of the next

Header → Image1 → Data *(→ Other Data)*
     ↓
    Image2 → Data
     ↓
    Image3 → Data
     ⋮

Figure 15.1 Conceptual Structure of a TIFF File

Size	Description
2	Byte order marker: II or MM
2	Magic number 42
4	File offset of first image

Table 15.2 TIFF Header

image in the file. An image is a directory containing 12-byte entries. Each directory entry contains a *tag*, indicating the purpose of the entry, and some data. For simple tags, the data is contained directly within the entry. For more complex tags, the entry indicates the position in the file of the associated data. Conceptually, TIFF files are structured as shown in Figure 15.1.

  The actual order in which data is stored in the file will vary depending on the application. The only piece that's stored at a particular location is the header, which is always stored at the beginning of the file.

TIFF Header

The TIFF header, shown in Table 15.2, is very simple, containing only three pieces of information. The first two bytes indicate how multi-byte values are stored in the file. II here indicates that two- and four-byte integers are stored starting with the least significant byte (the format used by the Intel 80x86 processors), while MM indicates the opposite order (the order used by the Motorola 68000-series processors). The two-byte value 42 provides a double-check that the application is reading data with the correct byte order.

Size	Description
2	Number of entries in directory
12×n	Entries
4	File offset of next image directory

Table 15.3 TIFF Image Directory

The last four bytes hold the file offset of the first image. Notice that the first image might immediately follow the header, it might be at the end of the file, or it could be anywhere in between.

TIFF Image

An image in a TIFF file is stored as a *directory* containing a number of *entries*. Each 12-byte entry holds a different piece of information about the image. For example, the ImageWidth entry contains the width of the picture. Table 15.3 shows the layout of this directory.

Each directory entry contains a *tag* that describes the purpose of the data, a *type* that describes how numeric data is stored, a *length*, and four bytes for the actual data.

Notice from Table 15.4 that the actual size of the data (in bytes) is the product of the number of elements times the size of each element. If the total size is four bytes or less, the data is stored directly in the directory entry; otherwise, the directory entry holds the file position of the actual data.

TIFF Image Data

TIFF was originally developed to handle large images, and this emphasis has been retained and expanded with TIFF 6.0. No single tag refers to the image data. Rather, the image data is stored in *strips* or *tiles*.

Strips have been an integral part of TIFF since the beginning. The idea is that, rather than storing the entire image as one monolithic chunk, you divide the image into more manageable pieces by storing horizontal strips that span the picture.

Size	Description		
2	Tag; purpose of data		
2	Type of numeric data		

Type	Size	Description
1	1	Unsigned integer
2	1	ASCII character
3	2	Unsigned integer
4	4	Unsigned integer
5	8	Fraction: two four-byte unsigned integers
6	1	Signed integer
7	1	Raw (non-numeric) byte
8	2	Signed integer
9	4	Signed integer
10	8	Fraction: two four-byte signed integers
11	4	IEEE single-precision floating point
12	8	IEEE double-precision floating point

Size	Description
4	Number of elements
4	Data or file offset of data

Table 15.4   TIFF Directory Entry

Images stored as strips use three directory entries to indicate where in the file the actual image is stored. The RowsPerStrip directory entry specifies how many pixel rows are stored in each strip. The StripOffsets directory entry contains a list of file offsets, one for each strip. The StripByteCounts directory entry contains a corresponding list of sizes for each strip.[1]

The reason for storing images as strips is to make it easier to handle very large images. For example, a TIFF file might store a full color image destined for an 8 1/2 by 11 inch piece of paper at 300 dots per inch. Uncompressed, such an image requires just over 24 megabytes of storage. Manipulating such an image requires either a very large amount of memory or the ability to quickly find and manipulate parts of the image on disk. A single row of pixel data from such a picture is less than 8000 bytes. By storing each row as a

---

[1]Remember that every directory entry "contains" either the actual data or else the file offset where the data is stored. If the image data can be stored as a single strip, the single file offset of the complete image data will be within the directory; otherwise, the directory entry will hold the offset of a part of the file where the offsets of each strip are held.

separate strip, an application that wants to edit a part of the picture can read, update, and alter just the necessary data, without requiring excessive amounts of memory.

Even strips can go only so far, however. Using strips requires always working with the full width of the image, which can require reading and writing a lot of unneeded data. It's much faster if you can read and write small rectangles of image data. For this reason, TIFF 6.0 has added tiles. Tiles work much like strips, except that the picture is divided into a two-dimensional grid. Tiles are especially useful for people working with images that: are very large (poster or billboard size), have a very high resolution (2400 dpi), or have demanding color requirements (48 bits or more per pixel).

Of course, simply knowing how to locate the data in the file isn't enough. You also have to know how it's compressed and what the data means when it's uncompressed. TIFF supports many different options. Compression options include:

- No compression at all (which allows the fastest possible reading and writing of small parts of large images),

- The simple PackBits compression scheme,

- T3 and T4 compression (the same as used by fax machines), and

- Several optional compression methods, including LZW and JPEG.

The uncompressed data can range from bilevel (for fax software) to 96 bits per pixel full color data (for high-end image processing). Alpha data can be included, and TIFF contains tags to specify a variety of different color models and additional information required for accurate color reproduction.

Again, the most important point about TIFF files is that, as far as the program reading the file is concerned, the actual data (picture data, palette data, image directory, and so on) is randomly ordered within the file. In particular, individual strips or tiles of image data may appear in any order at any location in the file. Programs that update a TIFF file must be very cautious not to move or overwrite any other data in the file.

For example, consider a program that simply adds comments to images in a TIFF file. Adding a comment to an image requires extending that image's directory. Because the program cannot know if important data follows the directory, it must use something like the following procedure:

1. Add the new comment to the end of the file.
2. Copy the entire image directory to the end of the file, adding the new entry for the comment.
3. Update the previous image directory so that it holds the new file offset of this image directory.

Similar gymnastics must be performed when *any* data within a TIFF file is lengthened. You can see that often-updated TIFF files can have their different components in an essentially random order within the file. Furthermore, it's not generally possible to "squeeze" a TIFF file to remove any holes that have developed in the process. Private tags can refer to blocks of data in the file that themselves refer to other blocks of data. If you don't understand the private tag in the first place, you can never be certain that a block of data isn't being used by a reference within that private data.

More Information

The official TIFF 6.0 specifications have been maintained by Aldus Corporation, now a part of Adobe Systems. The complete specifications are currently available using anonymous FTP from `ftp.adobe.com`, under the filename `pub/adobe/DeveloperSupport/TechNotes/PDFfiles/TIFF6.pdf`

JPEG (JFIF) **16**

As graphics hardware improves to support higher resolutions and a wider color range, graphics files are becoming significantly larger. Professional graphic artists now routinely deal with graphics files that contain 10 or more megabytes of data for each image. Even less sophisticated users have become used to dealing with 640 by 480 pixel images in 256 colors (over 300 kilobytes). They are beginning to work with 1024 by 768 pixel direct color images (over 2.3 megabytes of data). As these high-quality images become more common, the limitations of general-purpose compression methods such as LZW have become more apparent.

Two influential international standards bodies, the International Telecommunications Union (ITU)[1] and the International Organization for Standardization (ISO) created the *Joint Photographic Experts Group* (JPEG) to find a better way to compress photographic-quality digital images.

---

[1] The ITU was formerly known as the International Consultative Committee for Telephone and Telegraph (CCITT).

JPEG at a Glance	
Names:	JPEG, JFIF (JPEG File Interchange Format)
Extensions:	`.jpeg`, `.jpg`, `.jfif`
Use For:	High-resolution photographic images
Reference:	*JPEG: Still Image Data Compression Standard* [PM93]
On CD:	Various graphics viewers, converters

The JPEG committee considered a half-century's worth of research into human vision and computer graphics, drawing on expertise developed by television engineers, computer scientists, and many other disciplines. The final report of the JPEG committee contained a detailed recommendation for a technique to dramatically reduce the size of photographic-quality digital images. The name "JPEG" has since been used to refer to this compression technique as well as several different file formats that use this technique. The most widespread of these file formats is the *JPEG File Interchange Format* (JFIF), which essentially standardizes one simple way to wrap a JPEG compressed image into a file. In fact, many images referred to as "JPEG" are more properly called "JFIF" images.

The name "JPEG" refers to a *compression method*, not a particular file format. A number of slightly different file formats are commonly referred to as "JPEG" and a few radically different file formats (such as TIFF and QuickTime) may use JPEG compression. Fortunately, the most common file formats referred to as JPEG are all quite similar, and you probably won't run into problems, but you should be aware of this possible complication.

When to Use JPEG

JPEG differs from the other graphics formats I've considered by being a *lossy* approach. JPEG selectively identifies and removes information to which the human eye is less sensitive. As a result, JPEG can achieve much higher compression without a noticeable loss in picture quality.

This lossy approach has a number of implications. JPEG achieves its impressive compression abilities by discarding the kind of graphic information that doesn't typically appear in *natural images*. The sharp edges that appear in line art or cartoons produce "ripples" when compressed with JPEG. If you see images produced with JPEG that have text overlaid, look carefully around the text characters and you'll see this effect. This effect can be minimized by keeping the quality setting very high, but that keeps the image from compressing well. Future additions to JPEG may allow different quality settings in different parts of the image, which would allow high quality (with no ripples) in areas with sharp edges, while using reduced quality (and better compression) for the bulk of the image.

JPEG discards some information every time it is used. This fact makes JPEG a poor candidate for storing intermediate images. Graphic artists often store intermediate images that will later be subject to additional manipulation. If you store these intermediate images with JPEG, you'll lose more detail each time you touch the image. You should instead store the intermediate images using a lossless format such as TIFF and only compress the final result with JPEG.

Because of the way JPEG stores varying color, it works best for full color images with 24 bits or more per pixel (sometimes referred to as "millions of colors"). It also works well for high-resolution images. If you need to store low-resolution images or images with a restricted set of colors, you should consider other file formats. You'll find that GIF or PNG compress many eight-bit images better than JPEG, without the side effects of JPEG's lossy approach.

Generally, JPEG is best for high-resolution full color images that will be displayed on 24-bit color displays. If you know that you'll never use this type of display, you may be able to do better by storing the image using GIF or another eight-bit format. Simply converting from 24 bits to eight bits per pixel reduces the amount of data by two-thirds. On the other hand, if you know that your images will be displayed on a variety of different monitors, storing them in a full-color format such as JPEG allows them to look as good as possible on a wide variety of displays.

How to Use JPEG

Because JPEG is lossy, you have to be careful when creating JPEG files. Most programs that create such files allow you to set the *quality* of the picture. Typically, this value ranges from zero to one hundred. A low quality setting allows the JPEG compressor to discard more information, resulting in a much smaller file. Conversely, a high quality setting restricts the amount of information that the compressor will discard.[2]

The trick, then, is to use the lowest quality setting that doesn't result in *visible* deterioration of the picture. Usually, you'll start with a moderately high

---

[2]One common error is to interpret the zero to one hundred quality scale as the percentage of data that is preserved. To reduce this misunderstanding, some newer JPEG software simply provides a handful of settings, ranging from "best compression" to "best quality."

setting, then carefully look at the result. If you can see visible deterioration, try a higher setting; if not, try a lower one. Look for the following when inspecting the picture:

- Look for problems near sharp edges and corners, for example, around text or a foreground image that has a sharp edge against the background. Such sharp edges often produce "smears" or "ripples" that can be quite visible.

- JPEG compresses tiles of eight pixels by eight pixels at a time. At low quality settings, the edges of these tiles will be noticeable.

If you already have images in GIF or some other eight-bit format, you may be tempted to convert them into JPEG. While this sometimes results in significant space savings, such conversions often require more work than they're worth. If you do want to try it, begin by checking the number of colors used by your GIF images. A GIF image with only 64 colors will rarely benefit from conversion to JPEG, because an image with so few colors doesn't have the kind of gradual color variation that JPEG compresses so well. Conversion to JPEG will simply damage the image with no significant space savings.

One of the most serious problems converting GIF images into JPEG is that GIF images have already been limited to 256 or fewer colors, often by *dithering* or *halftoning*, in which two different colors of pixels are mingled to produce the effect of a third color. These techniques create detailed patterns that prevent them from being effectively compressed by JPEG. Better software will allow you to "smooth" the picture to average out these patterns before conversion, which can help to improve the compression achievable by JPEG.

Recognizing JPEG and JFIF Files

Any JPEG *data stream* begins with the two bytes 255 and 232. Many JPEG file formats add a header before the JPEG data stream, so this marker won't always appear at the beginning of the file. JFIF files are JPEG data streams, so they always begin with this marker. In addition, the letters JFIF appear starting at the seventh byte of a JFIF file.

$$Y = 0.299R + 0.587G + 0.114B$$
$$C_b = -0.1687R - 0.3313G + 0.5B + 128$$
$$C_r = 0.5R - 0.4187G - 0.0813B + 128$$

Figure 16.1   Converting from RGB to JFIF's Color System

How JFIF Works

The final report of the JPEG committee was extensive, but omitted a handful of details. These omissions prompted a variety of minor extensions. Fortunately, most of the file formats built around JPEG compression simply use the "Baseline JPEG" defined by the JPEG committee and add a header to carry some additional information. Better JPEG software knows how to search through a file for the start of the Baseline JPEG data, ignoring any additional header that it doesn't understand.

Because an additional header is likely to be ignored anyway, the most popular JPEG file format is also one of the simplest. The JPEG File Interchange Format (JFIF) defined by C-Cube Systems simply nails down some of the ambiguities in the standard, and takes advantage of the modular format of Baseline JPEG.

JFIF specifies a few things that Baseline JPEG leaves undefined. One of these is the color model. As I'll describe later, JPEG takes advantage of certain kinds of color models to provide good compression. JFIF uses the YC_bC_r color model, which describes a color in terms of *lightness* (Y) and two *chromaticities* (C_b and C_r). Figures 16.1 and 16.2 show how to convert between eight-bit RGB and the color model used by JFIF.

Baseline JPEG uses a number of *markers* to store specific data. These markers all start with a two-byte code beginning with 255. Some markers include data, in which case the code is followed by a two-byte count and corresponding data. (Note that the count value includes the two count bytes but does not include the two-byte code.)

Rather than wrap a Baseline JPEG compressed data stream inside of another structured data file, JFIF simply uses a Baseline JPEG compressed data stream and embeds additional information in markers. JFIF files use Base-

$$R = Y + 1.402(C_r - 128)$$
$$G = Y - 0.34414(C_b - 128) - 0.71414(C_r - 128)$$
$$B = Y + 1.772(C_b - 128)$$

Figure 16.2   Converting from JFIF's Color System to RGB

Size	Description
2	APP0 marker (255, 240)
2	Length of remaining data + 2
4	Identifier: JFIF
1	Zero byte
2	Version (1, 2)
1	Units for X and Y densities
2	X (horizontal) density
2	Y (vertical) density
1	Width of thumbnail: x
1	Height of thumbnail: y
$3 \times x \times y$	Raw RGB values for thumbnail

Table 16.1   The JFIF APP0 Marker

line JPEG's *Application Marker 0* (APP0) to embed this extra information. The data within an APP0 marker begins with a zero-terminated string that indicates the purpose of this marker.

Currently, two such APP0 markers are defined. The first marker is the *JFIF APP0* marker (see Table 16.1), which gives the JFIF version, picture resolution, and an optional thumbnail image. The *JFXX APP0* marker (see Table 16.2) is a recently-introduced marker designed to hold other optional JFIF information. Currently, the JFXX extension is used to hold thumbnails. This extension allows a single image to have multiple thumbnails (at different sizes) and allows thumbnails to be compressed with JPEG or by storing a palettized image. (The JFIF APP0 marker only supports a single uncompressed thumbnail).

Size	Description
2	APP0 marker (255, 240)
2	Length of remaining data + 2
4	Identifier: JFXX
1	Zero byte
1	JFIF extension code
	16 JPEG compressed thumbnail
	17 Eight bit per pixel thumbnail
	19 24 bit per pixel thumbnail
n	Extension data

Table 16.2   The JFXX APP0 Marker

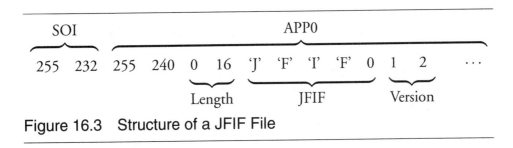

Figure 16.3   Structure of a JFIF File

Because a JFIF file is a JPEG data stream, it starts with a JPEG *Start-of-Image* (SOI) marker (255, 232) and ends with an *End-of-Image* marker (255, 233). The JFIF APP0 marker immediately follows the SOI marker in a JFIF file. Figure 16.3 shows the beginning of a typical JFIF file.

How JPEG Compression Works

To do good data compression, you must understand your data. JPEG compresses graphics data by understanding how humans see, and I can't explain JPEG without delving into some basic facts about human vision.

JPEG compression is done in several stages. The purpose of these stages is to convert the graphics data into a form where unimportant visual information can be easily identified and discarded. This lossy approach differs from most graphics formats, which attempt to preserve the exact pattern of bits in the image.

Color Model

The first step in JPEG is to choose an appropriate way to represent colors. Colors are usually described using a three-dimensional coordinate system. The system familiar to most computer programmers describes each color as a combination of red, green, and blue. Unfortunately, this system isn't the best way to describe colors if you're interested in compression. The problem is that all three of red, green, and blue are equally important. By changing to a different color system, you can concentrate some of the important information.

Two color models used by graphic artists are the *HSL* (Hue-Saturation-Lightness) and *HSV* (Hue-Saturation-Value) models. Intuitively, *lightness* and *value* are different ways of measuring how light or dark something is. *Saturation* measures how "pure" a color is; unsaturated colors are often informally described as "grayish." *Hue* is what we think of as color, such as red or greenish-blue. The important fact is this: Human vision is more sensitive to changes in lightness than in color.

Different implementations of JPEG compression use different color systems. JFIF uses a system called YC_bC_r, which is similar to the one developed many years ago for color television.

Subsampling

The basic reason for converting to a different color model is to isolate information that's less important to the image. JPEG reduces the resolution of the color information. While the lightness is stored at the full resolution of the picture, the two color components are usually stored at only half the resolution. This simple step alone reduces the amount of data by one-half.

This *subsampling* corresponds to the way that color television handles color. Color television is actually a black-and-white television image (lightness) with additional color information sent separately. The separate color information is transmitted in a less exact form than the black-and-white information.

Discrete Cosine Transform

After subsampling, each of the color components is handled separately, as if they were three grayscale images instead of a single color image. If you look at a detailed image from far away, all you can discern is the overall color of the image, whether it's "mostly blue" or "mostly red." As you get closer, finer and finer details become evident. JPEG uses a mathematical trick to simulate this effect. This trick, called the *Discrete Cosine Transform* (DCT), converts a group of pixels to a description of how those pixels vary. The first thing the DCT tells you is the average color of an area; then it tells you increasingly more detailed information about how the color changes.

Just like a picture seen from far away, the average color is the most important fact about an area. Your eyes are less sensitive to rapid changes, so those are less important. By rearranging the color information in this way, we've isolated information that can be safely sacrificed.

The DCT stage is usually described as being inherently lossy. If you use just a DCT to encode a picture and then do an inverse DCT to recover the original picture, you won't have the exact same bits. However, the errors occur only because of rounding errors in the arithmetic, and are generally very small. I prefer to think of the DCT stage as "mostly lossless."

Computing a DCT or an inverse DCT is very time-consuming for large images. To save time, JPEG breaks the entire picture into tiles that are eight pixels wide and eight pixels high. Each of these tiles is handled separately, which greatly reduces the amount of computation needed by the DCT stage. One problem with this approach is that after the quantization stage (which I'll describe in the next section), the tiles may no longer "line up" perfectly; noticeable edges can appear between the tiles at low quality settings.

Quantization

The designers of JPEG were primarily interested in photographic images, which are often described as "continuous tone," meaning that they tend to have smoothly varying regions of color. For these images, the low-frequency (slowly changing) components of the DCT are more important than the high-frequency (quickly changing) components.

The term *quantization* simply means "rounding." JPEG discards graphics information by rounding each DCT term by a different factor. Higher-frequency components are rounded more than lower-frequency components. For example, the lowest-frequency component, which simply stores the average lightness, may be rounded to the nearest multiple of three, while the highest-frequency component might be rounded to the nearest multiple of 100.

This quantization explains why JPEG compression produces ripples near sharp edges. Sharp edges are defined by high-frequency (quickly varying) color information. Because that high-frequency information is rounded, you get a ripple near the sharp edge. (At first glance, it might seem that you should get a blurred edge, but remember that the C in DCT stands for *Cosine*.)

Typically, the color planes are quantized more aggressively than the lightness plane. This is another place where the selection of an appropriate color model helps to selectively discard information.

Compression

Thus far, no compression has occurred, except for the subsampling of the two color channels. All of the other steps—converting color models, DCT, and quantization—leave the data exactly the same size. The last step is to use a standard lossless compression technique to actually reduce the size of the data.

The result of the preceding steps is a collection of data that can be compressed much more effectively than a raw RGB graphics dump. Each of the preceding steps altered the data in a way that allows the final data to be compressed very effectively.

The change in color model allowed certain channels to be subsampled and then quantized more aggressively.

The DCT isolated high-frequency information. This high-frequency information is usually quite small in value, so the output of the DCT stage has a disproportionate number of small values, which makes it easier to compress.

The quantization step rounded most of the high-frequency information to zero, and the rest to a small number of distinct values. Reducing the number of different values also makes the data easier to compress.

The JPEG standard specifies two different lossless compression methods that can be used for this final step. *Huffman compression* (see page 185) is simple to program, and it is an old compression method with no patent complications. *Arithmetic coding* (see page 186) is a newer technique that is the subject of a number of patents. (Not surprisingly, many JPEG compressors support only Huffman compression.)

Decoding a JPEG image requires reversing each of these steps. The data stream is first decompressed, then each 8×8 block is recovered by an inverse DCT, and finally the image is converted into the appropriate color space (usually RGB). Note that the information that was deliberately thrown away by subsampling and quantization is never recovered. When done correctly, however, this lost information does not cause any visible degradation of the image.

Future Lossy Compression Methods

JPEG is not the only lossy compression technique for graphics. Many others have been proposed, and new research into human vision is discovering facts that may make future compression techniques even more effective.

One weakness of JPEG is that it tends to throw out high-frequency information that defines edges in the picture. The loss of this information causes visible smears and ripples at lower quality settings. One area of research is to find ways to identify and separately compress the edge information. Such a technique may allow a future lossy compression algorithm to obtain even better compression.

Lossless JPEG

The report of the JPEG committee actually specified two completely different compression techniques. The best-known is the lossy technique I described earlier. The report also describes a lossless technique that has received little attention. The lossless technique uses a simple "filter" followed by either Huffman or arithmetic encoding.

For photographic images, standard JPEG offers much better compression, even at high quality settings. For other types of images, there are many popular and effective lossless compression methods, and hence there is little need for another. Generally, you should use standard lossy JPEG for photographic images, and look to other formats if you require good lossless compression.

More Information

The report of the JPEG committee is available from the ISO or ITU. You can also get detailed information from William B. Pennebaker and Joan L. Mitchell's book *JPEG: Still Image Data Compression Standard* [PM93].

Most better graphics viewer programs support JPEG images, check the archive sites listed in Chapter 2 to find software for your particular platform. If you're a programmer, you may be interested in the JPEG compression and decompression code available from the Independent JPEG Group at `ftp://ftp.uu.net/graphics/jpeg`.

There is also a JPEG FAQ available from `ftp://rtfm.mit.edu` in the directory pub/usenet/news.answers.

VRML

17

The *Virtual Reality Modeling Language* (VRML) can be viewed as many different things. Most simply, it's a graphics format based on a subset of Silicon Graphics' *Open Inventor*. However, instead of flat, two-dimensional images, VRML *worlds* are three-dimensional. VRML browsers display these worlds and let you walk around and explore them. As used on the World Wide Web, you download the world to your computer and then display and explore it there. A VRML world can be a single three-dimensional object (such as a car or airplane) or a simulated city with buildings and sidewalks.

Some of the worlds that have been created are quite impressive, such as Planet9's *VirtualSOMA*, which lets you walk around several blocks of San Francisco's "South of Market Area." However, impressive graphics don't quite explain the excitement that VRML has generated. The two evolving features of VRML that make it most interesting are its connections to the World Wide Web and the emerging possibilities of multiple people interacting in a single world.

VRML at a Glance	
Name:	VRML, Virtual Reality Modeling Language
Extension:	`.wrl`
Use For:	Exchanging three-dimensional models
Reference:	*VRML: Browsing and Building Cyberspace* [Pes95]
On CD:	Viewers for Windows, Macintosh

Size constraints place some practical limits on how complex a single world can be. VRML skirts this limit by including HTML-style links to other worlds. For example, VirtualSOMA lets you click on a storefront to access a new world modeling the inside of a building. In this way, worlds developed by different people are being linked together into larger metropolises. It's also possible to link from a VRML world to other types of data. For example, you might browse the bookshelves of a VRML library and click to view an HTML version of a particular book. Many of the VirtualSOMA storefronts are links to the home pages of the respective companies.

A more experimental facility is being developed to allow multiple people to interact within one VRML world. The basic idea is that each person's VRML browser broadcasts a location in the VRML world using the well-established *Internet Relay Chat* mechanism.[1] This technique allows your VRML browser to display the other people currently visiting that world.

VRML promises to transform the flat, static World Wide Web into a three-dimensional interactive space.

How to Use VRML

To use VRML, you'll need a VRML browser. Typically, you'll configure your World Wide Web browser to automatically run your VRML program whenever you receive a world file. Depending on the setup, the VRML browser will often use your World Wide Web browser to access any other pages needed. VRML worlds can then link to HTML pages or any other data type supported by your World Wide Web browser.

You should be aware that, in theory, VRML precisely specifies the appearance of a three-dimensional model. In practice, subtle variations between browsers cause the results to vary. One obvious variation is that different browsers interpret lighting and color differently; a model that looks subtly shaded in one browser might look flat and dark in another. Also, browsers make many concessions to speed, which in practice means that many models

---

[1] Internet Relay Chat (IRC) allows multiple people to hold live discussions by relaying typed comments to all of the other participants. When combined with VRML, the browsers use this to relay encoded information to the other browsers.

will look better in certain browsers. (In particular, texture mapping and shading are time-consuming options that are handled quite differently by different browsers.)

One optimization causes a few strange effects for people using PC-based browsers. In practice, solid objects are defined by listing flat polygons that define the surface of the object. For efficiency, most PC browsers assume that one side of each face is "facing out" and the other side is "facing in." This assumption makes the browser much faster, because it can ignore about one-half of the faces at any given time. The problem is that not all faces are on the surface of some object. Sometimes a single face is used by itself as part of a sign, for example. In this case, the sign may disappear when viewed from the wrong side. More problematically, large objects are sometimes created by placing individual faces without connecting them. In this case, it's very difficult for the browser to correctly identify which side of a face is which. A wrong guess will result in visible holes in the object.

This problem is common because the optimization is often not done on high-end workstations that have hardware-assisted graphics. Many of the more impressive VRML models have been created on such workstations, where faces appear solid from both sides. Sometimes, transferring such models to a less sophisticated PC causes some of the faces to disappear. Most PC viewers provide an option to synthesize the back of each polygon. This option causes the viewer to duplicate each polygon so that you'll always see the front of one of them. Enabling this option allows these problematic models to display correctly, but at a noticeable cost in speed.

Because VRML files use a text-based graphics format, they tend to be fairly large. Fortunately, they compress very well, and are frequently stored and transferred in a compressed format.

How VRML Works

VRML files are text files with a list of *nodes*. Some of these nodes define new visible objects on the screen. For example,

```
Sphere { radius 2.3 }
```

creates a sphere with the indicated radius. Note that nodes contain a *type* followed by curly braces containing some *fields*. If you don't specify any fields, some reasonable defaults will be used. For example, Cube{} defines a cube one unit long on each side at the current position, with the current orientation and color. Other nodes change the way later nodes are drawn. The Translation node moves the current position, affecting where the following objects will appear; the Material node affects the surface appearance of subsequent objects.

Figure 17.1 shows a simple VRML model. This model was created by the listing in Figure 17.2. This fairly simple model illustrates a few aspects of VRML. The first thing you should notice is the use of Separator to enclose the entire file and certain collections of nodes. Separator nodes isolate changes to the current position and other rendering variables. Placing the whole file within a Separator makes it easier to include this file into another file.

Within the outermost Separator, the first two nodes set a light and a camera. The camera is also called the *viewpoint*; it's where you are when you first look at the model. As you'll see in a moment, the center of the table is at (0,0,0). The location (-2, 2, 8) for the camera places the camera slightly to the left (*x* is -2), slightly above (*y* is 2), and in front of (*z* is 8) the model. Notice that positive *z* coordinates are towards you, out of the screen. The orientation specifies the line through the points (0,0,0) and (1,.7,0) and a rotation about that line. The numbers listed here were determined pretty much by trial and error.

The Material node defines the appearance of the surface of the following objects. To keep this example simple, I've only specified a color, and omitted reflection and transparency information.

I then proceed to define the different objects that make up the table. By enclosing each object in a Separator, I can move the current position and change the current material for just that object, without complicating anything else. The first object is the table top itself, which is a rectangular solid created by the Cube node. The Translation places the center of the table top slightly below the origin, to simplify placing the objects that will rest on top of the table. The sphere and cube are created similarly, but each of those also specifies a new color. The legs take advantage of VRML's DEF and USE features. The DEF LEG preceding the Separator defines a LEG object as a tall thin cylinder with its center moved down below the current position. The following statements move the current position to the remaining three corners

Figure 17.1   Example VRML Table

of the table and re-USE the LEG object. Judicious use of this technique can make VRML files much smaller.

Many of the more elaborate VRML files don't look very much like my example. Many worlds are created in modeling programs that don't work with cubes and spheres internally. Rather, they store the surfaces of objects as collections of flat polygons, usually triangles. In VRML, solids defined from groups of triangles are expressed by first listing many points inside of the PointSet node. These become the *current points*, and can then be used much as the current material or position is used. In particular, an IndexedFaceSet node defines a single solid by listing the points on the edge of each polygon. Each point is described with a single number identifying one of the current points. Typically, the faces are all triangles, so the IndexedFaceSet will contain a long list of numbers arranged in threes. (There are actually four numbers in each group; a -1 is included to mark the end of each face.)

For increased realism, many VRML worlds also make extensive use of *texture mapping*. Rather than simply specifying the color of a cube, a *texture map* is a graphic image that is shown on the outside of a solid. This image can be used, for example, to simulate a stone or brick wall. Texture maps are usually stored in GIF or some similar graphics format, and are often quite modestly sized. A brick wall only requires a small image of a few bricks. The VRML browser will then *tile* the image, duplicating it to cover the entire solid. In this way, a few small GIF images can greatly enrich a VRML world.

More Information

As a new and rapidly evolving standard, the best sources of VRML information are on the World Wide Web. Searching Yahoo (see page 14) for `vrml` returns a manageable number of references, many of which are references to worlds that people have created or to people marketing VRML browsers (often free for personal use).

The VRML standard on `http://www.virtpark.com/theme/vrml` is a particularly good reference. It includes many examples in source code form, with links to the examples themselves. If you have a VRML browser, you'll be able to compare the source code to the final effect.

The *VRML Repository* at `http://sdsc.edu/vrml` contains lots of pointers to the VMRL standards, a bibliography, mailing lists, research projects, and other information.

The VirtualSOMA project is a VRML gateway to a group of San Francisco multimedia companies. The HTML home page has several images of VirtualSOMA viewable by people without VRML browsers, as well as links to the model itself (`http://www.hyperion.com/planet9/vrsoma.htm`).

Mark Pesce's *VRML: Browsing and Building Cyberspace* [Pes95] provides a good look at VRML and many of the tools and techniques used to build VRML worlds.

```
#VRML V1.0 ascii
Separator{
    PointLight{
        location 10 10 30
        intensity .7
    }
    PerspectiveCamera {
        position -2 2 8
        orientation 1 .7 0 -.4
    }
    Material { diffuseColor .2 .2 .2 }
    Separator{ # Table top
        Translation{ translation 0 -.1 0 }
        Cube{   width 6.5
                height .1
                depth 6.5
        }
    }
    Separator { # yellow-brown sphere
        Translation { translation -2 1 1 }
        Material {diffuseColor 1 .4 0}
        Sphere{}
    }
    Separator { # bluish cube
        Translation { translation 1 1 -2 }
        Material {diffuseColor .3 .5 .8}
        Cube{}
    }
    Separator { # Four legs
        Translation { translation 3 0 -3 }
        DEF LEG Separator { # One leg
            Translation { translation 0 -1.6 0 }
            Cylinder { radius .1
                       height 3
            }
        }
        Translation { translation -6 0 0 }
        USE LEG
        Translation { translation 0 0 6 }
        USE LEG
        Translation { translation 6 0 0 }
        USE LEG
    }
}
```

Figure 17.2   Source for VRML Table

Other Formats

The graphics formats I've discussed so far cover the majority of files exchanged on the Internet, but you may stumble across many other types of files. I'll briefly mention a few other graphics formats in this chapter.

XBM and XPM

X is the name of a windowing system for Unix, originally developed at the Massachusetts Institute of Technology and now a widespread standard for Unix workstations. Much of the original work for the World Wide Web was done on Unix systems, so it's no surprise that most browsers support the *X BitMap* (XBM) format. XBM is a simple bilevel format that provides a list of numeric byte values, each byte holding eight pixels. It uses C language notation to simplify compiling pictures directly into a program. As a simple text format, XBM files are very easy to understand and use, which also helps explain why it was supported by many early World Wide Web browsers. The glaring disadvantage is that these files are quite large.

The *X PixMap* (XPM) format is a similar text format that also supports grayscale and color images. Rather than storing numeric values, XPM files use character sequences to represent colors. The image is stored as a collection of quoted strings, each representing a single row of the picture. The character sequences can be defined to represent different colors in different environments, so that the same image data represents both a grayscale and color image.

BMP

The *BMP* format is the native graphics format for both OS/2 and Windows. A lot of images are available in this format. BMP has two practical limitations that have restricted its widespread adoption. First, although BMP is used both by OS/2 and Windows, the current versions of OS/2 and Windows support slightly different versions of BMP. Second, BMP only supports very simple compression methods, which are rarely used. This makes BMP a good candidate for reading and writing small images very quickly (BMP is often used by people experimenting with simple animation techniques). However, BMP is not very well suited for exchanging files between different systems.

PICT

PICT images are used primarily on the Macintosh. The Macintosh clipboard uses PICT format to exchange graphics data between different programs. This format is also used in the "resource fork" of a Macintosh file to attach a variety of graphical images to files. PICT images can contain graphics data in a variety of sub-formats, including bilevel bitmaps, full color JPEG images, or a list of drawing commands for reproducing an image.

On the Macintosh, PICT format is supported directly by the system. However, internally, PICT is fairly complex, so it's not widely supported on other platforms. Some versions of the NetPBM utilities for Unix or MS-DOS can convert PICT files into other formats for viewing.

IFF

The Commodore Amiga was one of the first personal computer systems to include sophisticated video and audio capabilities. It rapidly became a standard part of inexpensive video editing systems. It also provided fertile ground for early experiments with the mixture of sound, graphics, and computer interface that later became known as *multimedia*. *Interchange File Format* (IFF) is a flexible format that started on the Amiga and has become common outside of the Amiga community. Like Microsoft's RIFF (Resource Interchange File Format, see page 299), IFF allows a wide variety of different kinds of data to be stored in the same file. IFF files can include bitmapped graphics, text, sound, and many other types of data.

Outside of the Amiga world, IFF files are used primarily for bitmapped images and sound.

PBM, PGM, PPM, and PNM

Many programs convert between different graphics formats. Unfortunately, if you want to build a collection of such programs to convert between any two formats in a single step, you need a lot of programs.

One way to reduce the amount of work is to choose a single intermediate format, and develop conversions between this intermediate format and all the others. Using this approach, you only need twice as many programs as formats. A good intermediate format for this scheme should be very simple, because every converter will have to read or write it.

Jef Poskanzer's PBM system does exactly this. Poskanzer designed a very simple graphics format with three different variants: *PBM* (Portable BitMap) for black and white images, *PGM* (Portable GrayMap) for grayscale images, and *PPM* (Portable PixelMap) for color images. Each of these formats is nothing more than a list of the pixels in the picture (either binary or ASCII), with no compression or special encoding. Because they are so simple, many programs convert to and from these formats and do various picture manipulations on images in these formats.

For example, to convert a GIF picture to TIFF format, you would first use `giftopnm` to convert the GIF picture into PPM format, then `pnmtotiff` to convert it into TIFF format. ("PNM" stands for "Portable aNyMap" and indicates a program that supports all three of PBM, PGM, and PPM.) Once you have the picture in PPM format, you could scale the picture (with `pnmscale`), smooth it (with `pnmsmooth`), and add a border (with `pnmmargin`) before converting it into TIFF.

Poskanzer's original PBM utilities have grown extensively, both from his own work and contributions by many people. The NetPBM collection, which combines many of these tools, has been ported to many different systems. It is a useful set of tools for anyone who must deal with many different graphics formats.

Because the PBM formats are so simple, they're supported by many viewing utilities. If you're interested in the PBM utilities, the source code is available using anonymous FTP from the archives at `ftp.x.org`. Ports of the PBM utilities to MS-DOS are available from both the SIMTEL and *Garbo* archives.

Part Three
Compression and Archiving Formats

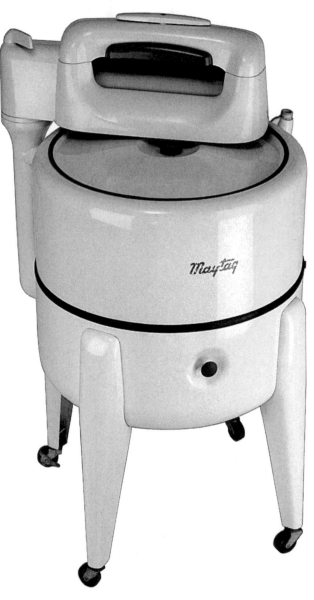

About Archiving and Compression 19

It's a fact of life that even computers sometimes break. When they do, the information stored on them becomes inaccessible. Sometimes the situation can be remedied quickly (say, by plugging the computer back in after you trip over the power cord), but other times there's no easy fix (such as when lightning strikes the powerlines near your house).

To guard against the havoc caused by this loss of information, cautious people *back up* the critical data on their computers, usually by copying it to floppy disks, tape, or some other removable media, so it can be stored apart from the computer.[1]

About Archiving

Copying thousands of individual files is inconvenient at best, so most backup schemes involve *archiving*—wrapping up many files into a single file. The resulting *archive file* can later be burst into its separate components to retrieve the files that are stored within it.

Archiving is also useful in other situations. When transferring files by modem or mail, it's usually simpler to send a single file. Similarly, software distributed on floppy disk or CD-ROM is often archived to simplify the installation software.

---

[1]Some people think a second hard disk is a good form of backup. Unfortunately, many of the causes of system failure—such as power supply problems—will damage every connected drive, which is why the "removable" aspect is so important.

One less obvious benefit to archiving is that simply combining files saves some space. All computer systems waste a small amount of space for each file. This wasted space may only be a few thousand bytes per file, but it adds up when you have several hundred or several thousand files. Archiving also allows you to preserve filenames. If you send a single file through mail, you have no guarantee that the recipient will save the file under the correct name. Files sometimes need to refer to one another by name, such as a program and a configuration file for that program. If the recipient unwittingly changes the name of the configuration file, the program may not work. By storing the files in an archive, the files will automatically end up with the correct names when the recipient de-archives them. Similarly, most archiving methods can preserve the directory structure, so that when the archive is burst, not only will the files be extracted, but they will be extracted into appropriate directories.

Stringing together a few thousand files gives you a pretty large archive file. As a result, archiving programs often incorporate file compression techniques. These techniques encode data in such a way that the result is frequently smaller than the original data. While specialized compression techniques geared to specific types of data are an important part of graphics, audio, and video file formats, archiving programs must use more general techniques that attempt to give good compression on a wide variety of data.

On Unix, the TAR program was developed to archive files to tape (hence the name "*t*ape *ar*chive"). It does no compression, so Unix users have become accustomed to first archiving files using the TAR program, and then compressing the resulting archive file with a separate program.

Archive programs for microcomputer systems usually take a slightly different approach. The archiver program compresses each file as it is included in the archive. This approach makes the archiver program faster and easier to use because single files can be extracted without having to first uncompress the entire archive. On the other hand, compression techniques are generally more effective when used on larger files, so compressing the entire archive at once usually results in a somewhat smaller overall result.

A Brief History of Compression

In the 1940s, computer scientists realized that it was possible, for most data files, to develop ways of storing that data in less space. Much of the basic theory was developed by Claude Shannon, who explored the subtle distinction between *semantics* (what something means) and *syntax* (how something is expressed). Once you realize that the same meaning (semantics) can be expressed in many different ways (syntax), you can ask the question: What's the smallest way to express something? This question led Shannon to define the idea of *entropy*, which is (loosely speaking) the relative amount of information contained in a file. Compression techniques attempt to increase the entropy of a file, that is, make the file shorter while still containing the same information.

For example, in most files, some byte values occur more often than others. By using different-sized codes for each byte, you can significantly reduce the total size of the data. This basic idea led to the *Shannon-Fano* and *Huffman* compression algorithms. These algorithms choose shorter codes for common byte values, and longer codes for less-common byte values. They usually compress text files (which use certain byte values much more heavily than others) fairly well.

For over 30 years, Huffman compression and its variants were the most popular compression methods around. In 1977, two computer researchers in Israel developed a completely different approach. Abraham Lempel and Jacob Ziv had the idea of building a "dictionary" of common sequences in the data to be compressed, and then compressing the data by using a code for each entry in the dictionary. Their two algorithms, now known as *LZ77* and *LZ78*, managed to arrange things so that you don't need to include the dictionary with the data; if you build your dictionary in a certain way, the decoder can reconstruct the dictionary directly from the data. Unfortunately, LZ77 and LZ78 weren't very fast at building an effective dictionary. Lempel was hired by Sperry to help them develop ways to pack more data onto computer tapes. There, Terry Welch was able to extend LZ78 into an algorithm that became widely known as *LZW*.

A group of Unix programmers noticed Welch's work and implemented LZW compression in their aptly-named *compress* program. They added several refinements and published their public domain program in an Internet newsgroup, where many other people saw it and began to use it.

The popularity of the LZW algorithm is due in large part to the success of the compress program. The most recent version of the program handles both compression and decompression in a modest 1200 lines of source code. The core compression code is a mere 100 lines, and the decompression code is only slightly larger. Programmers found it easy to read and understand the algorithm and adapt it to a wide variety of purposes.

LZ-style algorithms (including LZW, LZ77, LZ78, and many variations) are very popular wherever general-purpose compression is needed. LZW is used in the V.42bis modem standard, the ZModem file transfer protocol, GIF, TIFF, ARC, compress, and other applications. Other LZ algorithms are used in disk compression utilities such as DoubleSpace and Stacker, graphics formats such as PNG, as well as general-purpose archiving and compression utilities including ZIP, GZIP, and LHA.

While dictionary-based compression algorithms receive a lot of attention, there are other approaches. Huffman compression, which exploits statistical variations in the occurrence of certain bytes, led to a powerful compression method known variously as *arithmetic encoding, entropy coding*, or *Q-coding*. Arithmetic encoding improves Huffman compression in two ways. The first improvement is that it does not require the selected codes to be a whole number of bits. While Huffman compression might choose some two-bit codes and some four-bit codes, an arithmetic encoder can choose a code that is 6.23 bits long. (The precise definition of ".23 bits" is somewhat technical; see [Nel92] for another explanation of arithmetic coding.) The second improvement (which can also be applied to Huffman compression) is that arithmetic coding uses more complex statistics. Rather than simply looking at how often each byte occurs in the entire file, it looks at how often a byte occurs in a particular context. For example, with normal Huffman compression, the letter "u" might receive a fairly long code, since it doesn't occur very frequently. But in a sophisticated arithmetic encoding program, a "u" that followed a "q" would be encoded very compactly, since "u" is very likely to occur after a "q." The combination of these two improvements results in very effective compression.

Most other compression techniques are tailored for a specific type of data, so they aren't well suited for archiving. The three basic methods I've described here—Huffman compression, the various LZ techniques, and arithmetic coding—cover the bulk of what's used in practice. Many of the improvements in recent years have revolved around ways of combining these techniques (for example, using Huffman codes for the dictionary entries) or doing sophisticated preprocessing to change the data so it's more effectively compressed by one of these methods. (JPEG converts and selectively removes graphical data so it can be compressed with Huffman or arithmetic encoding; PNG uses a simple filter technique to convert graphics data so it can be more effectively encoded with a dictionary-based approach.)

Perhaps the single most significant development in compression algorithms over the last several decades is the appearance of software patents. Since 1981, the United States Patent and Trademark Office (USPTO) has accepted patent applications for software algorithms. Many patents have been awarded for compression techniques, of which the most publicized are Unisys' patents on LZW compression and IBM's patents on arithmetic encoding. Unfortunately, the USPTO did not initially handle such patent applications well; several patents have been awarded to different people for the same algorithm (sometimes with almost identical wording). Few of these patents have been challenged in court, and the high cost of patent lawsuits makes it unlikely that many will be challenged.

One positive result of these patents is the enormous amount of work that has been done to develop new compression algorithms (most of which are promptly patented by their inventors). Another effect, however, has been quite negative. Many compression algorithms were adopted for specific uses either as part of international standards (such as V.42bis and JPEG) or by companies or individuals who copied public domain code (the `compress` implementation of LZW was widely copied for various uses). The financial penalties for using these algorithms (in the form of royalties to the patent owners) has dissuaded support for these standards by authors of shareware, free software or "royalty-free" libraries. A few companies have publicly announced that they will not charge royalties for use of their patented algorithms in free software, but this policy is uncommon. It's unclear what effect this conflict will have on the free software industry or on patent law. At least one organization, the League for Programming Freedom, is opposed to software patents and is actively working to have software patents overturned.

Compression Isn't Perfect

Compression algorithms are useful, but they have limits. The most obvious limit is that no compression method (or combination of compression methods) is perfect; some data will become larger when you use that technique.[2]

---

[2]When you look carefully at how compression algorithms work, it's really quite remarkable that these algorithms do manage to reduce so many types of data.

Intelligent compression programs put a marker at the beginning of their output indicating how the data was compressed. If the data could not be made smaller, that marker indicates that the data is "uncompressed." In this case, the data has been enlarged only by the size of the marker, but it has still become larger.

Occasionally, a compression program claims to compress "*any* file down to 16 kilobytes," or "compress *every* file by at *least* 30 percent." Any such claim is simply wrong, although a few highly respected publications have been persuaded to publish announcements of such products. (See page 250 for the story of one product that claimed perfect compression.)

A few of these claims have been shown to be simple fraud: The data to be "compressed" was copied into a separate hidden file, leaving the original file obviously smaller. While such a scheme does look impressive in a directory listing, it hardly qualifies as "compression." Most "perfect compression" claims have been quietly withdrawn without public scrutiny of the proposed compression techniques.

A few perfect compression claims have turned out to be simple fraud. One such program, when asked to archive a file, would delete the file from your hard disk and the archive would only grow by a hundred bytes. De-archiving restored the file as you would expect, unless you were unlucky enough to use your hard disk before attempting to de-archive. The program actually stored only the filename and the location on the disk where the file data remained, and then deleted the file. It could properly restore the file to a directory only as long as that part of the hard disk had not been re-used for another file. If that area had been re-used, your data was simply gone.[3]

It's not difficult to see why any compression technique must make some files longer. Remember that these techniques are really "encoding" techniques, which take some information and store it in a different way. Once you sidestep the prejudice of using the word "compression," it's reasonable that any encoding method that makes some information smaller must also make some information larger.

---

[3]One simple way to test for this sort of hoax is to perform the following experiment: Copy several files onto a freshly formatted floppy disk, use the program to archive the files, then copy the archive onto another freshly formatted floppy disk and try to extract the files from the archive.

But the real proof is to think not of the encoding (compression) technique, but the decoding (decompression) technique. A compression method that doesn't allow you to recover the original data isn't very useful.

Here's a little thought experiment for you. Pretend that you actually have a compression program that makes every file smaller. Also pretend you have a computer with a *really* big hard disk, and you have on this hard disk a copy of every possible 10,000 byte file. Now, take your imaginary compression program and compress every one of those files. When you're finished, every one of those files is shorter than 10,000 bytes.

It may not seem relevant, but exactly how many files are there? Since a byte has eight bits in it, there must be $2^{80,000}$ files with exactly 10,000 bytes in them. So, our little thought experiment now has $2^{80,000}$ files, all of which are shorter than 10,000 bytes. What may not be entirely obvious is that all of those "compressed" files aren't different! The reason is that there aren't that many different files shorter than 10,000 bytes. If you add together the number of files exactly 9,999 bytes long, and the number of files exactly 9,998 bytes long, and so on, you end up with a number less than $2^{80,000}$.

The important consequence is that *two of the compressed files must be identical.* If this seems like a big jump, imagine that you have five face-down cards. Because there are only four possible suits, you know that two of those cards have the same suit (it's possible that all five have the same suit, but you can't be certain). The same principle applies: This thought experiment leaves you with $2^{80,000}$ files, and there are fewer possible different files, so two of them must be the same.

What does all of this mean? You started by pretending you had a perfect compression method, one that compressed every file. I then showed you that at least two files were different before they were compressed, but were the same after they were compressed. There's no way to decompress those two files to obtain the originals.

What this thought experiment shows is that it's perfectly possible to have some program that compresses every file, but only as long as you don't expect to have a corresponding decompression program. Of course, a compression program that doesn't allow you to retrieve the original data is not very useful. (Put slightly differently, one "perfect" compression method for paper files is incineration. Your files do indeed become much smaller, but recovering them is rather tricky.)

A Note About Encryption

Encryption is similar to compression in many ways. The goal of encryption is to encode data so that it is difficult for anyone to figure out what the data is. Usually, encryption requires a password for encoding, and the same password for decoding, although "public key" schemes such as pgp actually use different passwords for encryption and decryption.

Many archiving programs also support some form of encryption. The idea of such encryption is to make it difficult for anyone who doesn't know the password to extract the files from the archive. No encryption method is impossible to break, given enough resources. A few encryption methods (such as the algorithms used by some Unix crypt programs and the popular pgp program) are widely believed to require enormous resources to break, and are considered "secure" by experts. Generally, the encryption techniques used by archiving programs are not considered "secure" by experts. In fact, some freely available programs claim to be able to decrypt an encrypted ZIP file in a few hours, without requiring the password.

However, you rarely need more security than that provided by ZIP or similar programs. If all you want to do is deter a snoopy coworker from reading your personal files, the security provided by PKZIP or a similar archiving program may well be sufficient. (Of course, if you've inadvertently left the original, unencrypted file on the same disk, or left a printout sitting on your desk, then the encryption in the archive is useless.)

However, even the modest security provided by an encrypted archive *is* difficult to circumvent. If you forget the password, you may never recover the data.[4]

Which is Best?

Choosing an archiving and compression program is complicated by several factors. New compression methods are created almost weekly, each claiming marginally better compression or speed than its predecessors. You must often

---

[4]My advice for data that you want to protect is to store it, unencrypted, on a floppy disk in a locked drawer. This method probably is more secure than any easily available encryption, is easier to understand, and involves fewer risks.

decide between a newer program that offers better compression and an older, more established program that will be easily available to people with whom you may trade files. Another factor is that different archiving and compression programs have become popular on different platforms. If you need to move archived data between different types of computers, you have few real options. Finally, the reason for archiving data is often to give it to someone else or to store it away somewhere. You want to make sure that the necessary de-archiving program will be available.

For most users, the security of using a well-established product far outweighs the advantages of better compression in new programs. Stick with the established standards for your particular platform: StuffIt for Macintosh users, TAR/compress or TAR/GZIP for Unix users, and ZIP or PKZIP for MS-DOS users. If you need to exchange data across different systems, look at ZIP or ZOO, both of which are well-established and available on a wide range of different systems. Finally, the better archivers have a "free" companion de-archiver that you can give to your friends; include a copy on any floppy disk or hard disk directory that contains archived data. You'll be glad you did.

More Information

A good introduction to a variety of basic compression algorithms can be found in Mark Nelson's *The Data Compression Book* [Nel92]. If you have Internet access, the FAQ (Frequently Asked Questions) file for the `comp.compression` newsgroup is also a good source of general compression information. If you're curious about the absolute best compression available, a ranking of compression programs is published on `http://www.mi.net/act/act.html`.

A variety of MS-DOS archiving and compression programs are available from the SIMTEL archives in the `msdos/archiver` and `msdos/compress` directories.

The League for Programming Freedom (LPF) is an organization that opposes software patents and user interface copyrights. You can find out more from their World Wide Web site `http://www.lpf.org`, or by writing to: League for Programming Freedom, 1 Kendall Square #143, P.O. Box 9171, Cambridge, MA 02139.

TAR

20

TAR is one of the oldest archiving programs, and is still heavily used on Unix systems. A lot of the information on the Internet is archived with TAR, then compressed using one of two common Unix compression programs.

Because of this two-stage handling (archive with TAR and then compress with a separate program), these archives usually end up with two file extensions on Unix systems. For example, a group of files may be archived to form `files.tar`, and then compressed with the GZIP program to form `files.tar.gz`. Systems such as MS-DOS and Windows don't allow multiple extensions, so this name is frequently condensed to `files.tgz`. Similarly, an archive `files.tar.Z` compressed with the Unix compress program is typically named `files.tz` or `files.taz` on MS-DOS and Windows.

To recover such files, you need to first uncompress the file and then de-archive, although some programs perform both steps simultaneously. I'll talk about the GZIP and compress formats in later chapters.

TAR at a Glance	
Name:	TAR, Tape Archiving utility
Extensions:	`.tar`, `.tgz`, `.taz`, `.tz`
Use For:	Archiving files
References:	Unix man pages, *4.4BSD Programmer's Reference Manual* [PRM94]
On CD:	TAR programs for MS-DOS, Macintosh

Command Line	Description
tar tf *archive.tar*	List the contents of the archive
tar tvf *archive.tar*	Give a detailed listing
tar xvf *archive.tar*	Extract all the files
tar xvf *archive.tar files* ...	Extract only the named files
tar cvf *archive.tar files* ...	Create a new archive

Table 20.1   Common TAR Command Lines

How to Use TAR

TAR is an old format supported by many programs, including graphical archiving programs on some systems. I'll describe how to use the traditional Unix command-line version. Although there are many different versions of the command-line program, they are all used in the same way.[1]

The first item on the command line is a set of command letters that specify what the TAR program should do. These letters also determine how the rest of the items on the command line should be interpreted.

Here are a few examples. The command tar t means to give a listing (think "table of contents") of the current archive. What's the "current" archive? Well, remember that *TAR* stands for *tape archive*, and you can reasonably guess that the "current" archive is the one currently in the tape drive. Of course, you probably don't have a tape drive, so you'll almost always include the letter f, which means the archive should be read from the indicated file. The most common way to get a listing of the contents of a TAR archive is with the command tar tf archive.tar. The v modifier tells TAR to be *verbose* about whatever it's doing. A verbose listing tells you the sizes and other information about each file. Thus, tar tvf archive.tar gives a pretty thorough overview of the contents of the file archive.tar. Table 20.1 gives some other common uses of the TAR program.

Notice that the first letter is the command letter (t for *table* or x for *extract*) and the remaining letters are modifiers. Besides the common v and f modifiers, many others are of interest only if you're using TAR to back up a

---

[1] Even if you expect to use a graphical version, it's worth knowing how to use the command line version. Not only will it give you a feel for what TAR does, if you ever use a Unix Internet shell account, you'll have access to the text-based TAR program there.

First File		Second File		
Header	File Contents	Header	File Contents	· · ·

Figure 20.1   Organization of a TAR Archive

Unix system to a tape drive. The z modifier supported by the GNU version of TAR is quite useful.[2] The z modifier instructs TAR to compress the archive as it is being created, or uncompress it as it is being extracted. The result is the same as compressing the archive with GZIP (see page 223) after it is created, or uncompressing it with GUNZIP before it is extracted.

How TAR Works

Since TAR does no compression, it's a good place to start understanding how simple archiving programs work. Most archiving programs are fundamentally similar. As shown in Figure 20.1, a TAR file is created simply by appending the files to be archived, preceding each one with a 512-byte header containing information about the file. The end of the archive is marked by two blocks of 512 zero bytes each.

If 512 bytes of header for each file seems like a lot, that's because it is. In fact, the current standard format for TAR archives only uses 345 of those bytes, and most of that is usually empty. Table 20.2 lists the contents of the header. Unlike many programs, all of the information in the TAR header is in ASCII text format, with null bytes filling any unused space.

Although the format shown in Table 20.2 is currently the most widespread, there have been many slightly incompatible formats for the data in the header:

- The original TAR dates back to the early 1970s. It only stored the information identified in Table 20.2 as "Old."

---

[2]Type the command `tar --version` to see if you're using the GNU version of TAR. Yes, there are two dashes in that command.

Size	Origin	Description
100	Old	Name of file
8	Old	File mode in octal
8	Old	User ID of file owner in decimal
8	Old	Group ID of file owner in decimal
12	Old	File size in decimal
12	Old	File date in decimal. Seconds since 0:00 January 1, 1970
8	Old	Checksum of header
1	Old	Type of link
100	Old	Name of linked file
8	POSIX	Magic value `ustar` followed by 2 blanks and a null
32	POSIX	User name
32	POSIX	Group name
8	POSIX	Device major number in decimal
8	POSIX	Device minor number in decimal

Table 20.2   Header of a TAR File

- The *POSIX* standard extended the old TAR header with a few useful new fields, the most important being the magic string `ustar` ("Unix Standard TAR") which can be used to quickly identify TAR archives.[3]

- Prior to the POSIX standard for TAR, the Computer Science Research Group at the University of California at Berkeley developed another extension to the old TAR format as part of their 4.2BSD operating system. The 4.2BSD TAR format has been largely replaced by the POSIX format.

- Unix System V used another slightly incompatible extension to the TAR format. This extension has also given way to the POSIX format.

---

[3]"Unix" is the trademarked name of a specific operating system, originally developed by AT&T. However, the word is commonly used to refer to any similar system. The IEEE's Portable Open Systems standard (POSIX) was developed to maintain a high degree of compatibility between Unix-like systems developed by different groups. No operating system is actually called "POSIX." POSIX itself is defined only on paper. Most Unix-like operating systems now attempt to be "POSIX-compatible." Throughout this book, I'll succumb to the common error of using "Unix" to refer to any Unix-like system.

- The Free Software Foundation (see page 226) has spent many years developing a freely distributable collection of Unix software, with the intention of eventually developing a complete Unix-like system they call GNU. The GNU version of TAR includes several extensions to the POSIX standard, most notably support for *sparse files*. (Sparse files use less disk space than the official length of the file; these files often are created database programs that only store a few records in a large file. Many Unix-like systems will only allocate disk space to the part of the file that currently holds data.)

Unless you're transferring data between Unix systems, only the original TAR header fields are important. The extensions added by POSIX, 4.2BSD, System V, and GNU are probably of interest only if you're actually backing up Unix file systems to tape.

All of the information in a TAR header is stored as ASCII strings. The file size, for instance, is stored as an ASCII string with the decimal number, rather than in binary. You can (if you're careful) manually disassemble a TAR archive by using a binary editor program: Just read the name and size of the file, shave off the 512-byte header, and store the appropriate number of bytes into the desired file.

Any unused part of the 512-byte header is filled with zero bytes. (In particular, all strings are terminated by zero bytes.) This convention helps distinguish the different TAR header formats. If a particular part of the header is filled with zero bytes, that part is not being used and can be ignored.

The POSIX standard added a "magic string" that can be used to rapidly tell if a file is a TAR file. Unfortunately, this string doesn't help detect old-format TAR files. If a file lacks the magic string, you can tell if it's a TAR file by verifying the checksum:

- Read the decimal number from the checksum part of the header.

- Fill the checksum part of the header with eight blanks (ASCII 32).

- Add together the value of every byte in the header.

- If the result matches the number you read from the checksum part, the header is valid.

Obviously, this procedure isn't something you'd want to do by hand, but it is useful if you want to write a program that recognizes TAR files.

The TAR format also supports "links." Unix systems allow a single file to appear under multiple names. This feature is used in a variety of ways, both to conserve disk space and to maintain compatibility when different programs expect to find certain files in different locations. It's wasteful to store the same file data multiple times in the TAR file, so TAR includes the ability to explicitly store a link, which specifies another name for the same file data. This approach both saves space in the TAR file (since the file data isn't duplicated) and helps preserve the link status when the TAR file is de-archived. The link type field is also used to indicate a file stored in a special format.

Also note that the name of the file can be up to 100 bytes long. This name is the full path name of the file, with / characters separating directories. It's quite common for the names in a TAR file to begin with ./, where the period indicates the current directory.

More Information

Most Unix-like systems already have some form of TAR. If you're on an old system, the native TAR program may not support the newer POSIX, 4.2BSD, or GNU extensions. In that case, you may want to obtain the GNU version.

The GNU TAR program is available from any GNU archive site, including `ftp://prep.ai.mit.edu/pub/gnu`.

The Windows WinZip program supports TAR and many other formats. It's available from `http://www.winzip.com/winzip`.

Several TAR programs for MS-DOS are available from the SIMTEL collection in the `pub/archiver` directory.

The Macintosh `suntar` program is available from the Info-Mac archives.

Compress

In the previous chapter, I mentioned that TAR archives are usually compressed with a separate program. Over ten years after its creation, the *compress* program is still the most popular choice for this separate compression. Perhaps more importantly, its source code was placed in the public domain, which allowed many programmers to adapt its compression code to other purposes. The compression algorithm from compress was used in the popular MS-DOS ARC archiving program, CompuServe's GIF graphics format, and ZModem's compression extension. Compress itself has been ported to a variety of different systems.

The popularity of compress source code has led to a number of conflicts with Unisys' patent on the LZW algorithm used by compress. Although Unisys has not tried to restrict the use of compress, it has charged licensing fees for other software implementations of the LZW algorithm. As a result, the use of compress is being discouraged by some groups. This patent issue was one of the major motivations for the development of GZIP (see page 223).

Compress at a Glance

Name:	(Unix) Compress
Extensions:	.Z, .??Z
Use For:	Compressing a single file
Reference:	Unix man page, reproduced in [URM94]

How to Use Compress

The compress program does one thing, and it does it very simply: Type compress *filename* to compress the indicated file. If compress is successful, it changes the filename by adding .Z to the end of the file.[1] If compress cannot make the file smaller (see page 187), it leaves the file unchanged.

To uncompress a file, type uncompress *filename* or compress -d *filename* if you don't have a separate uncompress program. The file will be uncompressed and restored to its original filename.

These programs have few options. Besides -d (decompress), there are -v (verbose), -f (force compression, even if the result is larger), -c (list the data to the screen, rather than replacing the file[2]), and -b (use the specified number of bits). The default for -b is 16 bits, which requires over 400 kilobytes of memory for compression or decompression. When compressing something to be decompressed on a machine with limited memory, use -b 12 (which only requires about 30 kilobytes of memory to decompress).

How Compress Works

Compress' LZW algorithm works by listing all of the sequences it has seen so far in a *dictionary*. Whenever it sees a sequence in the data to be compressed, it looks in the dictionary:

- If the sequence is in the dictionary, the compressor outputs the code for that entry.
- If the sequence extends a sequence already in the dictionary, it's added to the table.

For example, if the compressor already has Kientz in the dictionary and it sees Kientzl, it will output the code for Kientz, then output l, and then add Kientzl to the dictionary. If it later sees Kientzle, it will output the code for Kientzl followed by e and add Kientzle to the dictionary. Each time it sees something that's in the dictionary, it spits out the code from the

---

[1]On Unix systems, note that this is an *uppercase* Z. On MS-DOS, filenames can only have a single period, so rather than add a new extension, the last letter of the current extension will be changed to Z.

[2]The letter c is suggestive of the Unix cat program, which simply lists a file.

dictionary and adds a new entry that's one byte longer. In this way, each time a sequence of bytes is repeated, the dictionary grows to include a longer part of that sequence. Note that it has to see the string `Kientzle` at least eight times before it creates a dictionary entry containing the entire string.

Actually, the prior paragraph is a bit misleading. The compressor works one byte at a time, not by grabbing a bunch of bytes, although the end result is still the same. Initially, the dictionary contains every single-byte sequence, numbered 0 through 255, and one extra entry numbered 256, which I'll discuss later. Let's walk through as the LZW compressor reads each byte of `abcabc`.

a This is already in the dictionary, so the compressor remembers it and gets the next byte.

b Since `ab` isn't in the dictionary, it gets added as code 257. The compressor outputs `a` and starts looking for sequences starting with `b`.

c Since `bc` isn't in the dictionary, it gets added as code 258. The compressor outputs `b` and starts looking for sequences starting with `c`.

a Again, `ca` isn't in the dictionary, so it gets added as code 259. The compressor outputs `c` and starts looking for sequences starting with `a`.

b Now `ab` is in the dictionary, so the compressor remembers it (actually, it remembers the code for it: 257) and keeps going.

c Now the compressor has 257 (the code for `ab`) and `c`. Since `abc` isn't in the dictionary, it gets added (code 260), 257 is output, and the compressor looks for sequences starting with `c`.

Table 21.1 summarizes a longer example in a more compact form. Notice that at every step, either the current sequence is already in the table (indicated by a number in parentheses) or is added to the table. Also notice that the sequences being added to the table grow longer and longer, and the entries in the output column become less frequent.

If you follow these steps carefully, you'll get a good feel for how LZW compression works. Besides the dictionary, the compressor actually uses very little data. It only needs to keep the code for the sequence matched so far and the current byte.

Previous Code	Current Byte	Current Sequence	Add to Dictionary	Output
None	a	a		
a	b	ab	257	a
b	c	bc	258	b
c	a	ca	259	c
a	b	ab (257)		
257	c	abc	260	257
c	a	ca (259)		
259	b	cab	261	259
b	c	bc (258)		
258	a	bca	262	258
a	b	ab (257)		
257	c	abc (260)		
260	a	abca	263	260
a	b	ab (257)		
257	c	abc (260)		
260	a	abca (263)		
263	b	abcab	264	263

Table 21.1   An Example of LZW Compression

As I discussed on pages 187–189, no compressor is very useful without the corresponding decompressor, so let's take a look at how the LZW decompressor works. Actually, you've already seen most of it; the decompressor works pretty much the same as the compressor. Whenever the compressor finds a long sequence that needs to be added, it outputs the previous code, rather than the one it just added to the dictionary. The decompressor can just follow along, building the same dictionary as the compressor. Whenever the decompressor reads a code, it decodes it from the dictionary and then mimics the compressor's operation to update the dictionary. Table 21.2 shows how the decompressor decodes the output of the compressor above. Notice that it builds the same dictionary as the compressor.

With one exception, Table 21.2 shows that the decompressor never sees a code until after that code has been entered in the dictionary. The one exception is for data that looks like *byte-sequence-byte-sequence-byte*, such as

Input	Output	Add to Dictionary
a	a	
b	b	ab (257)
c	c	bc (258)
257	ab	ca (259)
259	ca	abc (260)
258	bc	cab (261)
260	abc	bca (262)
263	abca	abca (263)

Table 21.2   LZW Decompression Example

abcabca. In this case, the code for *byte-sequence-byte* (263 in the example) will be seen by the decoder before it gets entered in the dictionary. Fortunately, the only way the decompressor will see a code that's not already in the dictionary is in this exact situation, so the decompressor can simply use the preceding code (260 in the example) to figure out what the code should be.

One part that requires some explanation is the reserved code 256 that I mentioned earlier. As you can tell from the examples so far, the dictionary grows steadily as the data is compressed. To do this sort of compression on very large files, you must somehow limit the amount of memory used to store the dictionary. The compressor places a fixed limit on the size of the dictionary (typically between 4,096 and 65,536 entries) and clears the dictionary when it reaches this size. That way, the memory usage can be limited. To keep from confusing the decompressor, the compressor inserts code 256 (which is called the *reset code*) whenever it clears the dictionary. When the decompressor sees code 256, it resets its dictionary.

When compress starts, it only has 257 entries in its dictionary, so only nine bits are required to represent any dictionary code. Once the dictionary grows to 512 entries, ten bits are required. Compress optimizes its output by only using as many bits as necessary to represent everything in the dictionary. After the 511th entry is made in the dictionary, it begins to output 10 bits for each code; after the 1023rd entry is made, it outputs 11 bits for each code; and so on. As long as the decompressor is building the same dictionary, it can switch code sizes at the correct time.

Compress implements some improvements on Welch's original LZW algorithm. The most interesting is *adaptive reset*. Rather than clearing the dictionary as soon as it fills, as I suggested earlier, compress actually continues to use the dictionary as long as the compression remains high. This approach is motivated by two observed facts about LZW compression. First, the amount of compression depends heavily on the size of the dictionary. A larger dictionary will have longer entries that can be compressed into a single code. Adaptive reset attempts to exploit a large dictionary by not throwing it away too soon. The other observation is that many files (especially TAR archives that contain different kinds of files within the archive) contain sections with very different kinds of data. As the LZW algorithm progresses, it builds a dictionary specifically tailored for a particular type of data. If the data changes significantly, the dictionary will no longer compress well. By monitoring how well the data is being compressed, the compress program can tell when this degradation occurs, and reset the dictionary at that point.

Other programs that use LZW actually use two reserved codes. In addition to the reset code, they use a special code to mark the end of the compressed data.

More Information

Many Unix systems have the compress and uncompress programs already available. If you have compress but not uncompress, just use `compress -d` instead. The source code is in Volume 2 of the `comp.sources.unix` archives.

A version of compress for MS-DOS systems is available from the SIMTEL archives as `msdos/compress/comp430s.zip`. It's also available from the *Garbo* archive as `pc/unix/comp430s.zip`.

A version of compress for the Macintosh is available from the Info-Mac archives as `cmp/maccompress-32.hqx`.

ARC

22

In 1985, Thom Henderson of Software Enhancement Associates (SEA) wrote a simple archiving utility, *ARC*, that attempted to compress each file as it was added to the archive. He gave it away with two interesting conditions:

- You can copy it and give a copy to anyone.
- Commercial users must pay for their use of it.

The primary goal was to distribute the program cheaply. Rather than sinking money into packaging and distribution to stores, SEA chose to rely on word-of-mouth and informal copying to make it available to users. This method of distribution proved to be quite successful, and ARC rapidly became a *de facto* standard.

Over the next several years, Henderson proceeded to experiment with a variety of different compression methods, eventually settling on LZW compression code copied from the Unix compress utility. Henderson's utility was very influential, and inspired the development of many later archivers.

ARC at a Glance

Names:	(MS-DOS) ARC, SEA ARC, PKARC
Extension:	`.arc`
Use For:	Archiving files with compression to exchange with MS-DOS systems
On CD:	*WinZip* program for Windows

Letter	Description
l	List contents
x	Extract files
a	Add files to archive
t	Test archive

Table 22.1   ARC Command Letters

Command Line	Description
arc l *archive.arc*	List contents of archive
arc x *archive.arc*	Extract files from the archive
arc x *archive.arc files ...*	Extract named files

Table 22.2   Sample ARC Command Lines

How to Use ARC

Two different ARC programs are widely available. Besides the original SEA ARC, the clone *PKARC* program, developed by Phil Katz, is also widespread. Both of these programs were originally for PC systems, but ARC has since been ported to a wide variety of systems. These programs are all compatible, except that PKARC adds a compression method not supported by the original SEA ARC. The portable version of ARC (based on the source code for SEA ARC) does support this additional compression method.

Like TAR, ARC is a command-line program where the first item on the command line is a series of letters specifying what the program should do and the second is the name of the archive file. Also like TAR, the letters begin with a command letter, and can include several options. Table 22.1 lists the most common commands. Table 22.2 gives some sample command lines.

How ARC Works

The basic organization of an ARC file is the same simple "header-data" arrangement used by TAR, as shown in Figure 22.1.

First File   Second File

| Header | File Contents | Header | File Contents | . . . |

Figure 22.1   Organization of an ARC File

Size	Description
1	Byte 26 (hex 1A) to mark the start of a header
1	Type of compression
13	File name with zero byte at end
4	Size of compressed file
2	File date, in 16-bit MS-DOS format
2	File time, in 16-bit MS-DOS format
2	CRC-16 of uncompressed file data
4	Size of uncompressed file

Table 22.3   Header of an ARC File

ARC's header, however, is much smaller. ARC was designed for MS-DOS, which is reflected in the header structure described in Table 22.3. The filename can only be 12 characters long, and the date and time are stored in compact MS-DOS formats.

The compression type field indicates how the file data is stored, according to Table 22.4. Compression type zero is used to indicate the end of the file. Compression type one indicates an old header format that omits the size of the uncompressed file. Compression type nine is not supported by the MS-DOS SEA ARC program. It was introduced by PKARC, and later added to the portable version of ARC. Note that the LZW compression went through several different versions before it adapted the code from compress.

ARC uses MS-DOS format for storing dates and times. The date is a single 16-bit number, where the high-order seven bits are the number of years since 1980, the next four bits are the month number (1–12), and the low-order five bits are the day number (1–31). The time is a 16-bit number where the high-order five bits are the hour (0–23), the next six bits are the minute (0–59), and the low-order five bits are the seconds divided by two (0–29).

Value	Compression Type
0	None: Marks end-of-archive
1	Uncompressed (obsolete, old header format)
2	Uncompressed
3	Packed (run-length encoding)
4	Packed, then Squeezed (Huffman compression)
5	crunched (early LZW attempt)
6	Packed, then crunched
7	Packed, then crunched (modified)
8	Crunched (compress-style 12-bit LZW)
9	Squashing (Packed, then compress-style 13-bit LZW)

Table 22.4   ARC Compression Type Codes

More Information

ARC has been largely supplanted by the newer ZIP format, but there are still many ARC files in older archives.

For MS-DOS, the `arca` and `arce` programs can be used to create and de-archive ARC files, respectively. They're available from the SIMTEL archives in the `msdos/archiver` directory.

The Macintosh `arcmac` program is available from the Info-Mac archives.

A Unix version of ARC is available from the CTAN archives (see page 75) in the `tex-archive/archive-tools/arc521` directory. It's also in Volume 26 of the `comp.sources.unix` archives.

ZIP

23

Phil Katz became well known first for his clone of SEA ARC (see page 205). Known as PKARC, Katz's program was faster and smaller than SEA ARC, and was a popular alternative.

After a legal conflict with SEA, Phil Katz abandoned PKARC to develop a new program which he called *PKZIP*. PKZIP was similar in many respects to ARC, but added a few nice features.

- It stores a centralized directory of all files at the end of the archive. If the archive is written to multiple floppy disks, PKZIP can prompt the user to insert the last floppy disk (which contains the central directory) and then insert only the floppy disks actually required to access a particular file.

- PKZIP's header and directory information support very long filenames and a variety of additional information. The PKZIP file format can be used on many different platforms, unlike the ARC file format, which can't handle long Unix or Macintosh filenames or other information.

ZIP at a Glance

Names:	PKZIP/PKUNZIP, ZIP/UNZIP
Extensions:	`.zip`
Use For:	Archiving files with compression
On CD:	ZIP programs for MS-DOS, Macintosh, Windows, Linux

• PKZIP uses different compression methods. In particular, Katz developed a compression technique called *Deflation*, which is believed to be completely free of patent restrictions. This compression method has been adopted by the PNG graphics format (see page 139) and GNU GZIP compression utility (described in the next chapter).

How to Use PKZIP/ZIP

Katz' PKZIP and PKUNZIP are standards among PC users. They're distributed as shareware: You can copy and test the programs for free, but are encouraged to pay for them if you do use them.

Because Katz was generous enough to allow free use of the PKZIP file format, ZIP name, and Deflation compression algorithm, several other programs support ZIP archives. For example, the *ZIP* and *UNZIP* programs are freely available for a variety of systems. These programs are functionally equivalent to the most recent PKZIP and PKUNZIP programs, although their options and capabilities differ slightly.

Unlike ARC or TAR, which handle both archiving and de-archiving in a single program, ZIP and PKZIP only create archives, while UNZIP and PKUNZIP only know how to extract archives. I'll describe how to use either set of utilities to perform standard archiving tasks.

The first task you will usually encounter is simply finding out what's in an archive. You can get that information with either `pkunzip -v archive.zip` (think "view") or `unzip -v archive.zip`.

The second task is extracting files from an archive. One important distinction needs to be made here. Frequently, if you're using an archive to transfer a small collection of files, the directory structure is unimportant. On the other hand, if you're archiving a large set of files (or an entire hard disk), restoring each file to an appropriate directory is necessary.

The problem is that sometimes, the person creating the archive will over-specify the directory. For example, if the archive has two files in it, stored as `C:\SOME\LONG\PATH\FILE1.TXT` and `C:\SOME\LONG\PATH\FILE2.TXT`, you'll probably want to extract them as `FILE1.TXT` and `FILE2.TXT` in the current directory. Fortunately, this situation is relatively rare, but you should keep this example in mind.

PKUNZIP and UNZIP differ in how they handle directory names stored in the archive. By default, PKUNZIP ignores all directory names. Typing simply `pkunzip` *`archive.zip`* will de-archive all the files in the archive to the current directory. This approach handles the example I gave in the previous paragraph. If you want to restore all files to the specified directory, you should give the -d option as in: `pkunzip -d` *`archive.zip`*.

UNZIP, on the other hand, always uses the directory names by default. If you have `FILE1.EXE` (some program) and `CONFIG\FILE1.TXT` (a configuration file for that program), UNZIP would create the `CONFIG` directory. If you want UNZIP to ignore ("junk") the directory names (mimicking PKUNZIP), use the -j option, as in: `unzip -j` *`archive.zip`*.

Both PKUNZIP and UNZIP allow you to specify which files to extract. Simply list the names you want to extract after the name of the archive. There's one caveat, though: PKUNZIP runs on MS-DOS, where case in filenames doesn't matter. UNZIP, however, is designed to run on many different systems, and case does matter. So, you need to either type the filename *exactly* as it is shown by `unzip -v`, or else use the -C option to make UNZIP mimic PKUNZIP's handling of case.

To create an archive, you use PKZIP or ZIP. If you just want to archive a bunch of files, use `pkzip` *`archive.zip filenames`* or `zip` *`archive.zip filenames`*.

Like their counterparts, PKZIP and ZIP disagree about how to handle directory names. PKZIP, by default, does not store directory names, just the names of the files. If you want to archive everything in a directory, use `pkzip -P` *`archive.zip directory`* (note that's *uppercase* P), which will store everything in the directory and include the directory names. Remember to either use UNZIP or use PKUNZIP's -d option when extracting.

ZIP does store the directory names, but won't look inside the directories unless you tell it to. Use `zip -r` *`archive.zip directory`* to archive everything in the directory.

PKZIP/PKUNZIP and ZIP/UNZIP all handle wildcards. The details vary from system to system.

Simply typing `pkunzip`, `unzip`, `pkzip`, or `zip` will yield a brief help message. ZIP and UNZIP are distributed with free documentation; PKZIP and PKUNZIP include documentation if you pay for them.

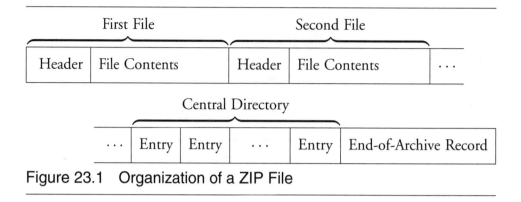

Figure 23.1   Organization of a ZIP File

ZIP File Format

ZIP files have the same general organization as TAR and ARC, but with a more sophisticated header, and with the addition of a central directory at the end of the archive, as shown in Figure 23.1.

ZIP files can be processed in two different ways. If a program needs to access a single file in a large archive, it can look at the end-of-archive record to find the beginning of the central directory, scan the central directory to find the desired file, and then go directly to the file. This approach is especially useful if the archive is split across many floppy disks; the user can be prompted to insert the last floppy (which probably contains the entire central directory) and then insert the floppy containing the desired file.

On the other hand, if a program wants to sequentially access all of the files in the archive, it can ignore the central directory and read each file in turn. This method makes it possible to read ZIP files on-the-fly.

I'll describe the different parts of a ZIP file starting from the end-of-archive record, to show you how a program might find and extract a single file from a multi-floppy archive.

The end-of-archive record is shown in Table 23.1. All binary numbers are stored starting from the least-significant byte (Intel byte order). Most of the information in the end-of-archive record is intended to help applications quickly locate the central directory. The disk containing the central directory and the position of the central directory on that disk are provided. The total size of the central directory (in bytes) allows an application to quickly copy the entire central directory into memory. Frequently, the entire central directory

Size	Description
2	Special code: PK
2	End-of-archive code: 5, 6
2	Number of this disk
2	Number of the disk where the central directory starts
2	Total number of central directory entries on this disk
2	Total number of files in archive
4	Number of bytes in central directory
4	Byte offset of central directory
2	Length of the archive comment
n	Comment

Table 23.1   ZIP End-of-Archive Record

will be on the same disk as the end-of-archive record, but if it's not, ZIP ensures that no central directory entry is split across two disks.

The central directory itself is composed of a number of entries that not only identify basic facts about the file (size and filename) and how it's stored (the type of compression used), but also provides an "extension" area that can be used to hold platform-specific information such as link information on Unix or OS/2 extended attributes.

The central directory entry, outlined in Table 23.2, holds a complete set of information about the file. The central directory has enough information to generate a list of the archive's contents or to locate any particular file in the archive. Some explanation of these fields might be helpful.

Version that Created this Archive   This eight-bit number encodes the version number. Version 2.0 is represented as 20, version 1.10 as 11.

System that Created this Archive   A few of the fields are interpreted differently on different systems. This code also provides a clue about the format of text files. Table 23.3 lists the codes that can appear in this field.

Version That Can Extract This Archive   This field partially depends on the type of compression used. If no compression was used, this field is set to 10, indicating that any version (1.0 or higher) can be used to extract this archive. Most de-archivers simply ignore it.

Size	Description
2	Special code: PK
2	Central directory code: 1, 2
1	Version that created this archive
1	System that created this archive
1	Version that can extract this archive
1	Reserved: always zero
2	General purpose bit flag
2	Compression method
2	File modification time
2	File modification date
4	CRC-32 of uncompressed file data
4	Compressed size of file
4	Uncompressed size of file
2	Length of filename
2	Length of extra data
2	Length of file comment
2	Volume number on which file begins
2	Internal file attributes
4	External file attributes
4	Position of file header on volume
n	Filename
n	Extra data
n	File comment

Table 23.2   ZIP Central Directory Entry Format

General Purpose Bit Flag   The lowest-order bit indicates whether the file is encrypted. The next two bits are used to indicate additional options with compression methods 6 and 8.

Compression Method   This field indicates how the file was compressed, using a code from Table 23.4. Generally, each successive compression method has provided somewhat better compression on typical data.

Date and Time Fields   The date and time are represented using standard MS-DOS formats (see page 207).

Code	System
0	MS-DOS and OS2 with FAT file system
1	Amiga
2	VAX/VMS
3	Unix-like systems
4	IBM VM/CMS
5	Atari ST
6	OS/2 HPFS
7	Macintosh
8	Z-System
9	CP/M

Table 23.3   ZIP System Codes

Code	Compression Type
0	No compression
1	Shrinking (modified LZW)
2	Reduced with factor 1
3	Reduced with factor 2
4	Reduced with factor 3
5	Reduced with factor 4
6	Imploded
7	Reserved
8	Deflated

Table 23.4   ZIP Compression Codes

CRC-32   The CRC-32 of the uncompressed data is provided so that the de-archiver can verify the integrity of the file.

Volume Number   This field indicates the disk on which the file header begins. Disks are numbered starting at zero.

Internal File Attributes   This bitmap indicates properties of the file that may be significant to an archiver or de-archiver. Currently, only bit zero is defined. If set, it indicates that the archiver believed this was a text file.

External File Attributes   ZIP puts MS-DOS attributes in the low-order byte and Unix-style attributes in the the two high-order bytes.

Position of File Header on Volume   This field indicates the byte position where the file begins, relative to the start of the archive file on the volume identified.

Filename   Unlike ARC, ZIP places no limits on the length of the filename, making it useful on a variety of systems. MS-DOS versions of ZIP store the filename in all uppercase.

Extra Data   The extra data section allows special system-specific information to be stored. Data in this field consists of a series of entries, each containing a two-byte ID (a binary number; 0–31 are reserved), a two-byte data size, followed by the data. To simplify reading an entire central directory entry into memory, the entire size of the central directory entry, including the filename, extra data, and comment, must be less than 64 kilobytes.

As you can see, the central directory entry serves two purposes. Besides serving as an index to help applications rapidly find a single file in a large multi-volume archive, it also duplicates all of the information stored in the per-file header. This duplication helps recover information from a damaged archive; even if the per-file header is damaged, it may be possible to recover the file contents using the information in the central directory.

The per-file header, described in Table 23.5 contains most of the information in the central directory.

ZIP's Compression Algorithms

Like many such archive programs, a number of different compression methods have been developed for use with ZIP. In theory, a ZIP program could try each different method and use whichever one worked best for a particular file. In practice, this time-consuming approach is never used. Usually, the newest compression method is the best for most types of files. As a result, most ZIP programs try only the newest method (possibly altered by command-line switches), reverting to an uncompressed format if the file grows.

Size	Description
2	Special code: PK
2	File header code: 3, 4 (multi-disk archives use 7,8 here)
1	Version that can extract this archive
1	Reserved: always zero
2	General purpose bit flag
2	Compression type
2	File modification time
2	File modification date
4	CRC-32 of uncompressed file data
4	Compressed size of file
4	Uncompressed size of file
2	Length of filename
2	Length of extra data
n	Filename
n	Extra data

Table 23.5   ZIP Per-File Header

I'll discuss these starting with the oldest format (rarely used today) and proceeding to the newer ones. The current Deflation algorithm has been adopted by other compression utilities (including GZIP and the PNG graphics format) in large part because it is believed to be completely free of patent restrictions.

How Shrinking Works

Shrinking is a modified version of the LZW algorithm used by compress (see page 200). The first change is that Shrinking only does a *partial reset*. Rather than completely emptying the dictionary at each reset, Shrinking only removes the longest strings. As I mentioned when describing compress, LZW compression relies on the existence of long strings in the dictionary. By only partially clearing the dictionary, some long strings are maintained, hopefully preserving a modest compression even after a reset.

Shrinking also optimizes compress' variably-sized output (see page 203) by only switching to a longer code when that longer code is needed for the output. For example, assume the compressor has just created entry number 511 in the dictionary. At this point, compress would switch to ten-bit codes so it would be prepared to output code 512. However, it may be some time before any code above 511 is actually used in the output. Shrinking defines a special sequence that it outputs just before switching to a longer code size. The decompressor switches code sizes only when it sees this special code.

How Reducing Works

Of course, since Shrinking is based on LZW, it may be subject to the patent on that algorithm, which explains why ZIP switched to variants of the (un-patented) LZ77 compression algorithm. Rather than output a code for each recognized sequence, LZ77 instead outputs an offset into the previous data. For example, abcdabc might be compressed as abcd followed by an offset of -4 and a length of 3, indicating to go back four bytes and copy three bytes.

Reducing, Imploding, and Deflation differ in how they store the offsets and lengths in the output and what kind of additional compression they use.

Reducing stores offsets and lengths by using an escape code. The encoder writes each uncompressed byte as-is, and precedes an offset/length pair with byte 144 (ASCII DLE with the high bit set). The offset and length together are either two or three bytes, divided between offset and length in different ways depending on the "compression factors" mentioned in the table on page 215. A larger compression factor allows larger offsets, while a smaller compression factor allows larger lengths.

After this LZ77 compression stage, the result is compressed again with a simple probabilistic method. This method builds a list that stores, for every byte value, the most common "follower" bytes. For example, the followers for t might include h and o. Reducing stores common followers using fewer bits than less-common followers. The table of common followers is attached to the beginning of the compressed data.

How Imploding Works

The two-stage compression used by Reducing, Imploding, and Deflation has two goals. The first is to take advantage of the strengths of two very different compression techniques (LZ77 and Huffman-style compression). The other goal is to optimize the output of LZ77 by using short codes for common offsets and lengths.

Imploding starts with LZ77 compression with a limit of either 4096 or 8192 on the offsets. It then uses Shannon-Fano compression to select variable bit-length codes for the literal (uncompressed) bytes, the offsets, and the lengths. These three Shannon-Fano trees are built separately; the compressed output includes an extra bit before each literal or offset to indicate whether the next bits encode a literal or an offset/length pair.

How Deflation Works

The Deflation algorithm handles LZ77 compression by keeping a table of all three-byte sequences that appear in the data. If three bytes match a table entry, it then looks at that point in the previous data to see if the match can be extended to more than three bytes. A parameter controls when the algorithm tries to find a better match. The "fastest" setting essentially means the compressor always uses the first match it finds. The "best" setting instructs the compressor to look at every match to find the one that works best. The decompressor just needs to keep the previous 32 kilobytes of decoded data available; the compressor will never use a larger offset.

Once this LZ77 compression is done, the result is evaluated in blocks of 32 kilobytes at a time, and three sets of Huffman codes are built. The first encodes the literals and offsets together (removing the need for the extra bit in the Implode algorithm), while the second encodes the length values. The third set of Huffman codes is used to compress the first two Huffman trees. The decompressor reads the first tree from the beginning of a compressed block, and uses it to decode the literal/offset Huffman tree and the length Huffman tree. These latter trees are used to decode the actual compressed data.

Overall, the Deflation algorithm is usually slightly better in terms of compression and slightly slower than the LZW compression used by the compress program.

Generally, combining two or more compression methods gains very little. However, this particular combination (LZ77 and Huffman) works reasonably well for two reasons: First, LZ77 and Huffman compress very different types of data. LZ77 compresses data that has repeating patterns of bytes, while Huffman compresses data that has an unequal distribution of byte values. The combination tends to compress more kinds of data than either one alone. More importantly, though, both LZ77 and Huffman have good "worst case" behavior. Neither one will ever lengthen the data very much, which makes it less likely that (unintended) expansion from one algorithm will cancel out any gains made by the other.

Drawbacks to ZIP

Overall, ZIP is a well-designed format, with only a few minor drawbacks. One drawback is that it's difficult to build ZIP archives on-the-fly. ZIP stores both the compressed and uncompressed data sizes in the file header. This means that ZIP must be able to do one of the following two things:

- Find the sizes before it writes the compressed data to the archive. This usually requires having enough temporary disk storage to store the compressed data. ZIP can then compress the data to a temporary file, then copy it to the archive. This isn't possible if the file to be compressed is extremely large.

- Edit the file header after writing the compressed file data. This requires that ZIP be able to seek back to the beginning of the file. This may not be possible if the archive is being sent to a tape drive or over a serial connection.

This restriction precludes ZIP from being used as one stage of a Unix pipeline. See page 224 to see how GZIP handles this issue.

A similar restriction occurs because of ZIP's central directory. As ZIP builds an archive, it needs to keep a list of all the files in the archive so that it can write the central directory at the end. This list must be kept either in memory or in a temporary file. If memory is limited and no temporary file can be created, then ZIP will not be able to build a very large archive.

These restrictions are rarely an issue, except for some Unix applications that require the ability to read data being generated by one program, compress it, and pass the result immediately to another program.

More Information

The PKZIP and PKUNZIP programs for MS-DOS are available from many locations, including the SIMTEL archives in the `msdos/zip` directory.

The Info-ZIP project has been developing their ZIP and UNZIP programs as portable, free clones of PKZIP and PKUNZIP. ZIP and UNZIP are available for many different platforms, including Macintosh, Amiga, OS/2, MS-DOS, and many Unix variants. The programs, source code, and information are available using anonymous FTP from `quest.jpl.nasa.gov`, in the pub directory.

The ZIP format has been fairly well documented in a series of notes included with PKZIP. The ZIP format is also a registered MIME format type. The full registration, which includes the most recent documentation of the file format, is available using anonymous FTP from `ftp://ftp.isi.edu` in the directory `in-notes/iana/assignments/media-types/application`.

GZIP

Because of the patent cloud surrounding compress (see page 199), there's been interest in an alternative compression program that could take its place. The *GZIP* program is a stand-alone compression program that can be used as a replacement for compress in most circumstances, provides marginally better compression, and is free of patent constraints. GZIP uses the Deflation compression algorithm developed for PKZIP (see page 219).

How to Use GZIP/GUNZIP

GZIP is used in essentially the same way as its predecessor compress: You type gzip *filename* to compress a file and gunzip *filename* or gzip -d *filename* to uncompress a file. GZIP compresses a file by reading the original and writing the compressed result to a file with the same name but the extension .gz. Table 24.1 lists a few additional options.

GZIP at a Glance	
Name:	GNU GZIP/GUNZIP
Extension:	.gz
Use For:	Compressing a single file
On CD:	GZIP program for MS-DOS

-d   Decompress. Useful if you have GZIP but not GUNZIP.

-c   Write the result to standard output, instead of replacing the file.

-r   Recursively visit each directory and subdirectory, compressing each file. This method is completely different from an archiver such as ARC or ZIP, which combines the compressed files into a single archive. This option simply compresses each file in place.

-l   List information about a compressed file, including the original (uncompressed) name and size.

-1, -2, ..., -8, -9   These options set the amount of compression desired. The option -1 is the fastest and usually offers the least compression, while -9 is the slowest and usually has the best compression. Depending on the data, the default -6 setting may actually compress better than -9.

Table 24.1   GZIP Options

One common point of confusion with the GZIP program is that, although GUNZIP is usually quite good at detecting damaged files, it will occasionally emit the somewhat cryptic error message "...is a multi-part gzip file — get newer version of gzip." Multi-part GZIP files are a planned addition that will allow a single file to be compressed into multiple parts (for example, to compress a large archive onto multiple floppies). This extension has not yet been implemented, however, so you should interpret this error message as indicating that the compressed file is damaged.[1]

How GZIP Works

GZIP is not an archiving program. It's intended to be used in conjunction with TAR or a similar archiver. It is frequently used as part of a Unix pipeline,

---

[1]Another point of confusion is that the GZIP documentation also uses the term "multi-part" to refer to a single GZIP file that contains multiple compressed files within it.

Size	Description
2	Identifying bytes: 31, 139
1	Compression method (currently always 8: Deflation)
1	Flags

Bit	Description
0	File is probably ASCII
1	This file continues a multi-part GZIP file
2	The extra field is present
3	The original file name is present
4	The file comment is present
5	The file is encrypted
6,7	Reserved

Size	Description
4	File modification time
1	Compression flags
1	Operating system
2	(optional) Part number
2	(optional) Length of extra field
?	(optional) Extra field
?	(optional) Original file name (null terminated)
?	(optional) File comment (null terminated)
12	(optional) Encryption information
?	Compressed data
4	CRC-32
4	Size of uncompressed data

Table 24.2   GZIP File Format

where data is sent into the GZIP program to be compressed (or decompressed), and the compressed data is immediately passed along. The output of GZIP can't require backing up to update data earlier in the file. The brief header at the beginning of the file cannot hold the size of the compressed data, since that's not known until the file is completely compressed. For that matter, the size of the uncompressed data may not be known until the complete file has been read.

Table 24.2 outlines the GZIP file format. Some of these fields are loosely based on corresponding fields in the ZIP file format. The fields marked "optional" appear only if the corresponding flag is set in the flags byte. All numbers are stored starting with the least-significant byte (little-endian). The Deflation compression algorithm was described in the previous chapter.

About the Free Software Foundation

The Free Software Foundation (FSF) is an organization working to produce a complete Unix-like operating system called GNU. The most interesting aspect of the FSF's work is the copyright notice included with all of their software. Among other things, the *GNU General Public License* (GPL) guarantees that end users of FSF software will always have access to the source code for that software.[2] Anyone who distributes programs based on FSF source code is obligated to make the complete program source available. One result of this restriction is that FSF software is rarely used as the basis for commercial products, although companies do sell FSF software.

The quality of FSF software is generally quite high, and many Unix-like operating systems include the GNU Emacs text editor and GNU GCC C compiler (with source, of course).

More Information

GZIP source code is available by anonymous FTP from `prep.ai.mit.edu`, in directory /pub/gnu. Look for `gzip-version.tar`. This distribution should compile on most Unix-like systems and several non-Unix systems. A text file in the same directory explains how to obtain versions of GZIP for other platforms.

GZIP for MS-DOS is available from the same location in a self-extracting archive named `gzip-msdos-version.exe`. It's also available from the SIM-TEL archives.

The Info-Mac archives have the `MacGZIP` program for Macintosh.

---

[2]The GNU GPL is colloquially known as "copyleft" to contrast it with more traditional commercial copyright notices. This nickname has caused much confusion among people who fail to understand the basics of copyright law. Despite the cute names, the GNU GPL *is* a copyright notice, and does place restrictions on the use of FSF software.

SHAR 25

One interesting fact about Unix systems and the Internet is that the vast majority of data shared between Unix systems is in text form. Unlike MS-DOS or Macintosh users, it's fairly unusual for Unix users to exchange compiled programs. Rather, they usually send the source code for that program, because different Unix-like systems have different kinds of processors and different ways of storing executable programs. The various standards that apply to Unix systems attempt to make sure that programs can easily be written that will compile on a variety of different Unix systems. Few standards concern themselves with binary compatibility.

For this reason, there's a real use for an archive format that can archive text files so that the resulting archive is itself a text file. This format makes it easy, for example, to bind a bunch of source files into a single mail message.

One way to build such an archive is to write a batch file that, when executed, creates the resulting files. In Unix, such batch files are typically executed by the shell, hence the name *shell archive*, abbreviated to *SHAR*. Note that the batch file itself is the archive. This technique is similar to the "self-extracting" archives that are popular on MS-DOS and Macintosh systems.

SHAR at a Glance	
Name:	Shell Archive, SHAR
Extensions:	`.shar`, `.sh`
Use For:	Archiving text files for transfer through mail or news

```
cat >Gettysburg <<END_OF_FILE
Four score and seven years ago, our fathers brought forth
upon this continent a new nation:   conceived in liberty, and
dedicated to the proposition that all men are created equal.
END_OF_FILE
cat >Constitution <<END_OF_FILE
We the people of the United States, in Order to form a more
perfect Union, establish Justice, insure domestic Tranquility,
provide for the common defence, promote the general Welfare,
and secure the Blessings of Liberty to ourselves and our
Posterity, do ordain and establish this Constitution for the
United States of America.
END_OF_FILE
exit
```

Figure 25.1   A Simple SHAR Archive

How to Use SHAR

A SHAR archive is a Unix batch file. Usually, you can tell when you have one by a series of comments at the beginning of the file. These comment lines begin with # and usually read something like the following:

```
# This is a shell archive.  Save it in a file, remove anything before
# this line, and then unpack it by entering "sh file".
```

If you're on a Unix system, you can simply follow the instructions. If not, there's an unshar program available for many systems that understands enough about Unix batch files to be able to unpack most SHAR files.

How SHAR Works

Figure 25.1 shows a simple example of a SHAR file. On Unix, typing sh file will invoke the standard Bourne shell program to interpret it as a batch file. The files are actually created with the cat program, which simply copies its input to its output. In this case, the > symbol instructs the shell to direct the output of the first cat command to a file named "Gettysburg." The << symbol directs the shell to feed the subsequent lines to the cat command,

```
# This is a shell archive.  Save it in a file, remove anything before
# this line, and then unpack it by entering "sh file".  Note, it may
# create directories; files and directories will be owned by you and
# have default permissions.
#
# This archive contains:
#
# Gettysburg
# Constitution
#
echo x - Gettysburg
sed 's/^X//' >Gettysburg << 'END-of-Gettysburg'
XFour score and seven years ago, our fathers brought forth
Xupon this continent a new nation:  conceived in liberty, and
Xdedicated to the proposition that all men are created equal.
END-of-Gettysburg
echo x - Constitution
sed 's/^X//' >Constitution << 'END-of-Constitution'
XWe the people of the United States, in Order to form a more
Xperfect Union, establish Justice, insure domestic Tranquility,
Xprovide for the common defence, promote the general Welfare,
Xand secure the Blessings of Liberty to ourselves and our
XPosterity, do ordain and establish this Constitution for the
XUnited States of America.
END-of-Constitution
exit
```

Figure 25.2   A Real SHAR Archive

until it sees a line containing END_OF_FILE. The second cat command similarly copies some text into a file named "Constitution."

Most SHAR archives are slightly more complex than this example. Typically, some shell commands are used to detect if the file exists before trying to create it, and often an additional check is made after the file is created to make sure the resulting file is the same as the original. A few SHAR files are quite complex, invoking a variety of Unix commands to recreate a complex hierarchy of files with a variety of checks on the result. Figure 25.2 is a more typical example of a SHAR archive. This particular example was created with the shar command in 4.4BSD.

Figure 25.2 is actually only slightly more complex than Figure 25.1. It has a series of comments at the beginning telling the human recipient how to unpack it. The echo commands provide some progress information to the person who runs this batch file. Finally, instead of simply using cat, this SHAR file uses the sed (stream editor) command to remove the X characters from the beginning of each line. Although usually unnecessary, the X characters here help prevent any initial spaces from being lost.[1]

More Information

SHAR archives can usually be easily disassembled in any ordinary text editor. Some can be fairly complex, though, so it's certainly convenient to have a program that can do this for you.

Unix users should already have shar available for building shell archives, and should also have the sh shell and other utilities (including cat and sed) available for unpacking them. If you lack the shar program, search for shar.sh on the http://ftp.digital.com archive to obtain a very short and simple version of the shar program. Versions of the sh shell and other utilities can be obtained from the GNU software collection.

The shar and unshar programs for MS-DOS are available from the SIM-TEL archives in the msdos/fileutil directory.

An unshar program for Macintosh is available from the Info-Mac archives in the _Compress_&_Translate directory.

---

[1]Amazing damage can be done to text sent through the Internet mail system. The more common abuses are the loss of spaces or certain punctuation at the beginning or end of lines. A discussion of other techniques used to guard against such mistreatment starts on page 255.

ZOO

26

Rahul Desi's *ZOO* is an old and well-known archiver on many platforms. Since the first version appeared in 1986, the author has been very careful to preserve compatibility with older versions of ZOO, and to make sure that ZOO will work well on many different platforms. As such, it is a good choice for archiving files when you need to access the archive on a variety of systems.

How to Use ZOO

ZOO's biggest drawback is the enormous number of options that it supports. These options are provided to allow expert users to control how files are stored in the archive. ZOO can maintain multiple *generations* of a file and access or retrieve any one of them. When a new file with the same name is added to an existing archive, you can ask ZOO to leave both files in the archive. You can then extract either one of them by specifying a *generation number*.

ZOO at a Glance	
Name:	ZOO
Extension:	.zoo
Use For:	Archiving files with compression
On CD:	ZOO programs for MS-DOS, Unix

Command Line	Description
`zoo -list` *`archive.zoo`*	List the archive's contents
`zoo -extract` *`archive.zoo`*	Extract all the files
`zoo -extract` *`archive.zoo files`* ...	Extract only the named files
`zoo -add` *`archive.zoo files`* ...	Create an archive or add files to an archive

Table 26.1   Common ZOO Command Lines

While this feature is quite useful to some people, most users don't need it. For that reason, the ZOO program includes two different modes of operation. Like most archivers, ZOO interprets the first argument as a set of instructions. Instructions beginning with a dash (-) are *novice* commands, which make it easy to perform the most common tasks. Table 26.1 describes some typical commands.

Using Generations

Suppose you have an archive `project.zoo` that has a file called `Q3.txt`. If you update your third-quarter estimates and add it to the archive with `zoo -add project.zoo Q3.txt`, ZOO actually goes through several steps. It first compresses `Q3.txt` and adds it to the archive. It then scans through the archive to see if another `Q3.txt` is already in the archive. If it is, ZOO marks that older version as deleted.

By default, ZOO then *packs* the archive to reclaim the space used by any deleted files. Packing an archive involves first renaming the old archive to `project.bak`, then copying all of the files to a new `project.zoo`.

All of the above steps are the default behavior of the `-add` option. By using the expert commands, you can control each of them. In this example, you might need to keep previous versions of your third-quarter estimates to show your boss. By enabling generations, ZOO will allow several different `Q3.txt` files to reside in the archive. You enable generations with a command similar to `zoo gA+ project.zoo`. ZOO will now allow multiple copies of `Q3.txt` to reside in the archive. By default, it will allow three copies before it starts deleting them. You can adjust the limit on an individual file with a command like `zoo gl=5 project.zoo Q3.txt`. When you list the contents of an archive, ZOO will append a semicolon and a number to indicate the generation. If your third-quarter estimates are updated frequently, you can use `zoo -list project.zoo Q3.txt;*` to list all the generations of `Q3.txt` that are currently in the archive (by default, ZOO will only list the most recent generation).[1] The output might look something like this:

```
Archive project.zoo:
Length   CF  Size Now  Date       Time
-------- --- --------  --------- --------
   19423 68%     6215  18 Aug 95 11:17:23 1641   Q3.txt;47
   21237 65%     7433  18 Aug 95 14:12:08 56e8   Q3.txt;48
   23088 67%     7619  18 Aug 95 16:37:45 d427   Q3.txt;49
   24046 72%     6733  19 Aug 95 10:04:01 2f60   Q3.txt;50
   23879 66%     8119  19 Aug 95 12:54:28 69e7   Q3.txt;51
-------- --- --------  --------- --------
  111673 69%    36119      5 files
```

How ZOO Works

ZOO has several features that make it possible to extract data from archives under a variety of less-than-ideal circumstances. ZOO tags each piece of critical data with *magic numbers* so that a quick scan through the file can locate much of this data. These magic numbers frequently make it possible to recover data from a damaged archive. New versions of ZOO store additional information in the archive, but in such a way that older versions will not notice this extra information. Older versions will often be able to successfully extract data from newer archives.[2] Finally, ZOO tries ensure that archives can be burst on platforms other than the one on which they were created. ZOO stores information in a platform-neutral format, or at least identifies the originating platform so the de-archiver can translate as necessary.

Figure 26.1 shows the logical structure of a ZOO file. Like TIFF, ZOO uses file position to locate various pieces of data. You can't predict the order in which this information will actually appear in the file. The archive header

---

[1] On Unix, you'll need to put quotes around the name, as in `"Q3.txt;*"`, to keep the shell from trying to interpret the filename before handing it to ZOO.

[2] The one fundamental obstacle is the compression method. Later versions of ZOO have added new compression methods, and files compressed with newer methods cannot be extracted with older versions of ZOO that don't support those methods.

Archive Header $\longrightarrow$ Directory Entry $\longrightarrow$ File Data
$\downarrow$
Directory Entry $\longrightarrow$ File Data
$\downarrow$
Directory Entry $\longrightarrow$ File Data
$\vdots$

Figure 26.1 Conceptual Structure of a ZOO File

always appears at the beginning of the file, but the various file headers, blocks of compressed data, and file comments can appear in any order. Unused gaps can exist in the file, caused by the "deletion" of files from the archive.

The archive header shown in Table 26.2 illustrates how this process works. Older versions of ZOO will only read and interpret the first fields; they will skip directly to the first directory entry without reading any data that remains in the archive header. Later versions can store additional information in the archive header while still allowing older versions to read files from the archive. A single archive may be manipulated by many different versions of ZOO during its lifetime.[3]

ZOO's archive header defies traditional wisdom in an interesting way. Most file formats try to place a signature value in the first few bytes of the file. This signature allows many programs to quickly identify a file format based just on the first few bytes. This trick is used by many graphics programs, and is an important feature of current Unix systems (which use the first few bytes to determine how to execute different types of programs). ZOO instead leaves the first twenty bytes of the file undefined. ZOO archivers place a brief text message there, indicating the version of ZOO that created the file. However, these twenty bytes could be used for a variety of other purposes.

The version numbering flags control ZOO's generational feature, which allows you to save many different versions of the same file in an archive. This

---

[3]There's one exception to the general rule that parts of a ZOO file can occur in any order: In old ZOO archives, the first directory entry was always located at position 34. This placement cannot happen in newer ZOO archives, because the archive header is now longer than 34 bytes. This fact is used to identify old ZOO archives. Such a trick is needed because the original archive header didn't include a version field. Later versions of the archive header can be distinguished by the value of this field.

Size	Description
20	Text identifier
4	Magic bytes: 220, 167, 196, 253
4	File position of first directory entry
4	Twos-complement of previous number
1	Major version needed to manipulate file
1	Minor version needed to manipulate file
1	Version of archive header
4	File position of file comment
2	Length of file comment
2	Version numbering flags

Table 26.2   ZOO Archive Header

feature is a simple way to keep track of old files without wasting too much disk space or having elaborate file naming schemes to separate different versions of the same file. However, you don't always want old versions occupying space in your archives. Rather than requiring you to specify whether to keep old versions in the archive on every update, ZOO lets you mark the archive itself. If you don't specify manually, ZOO will decide whether or not to keep old versions by examining flags in the archive. The version flag byte has the high bit set if old versions should be kept; the bottom four bits specify how many old versions should be preserved.

The directory entry shown in Table 26.3 uses the same approach as the archive header. It gives the specific byte positions of other data (the file data, file comment, next directory entry, and next subfile). One interesting aspect is that ZOO uses the system type to help deal with filenames. Filenames have different formats on different systems. A typical filename on a VAX/VMS system might look like sys$user:[kientzle.work]program.pascal;17.[4] ZOO attempts to deal with the multiplicity of different formats in two ways. Filenames can be stored in the native format, or they can be stored in a canonical "portable format." In either case, the system identifier indicates the format.

---

[4]Brief explanation: sys$user is a *logical name*, similar to environment variables on Unix or MS-DOS systems. In this case, the logical name indicates the disk used for user accounts. The square brackets hold a sequence of directories separated by dots. The filename and extension are separated by a period. The number following the semicolon is a version number.

Size	Description
4	Magic bytes: 220, 167, 196, 253
1	Version of directory entry
1	Compression method
	0 No compression
	1 LZW compression
	2 LZH compression
4	File position of next directory entry
4	File position of compressed file data
2	Date, in MS-DOS format (see page 207)
2	Time, in MS-DOS format (see page 207)
2	CRC of uncompressed file data
4	Uncompressed file size
4	Compressed file size
1	Major version needed to extract file
1	Minor version needed to extract file
1	1 if this file is "deleted"
1	File type
4	File position of comment
2	Size of comment
13	MS-DOS-format filename
2	Length of variable section
1	Timezone
4	CRC of directory entry
n	Variable section

Table 26.3   ZOO Directory Entry

If a ZOO de-archiver sees a system identifier (filename format) it doesn't understand, it can fall back on the short MS-DOS-style filename that is also stored in the file. Of course, every ZOO de-archiver should understand the portable format.

A few restrictions ensure that every system can understand and use the portable format. The portable format only allows lowercase letters, digits, and the underscore character (_) in names. The directory names are separated by slash characters (/) and may be preceded with ./ to start in the current

Size	Description
1	Length of long filename
1	Length of directory name
n	Long filename
n	Directory name
2	Filename format
	0 Unix-style system
	1 MS-DOS
	2 Portable format
3	File attributes
2	Version number
4	Next subfile
1	Sequence number

Table 26.4   ZOO Directory Entry Variable Section

directory. The filename can have a single period to separate the primary name from an extension.

The variable part of the directory entry, shown in Table 26.4, may be truncated at any point. This allows the archiver program to only store the information it needs. The de-archiver must be careful to check the length of this part.

Extracting data from a damaged archive is tricky business. ZOO attempts to simplify this process by tagging special points in the archive. You saw earlier that the archive header has a four-byte magic number, which is also used to tag each file header. In addition, the five bytes 64, 41, 35, 40, 0 ("@)#(" followed by a zero byte) appear immediately before the compressed file data. This latter marker is not seen by a ZOO de-archiver under normal circumstances. The file position in the file header indicates the beginning of the actual compressed data that follows this marker. If an error prevents data from being extracted normally, the *FIZ* program can be used to scan through the entire archive and locate the file headers and file data. FIZ uses these markers to identify the data. Once you have a list of the file positions of the file headers and file data, you can instruct ZOO (using special options) to extract single files from particular locations in the archive. In this way, you can extract the undamaged parts from a large archive.

Recovering Damaged ZOO Archives

The previous section showed that each file has two parts in the archive: The directory entry, which stores the filename and other information, and the actual compressed file data. The zoo program has an option @ that lets you specify the byte position in the file of these two components. To recover data from a damaged archive, you first use the fiz program, which scans through the file to locate the magic numbers marking these parts of the file, and simply prints the location of each one. For example, suppose you tried to extract some files from an archive with zoo -extract project.zoo and were greeted with the message Zoo: FATAL: Invalid or corrupted archive.

Often, such a message really only means that some part of the archive is damaged. If you can find a part that's undamaged, ZOO will usually be able to recover it. So, the first step is to type fiz project.zoo. FIZ will tell you something like the following:

```
***************
    112: DATA
***************
   2323: DIR  [Q1.txt] ==> 2394
   2394: DATA
***************
   5915: DIR  [Q2.txt] ==> 5986
   5986: DATA
***************
   8160: DIR  [Q3.txt] ==> 8231
   8231: DATA
***************
  16618: DIR  [Q3.txt] ==> 16689
  16689: DATA
***************
  25076: DIR  [Q3.txt] ==> 25147
  25147: DATA
***************
  33534: DIR  [] ==>     0
```

FIZ tells you the byte position of each directory entry or file data marker that it finds. For the directory entry, it tells you the name found in that location and the data to which it points. In this case, it looks like the first directory entry was damaged, but the rest of the data looks okay. You can list those files with zoo l@2323 project.zoo, or extract them all with zoo x@2323 project.zoo.

The tricky part in this example is extracting the data for the first file. You must give ZOO both a directory entry and file data position, as in: `zoo x@2323,112 project.zoo`. This command will extract the data for the first file under the name `Q1.txt`. ZOO will complain; each directory entry has a check to make sure the file data is correct, and since you're using the wrong directory entry, that check will fail. But, this procedure will often extract the data successfully. You'll have to manually check the data and decide what the actual filename should be.

ZOO's Compression Methods

ZOO stores files using either of two different compression methods. ZOO's LZW compression is based on Unix compress. ZOO's *LZH* method is similar to ZIP's Deflation algorithm (see page 219). It starts with LZ77 compression, and uses Huffman compression to reduce the offset and length codes.

More Information

The ZOO program can be found on the SIMTEL archives in the `msdos/zoo` directory.

A portable version of ZOO that compiles and runs under most Unix-like systems is available in Volume 17 of the `comp.sources.unix` newsgroup. Archives of this newsgroup are available from `http://ftp.digital.com`. They can also be accessed using anonymous FTP to `ftp.uu.net`, in the directory `usenet/comp.sources.unix`.

The `maczoo` program for the Macintosh is a simple, but functional, port of ZOO. It's available from the Info-Mac archives.

StuffIt

The original designers of the Macintosh system wrestled with a difficult problem for which they developed an interesting solution. The problem was how to juggle the various pieces of information that needed to be kept for each file. In addition to such mundane information as the name of the file and the time it was created, they also wanted to track the application that owned each file and a number of other details.

Their solution was to store each file as several distinct pieces. On MS-DOS or Unix, a file consists of only two pieces: the file data and the file directory information, which contains such trivia as the filename and the time the file was last modified. The Macintosh separates each file into three pieces. The directory information includes a variety of information, including the application associated with this file. The file data is stored as two separate pieces, called *forks*. The *data fork* is similar to files on MS-DOS or Unix, while the *resource fork* is a simple database used to store a variety of structured information.

StuffIt at a Glance	
Name:	StuffIt
Extensions:	.sit, .sea
Use For:	Archiving files with compression
On CD:	StuffIt Expander Lite for Macintosh

The extended directory information and the resource fork solve several problems. For example, many other systems attempt to decide what program to associate with a file based purely on the name of the file. This approach fails if the user who creates the file doesn't cooperate. For example, some people use their initials or the date as the file extension, foiling systems that rely on the file extension to determine the type of the file. (The files `chapter7.tbk` and `figure2.tbk` are probably not the same type of file, despite the common extension.) The Macintosh stores a separate code in the directory to identify the file format and the application that owns the file. Programs use the resource fork to store the text and images that they use internally. This makes it easy to customize a program's visual appearance (for example, to translate the text into a different language) without having to recompile the program. A *resource editor* can be used to browse the resource fork and examine and alter data in it.

As you can imagine, archiving a Macintosh file requires some additional attention. An archiver for Macintosh files must store all of the directory information and the resource fork in the archive, which must be a single stream of bytes that can be transferred using conventional serial protocols. Of the archivers I've examined so far, only ZIP and ZOO are capable of handling this additional information, and then only within limits. ZIP's "extra information" fields can be used to hold the additional Macintosh-specific directory information, but the limit of 64 kilobytes for this information makes it a poor candidate for storing the resource fork. ZOO is a better fit, since it allows a single file to be stored as multiple "subfiles," which can be adapted to store Macintosh files as three separate pieces. (In fact, Macintosh files are often stored on MS-DOS or Unix disks as three separate files.)

Aladdin's *StuffIt* program fills the bill nicely. Originally a shareware program developed by Ray Lau, StuffIt is freely available from many sources, offers good compression, and was designed specifically to handle the Macintosh's structured files.

How StuffIt Works

A simple StuffIt archive is organized as shown in Figure 27.1. Table 27.1 details the information in the archive header.

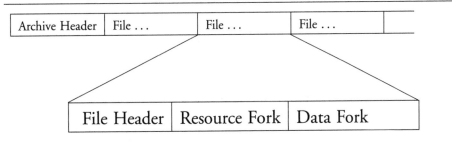

Figure 27.1   Organization of a StuffIt Archive

Size	Description
4	Magic value: SIT!
2	Number of files in archive
4	Length of archive, including this header
4	Magic value: rLau
1	Version number of archive
7	Reserved

Table 27.1   StuffIt Archive Header

The primary difference between StuffIt's file header, shown in Table 27.2, and the file header used by the other archivers we've examined is the additional information for the resource and data fork. The file type and file creator are four-character codes indicating the kind of data in the file and the application that currently owns the file. The compression codes that appear at the beginning of the file header are shown in Table 27.3.

Rather than storing the full name of a file, including the name of the folder, StuffIt indicates the folder containing a group of files by placing two special file headers before and after the group of files. The file header preceding the group of files uses compression code 32 to indicate the beginning of a new folder. The file header contains the name and other information about the folder itself. The file header following the group of files is identical, except that the compression type fields are set to 33 to indicate the end of the folder. By using these "start-of-folder" and "end-of-folder" markers, a StuffIt file can reproduce any set of nested folders without having to unnecessarily copy the folder name with every file stored in that folder.

Size	Description
1	Compression method for resource fork
1	Compression method for data fork
1	Length of filename
63	Filename
4	File type
4	File creator
2	Finder flags
4	Creation date. Seconds since 0:00 January 1, 1904
4	Modification date. Seconds since 0:00 January 1, 1904
4	Length of uncompressed resource fork
4	Length of uncompressed data fork
4	Compressed length of resource fork
4	Compressed length of data fork
2	CRC of resource fork
2	CRC of data fork
6	Reserved
2	CRC of file header

Table 27.2   StuffIt File Header

More Information

Aladdin Systems distributes commercial, shareware and freeware versions of StuffIt for Macintosh, MS-DOS and Windows. For further information, check http://www.aladdinsys.com or anonymous FTP to Aladdin Systems' archive site at ftp.aladdinsys.com.

Unix programs that are capable of packing and unpacking old-style StuffIt archives are available from the University of Michigan Macintosh archive (http://www.umich.edu/~archive/mac/util/unix).

Value	Description
0	No compression
1	RLE compression
2	LZW compression, *à la* compress
3	Huffman compression
32	Start-of-folder
33	End-of-folder

Table 27.3   StuffIt Compression Codes

Note: These are the compression codes used by the original shareware version of StuffIt. Newer versions support additional compression methods.

Other Formats

I've tried to cover the most important archiving and compression utilities, but there are literally hundreds of different programs available. This chapter briefly describes a few others.

SEA, SFX and EXE

It's a good idea to archive and compress a group of files before you send them to someone else. However, the recipient must be able to extract the files when she receives your archive, which generally means that she needs a copy of the corresponding de-archiving program.

If you're unsure what de-archiving programs she has, you can simplify things by providing a *self-extracting archive*. A self-extracting archive is a file that bundles a short de-archiving program with the archived data. The result is

Other Compression and Archiving Formats at a Glance	
Names:	LHA, ARJ, RAR, AR, Pack, Compact, Squeeze, CompactPro
Extensions:	`.lzh`, `.arj`, `.rar`, `.ar`, `.z`, `.C`, `.?q?`, `.cpt`, `.exe`, `.sea`, `.sfx`
Use For:	Archiving and/or compressing files
On CD:	Various archiving and compression utilities

a program that, when run, de-archives the data contained within the program. On MS-DOS, self-extracting archives always have the extension .exe. On the Macintosh, they can have a variety of different extensions; .sea and .sfx are common.

Of course, self-extracting archives are only self-extracting on the appropriate system. If you have an MS-DOS self-extracting file and you're using a Macintosh, you'll need an appropriate de-archiver to extract the data. There are two nasty complications. The first complication is that you need to figure out which de-archiver to use. An MS-DOS file with an .exe extension could have been created by any of a number of archivers. The second complication is that you may need a special version of the de-archiver to extract the data. Because self-extracting files have an executable program attached to the beginning of the file, many de-archivers won't be able to find the archived data within the file.

If you have a binary dump program, you can often puzzle out the format of the archived data by looking at the beginning of the program. There is usually a block of text identifying the archiver, or at least the manufacturer of the archiver.

How you create a self-extracting archive varies widely. In some cases, the normal archiving program can build one directly. In other cases, you use a separate program to attach the de-archiving code to the archive.

ARJ

Robert Jung's *ARJ* archiver has been gaining converts among many MS-DOS users. It offers good compression and speed, and the freely available version offers a number of features only available in the registered versions of its competitors, such as the ability to build self-extracting archives. ARJ archives have the extension .arj.

The ARJ program for MS-DOS is available in the SIMTEL archives in the msdos/archiver directory. A simple UNARJ extraction utility is available in source code form from the same source. UNARJ can be compiled on a variety of systems, and is capable of extracting both normal and self-extracting ARJ archives. An UNARJ program for the Macintosh is available from the Info-Mac archives.

LHA/LZH

LHA is an archiver similar to ARC and ZIP. It was originally named LHARC, but the name was shortened to avoid any confusion with the ARC program. (Some versions of the program are still called LHARC.) LHA is available for a number of platforms, and has been fairly popular. One confusing point is that LHA uses the file extension `.lzh`, unlike many other compressors whose name and extension are the same.

An LHA program for MS-DOS is available in the SIMTEL archives in the `msdos/starter` directory. The *MacLHA* program for the Macintosh is available from the Info-Mac archives.

RAR

RAR is another archiver that has been gaining some attention. Its primary feature is that it offers a "solid" archive option. With this option, RAR builds the archive and then compresses the entire archive at once, rather than compressing each file as it is added. Usually, this approach results in noticeably better compression, at the cost of making the archive slower to manipulate (extracting one file requires decompressing the entire archive). RAR archives have the extension `.rar`.

The MS-DOS version of RAR is available from the SIMTEL archives in the `msdos/archiver` directory. This file is a RAR-format self-extracting archive. The source code for a portable UNRAR de-archiving utility is included.

AR

There are (unfortunately) many different programs with the name *AR*. The Unix AR is an archiving program that does no compression, and is used primarily to maintain programming libraries. Haruhiko Okumura's AR archiver implemented the LZHUF compression algorithm that was later adopted by ZOO, ARJ, and several other programs. Carl Kreider's AR archiver is based on LZW code from compress, and has been a standard in the OS/9 community for many years.

Pack and Compact

Pack and *Compact* are two old Unix compression programs that are similar to compress, but have less effective compression. Pack uses an extension of .z, and Compact uses an extension of .C.

The GUNZIP program can uncompress Pack format. Compact is documented in [URM94].

Squeeze

Squeeze (also called *SQ*) is an old CP/M program that found its way to MS-DOS and a few other systems. Squeeze, like compress and GZIP, was a single-file compressor. It compressed a file and changed the second letter of the extension to Q to indicate this fact. For example, PROGRAM.COM would compress to PROGRAM.CQM.

CompactPro

Bill Goodman's *CompactPro* is another popular Macintosh archiving program. CompactPro archives have the extension .cpt.

WEB Compression

In 1992, WEB Technologies announced a new compression product called *DataFiles/16*. WEB made a number of claims. The most interesting one was "that virtually any amount of data can be squeezed to under 1024 bytes by using DataFiles/16 to compress its own output multiple times."[1]

This idea of repeatedly using a compression program to make a file smaller and smaller is quite appealing. In many ways, this idea is the software analog of the perpetual motion machine; people never seem to really believe that it's impossible. (See pages 187–189 for an explanation of why this is impossible.)

---

[1] *Byte Week*, April 20, 1992, quoting a WEB Technologies press release.

Many programs have claimed this feat. WEB was merely one of the best publicized.

In practice, running any file through a good compression program a second time will often reduce the size by an additional one or two percent. Beyond that, the compression program is as likely to expand the data as to compress it. The feat that WEB was attempting is impossible, although numerous tricks can make it appear to work.

Some of these compression claims can be attributed to programmers who fail to completely understand what they're doing. For example, many repeated compression ideas rely on altering the filename to indicate how many times the file has been "compressed." This method essentially boils down to transferring data from the file to the filename. The problem is obvious: Only so much data can fit in the filename.

WEB Technologies' perfect compression claim was silently dropped after several months.

Part Four
Encoding Formats

About Encoding

If you've ever accidentally listed a binary file to your computer screen, you know how unpleasant the results can be. Like your screen, many computer connections are designed to handle text files, and they get rather upset if you feed them raw binary data.

However, you often need to transfer raw binary data through mail or some other connection that's geared to handling text. To do this, you *encode* the data, converting it into a form that doesn't choke the computer connection and can be safely *decoded* on the other end.

Encoding is fairly simple. Many different programs perform suitable encoding. The most popular is the old UUEncode program. This program is simple and effective, but the output is not quite clean enough for a few unusually sensitive situations, which led to the development of alternatives such as XXEncode.

Encoding is increasingly being built into programs that access electronic mail. This allows you to send and receive binary data without having to worry about the actual mechanics of encoding and decoding. Systems such as MIME (which is used by many Unix, PC, and Macintosh mail readers, including the popular Eudora program) support this process nicely. They automate not only the encoding and decoding, but also mark the type of data, so that the recipient's mail program can show the data in an appropriate way.

UUEncode

UUEncode is still one of the most widely-used methods for encoding binary files to be transferred through mail. Unfortunately, some mail systems damage UUEncoded files, so UUEncode is slowly being replaced with more robust approaches.

When to Use UUEncode

Although UUEncode is very popular, it doesn't always work. UUEncode uses a lot of punctuation marks in the encoded output, and many of these punctuation marks are mangled or lost by certain mail gateways. You have no control over the path your mail takes through the Internet. If your message travels through one of these gateways, your UUEncoded data could get damaged. As a result, there are several incompatible versions of UUEncode floating around.

UUEncode at a Glance	
Name:	UUEncode/UUDecode
Extensions:	`.uue`, `.uu`
Use For:	Encoding files for transfer through mail or news
Reference:	Unix man page, reproduced in [PRM94]
On CD:	*UUDeview* for Unix and MS-DOS; *WinCode* for Windows

The original UUEncode program used spaces in its output. A space is the most common character that gets altered through certain mail gateways. Multiple spaces occasionally get reduced to a single space and spaces at the ends of lines can be lost. To avoid this problem, some versions of UUEncode use slightly different characters in their output. The most common variation is to use ` (ASCII character 96) instead of space; another variation uses ~ instead of space. Because of this variation, you may receive a UUEncoded file that your particular version of UUDecode can't decode.

You won't encounter either of these problems very often. As the Internet evolves, problematic mail gateways are slowly being replaced or upgraded, and the version of UUEncode that uses ` instead of space is the most common one in widespread use. Some versions of UUDecode recognize the output of several different UUEncode programs. But occasionally, you will find a file that has been mangled by a wayward mailer or was created with a different variant of UUEncode. In that case, you might want to try another encoding, such as XXEncode or MIME encoding. These encodings are very similar to UUEncoding, but avoid strange punctuation marks and spaces in their output.

How to Use UUEncode and UUDecode

UUEncoding converts a binary file into a file that consists only of text characters. You can then mail this file to someone, who can convert it back into a copy of the original binary file. On Unix or MS-DOS, you would use something like the following command to encode the file:

```
uuencode myfile <myfile >myfile.uue
```

The name following the UUEncode command is the name that will be placed inside the encoded file. Usually this name is the same as that of the file being encoded. By default, as with many programs that originated on Unix, the output is simply printed to the screen, and you must redirect it to a file to save it. The extension .uue is common.

You can mail the UUEncoded file the same way you would mail any text file. Details vary widely from system to system. On a Unix system, you might use the following command:

```
mail -s "A file for you" tim@humperdinck <myfile.uue
```

Other mail systems also allow you to mail a pre-existing file; check the documentation for your mail program. For many newer mailers, you simply begin a new message, and then read the pre-existing file into the mail editor.

At the other end, this process must be reversed, first saving the UUEncoded text into a file, and then using the `uudecode` command to decode the result. The common UUDecode program uses the filename specified by the sender.

UUEncoding and UUDecoding are now widely supported by archiving and mail reader programs.

How UUEncode Works

The output of UUEncode begins with the word `begin` and ends with the word `end`. These words let the UUDecode program ignore any text that may precede (such as mail headers) or follow (such as signatures) the encoded information. The `begin` line also specifies a three-digit number and the name of the file. The three-digit number specifies the file permissions using a common Unix notation; usually this number is 755 or 700 for executables, or 644 or 600 for other types of files. The remaining lines contain the actual encoded data.

```
begin 644 test
45&AI<R!I<R!A('1E<WO@9FEL90JD
'

end
```

Each line of the encoded data starts with a character indicating the number of bytes in the decoded data for that line. The number of bytes in the decoded line is added to 32 to obtain an ASCII character. In this example, the first line of data starts with 4 (ASCII 52), indicating the line decodes to 20 bytes of data. The second line of data starts with ', which is substituting for space (ASCII 32), indicating there are no bytes of data. By tradition, a line containing zero bytes of data is included at the end of the file. (Typically, a long UUEncoded file will have M at the beginning of most lines, because a full line encodes exactly 45 bytes of data.)

The actual encoding uses an algorithm known as *base 64* or *four-for-three* encoding. Three bytes of data are a total of 24 bits. Taking these bits six at a time gives four numbers between 0 and 63. UUEncode converts these numbers into characters by adding 32 to get a character value ranging from space for zero to underscore (ASCII 95) for a value of 63. Newer versions of UUEncode replace a space wherever it occurs with '.

UUEncode Program

UUEncode is actually fairly simple to implement; here's a C implementation:

```
/* Simple implementation of UUEncode */
#include <stdio.h>
static char encode[] =
"'!\"#$%&'()*+,-./0123456789:;<=>?@ABCDEFGHIJKLMNOPQRSTUVWXYZ[\\]^_";
#define WRITEBITS(n)    putc(encode[(n)&0x3f],outfile);

EncodeLine(length, line, outFile)
int length; char *line; FILE *outFile;
{ char *p;
  putc(ENCODE(length),outFile);
  for (p=line;length > 0;p+=3,length-=3) {
    long l = (((long)p[0] & 0xff) << 16)    /* collect 3 bytes */
             | (((long)p[1] & 0xff) << 8) | (((long)p[2] & 0xff));
    WRITEBITS(l>>18); WRITEBITS(l>>12);  /* Output 4 characters */
    WRITEBITS(l>>6);  WRITEBITS(l);
  }
  putc('\n',outFile);
}

EncodeFile(name, inFile, outFile)
char *name; FILE *inFile, *outFile;
{ char line[80];  int i;
  fprintf(outFile,"begin 644 %s\n",name);
  while ((i=fread(line,1,45,inFile)) > 0) /* At most 45 bytes/line */
    EncodeLine(i,line,outFile);
  EncodeLine(0,0,outFile); /* Encode one final zero-length line */
  fprintf(outFile,"end\n");
}

int main(argc,argv)
int argc; char **argv;
{ if (argc != 2) { /* Exactly one argument */
    fprintf(stderr,"Usage: %s name <infile >outfile\n",argv[0]);
    return 1;
  }
  EncodeFile(argv[1],stdin,stdout);
  return 0;
}
```

UUDecode Program

UUDecode is only slightly more complex:

```
/* Simple implementation of UUDecode */
#include <stdio.h>
#include <string.h>
#include <stdlib.h>
int decode[256]; /* Use a look-up for faster decoding */
#define VALID(c)  (decode[(int)(c) & 0xff] >= 0)
#define DECODE(c) (decode[(int)(c) & 0xff])

Init() /* Build decoding array */
{ int i;
  for (i=0;i<256;i++) decode[i] = -1; /* Make everything invalid */
  for (i=0;i<64;i++) decode[i+' ']=i;
  decode[(int)'`'] = 0; /* Decode both ` and space to 0 */
}

DecodeLine(line, length, outFile)  /* Decode one line of data */
char *line; int length; FILE *outFile;
{ long l; int i;

  while (length > 0) {
    l = 0;
    for (i=0;i<4;i++) { /* Collect four characters */
      if (!VALID(*line)) fprintf(stderr,"Illegal char '%c'\n",*line);
      l = (l << 6) | DECODE(*line++);
    }
    putc((l >> 16) & 0xff, outFile); /* Output three bytes */
    if (length > 1) putc((l >> 8) & 0xff, outFile);
    if (length > 2) putc(l & 0xff, outFile);
    length -= 3;
  }
}

DecodeFile(inFile, outFile)
FILE *inFile, *outFile;
{ char line[80];  int length;

  do {  /* Decode each line */
    if (fgets(line,80,inFile) == NULL) { /* Read the line */
      fprintf(stderr,"Error reading input.\n");
      exit(1);
    }
    if (!VALID(line[0])) /* Is count character valid? */
      fprintf(stderr,"Illegal line count character '%c'\n",line[0]);
```

```
    else /* Valid count, decode the line */
      DecodeLine(line+1,length = DECODE(line[0]),outFile);
  } while (length > 0); /* Stop at a zero-length line */
  fgets(line,79,inFile);
  if (strncmp(line,"end",3) != 0)
    fprintf(stderr,"Final ''end'' missing.\n");
  return;
}

/* Scan input looking for ''begin'' line */
FILE * FindBegin(inFile)
FILE *inFile;
{ char line[80], fileName[80];
  int mode;

  do {
    if (fgets(line,80,inFile) == NULL) {
      fprintf(stderr,"No 'begin' found.\n");
      exit(1);
    }
  } while (strncmp(line,"begin",5) != 0);
  sscanf(line,"begin %o %79s",&mode, fileName);
  printf("Decoding file '%s'\n",fileName);
  return fopen(fileName,"w");
}

int main(argc, argv)
int argc; char **argv;
{ FILE *f = FindBegin(stdin);

  Init();
  if (f != NULL) {
    DecodeFile(stdin,f);
    fclose(f);
  } else {
    fprintf(stderr,"Couldn't open file.\n");
    exit(1);
  }
  return 0;
}
```

XXEncode

The problems with UUEncode and UUDecode (see page 257) led to the creation of similar programs called *XXEncode* and *XXDecode*. These programs are used identically to UUEncode and UUDecode, but files encoded with XXEncode are much less susceptible to damage.

How to Use XXEncode

Two programs, called XXEncode and XXDecode, are used to encode and decode binary files. XXEncode converts a binary file into one that consists only of text characters. You can mail the encoded file in the same way you would mail any text file. The recipient can use the XXDecode program to convert it back into a copy of the original binary file. The syntax is identical to UUEncode.

```
xxencode myfile <myfile >myfile.xxe
```

XXEncode at a Glance

Name:	XXEncode/XXDecode
Extensions:	`.xxe`, `.xx`
Use For:	Encoding files for transfer through mail or news
On CD:	*UUDeview* for Unix and MS-DOS; *WinCode* for Windows

At the other end, this process must be reversed, first saving the encoded text version into a file, and then using the `xxdecode` command to decode the result. The XXDecode program puts the result into a file whose name was specified by the sender.

When to Use XXEncode

XXEncode is more reliable than UUEncode, but is still not very well known and not everyone has access to it. For that reason, it's probably best to stick with UUEncode unless you encounter problems with files that cannot be properly decoded. In that case, if XXEncode is available, it's a good choice.

How XXEncode Works

XXEncode works identically to UUEncode with one important change. Instead of simply adding 32 to obtain a character value, XXEncode takes the value from 0 to 63 and uses the values in Table 31.1 to convert it into a character.

XXEncode and XXDecode Programs

XXEncode is the same as UUEncode except for the string used to encode the actual digits. Here are the only two lines that needs to be changed in the source code on page 260:

```
static char encode[] =
"+-0123456789ABCDEFGHIJKLMNOPQRSTUVWXYZabcdefghijklmnopqrstuvwxyz";
```

Similarly, because UUDecode uses a look-up table to convert characters into the corresponding digit, only the `Init` function needs to be changed for XXDecode. The rest is the same as page 261:

```
static char encode[] =
"+-0123456789ABCDEFGHIJKLMNOPQRSTUVWXYZabcdefghijklmnopqrstuvwxyz";

Init() /* Build decoding array */
```

Code	Char	Code	Char	Code	Char	Code	Char
0	+	16	E	32	U	48	k
1	-	17	F	33	V	49	l
2	0	18	G	34	W	50	m
3	1	19	H	35	X	51	n
4	2	20	I	36	Y	52	o
5	3	21	J	37	Z	53	p
6	4	22	K	38	a	54	q
7	5	23	L	39	b	55	r
8	6	24	M	40	c	56	s
9	7	25	N	41	d	57	t
10	8	26	O	42	e	58	u
11	9	27	P	43	f	59	v
12	A	28	Q	44	g	60	w
13	B	29	R	45	h	61	x
14	C	30	S	46	i	62	y
15	D	31	T	47	j	63	z

Table 31.1   XXEncode Encoding

```
{
  int i;
  for (i=0;i<256;i++) decode[i] = -1; /* Make everything invalid */
  for (i=0;i<64;i++) decode[(int)encode[i] & 0xff]=i;
}
```

BtoA

One common complaint about UUEncode and similar programs, such as XXEncode, is that the encoded file is 33 percent larger than the binary file. The *BtoA* (Binary-to-ASCII) program encodes binary files into an ASCII form that is only 25 percent larger than the original. The *AtoB* (ASCII-to-Binary) program decodes this format.

When to Use BtoA

The encoded output of BtoA is noticeably smaller than the output of either UUEncode or XXEncode. As a result, BtoA is a good choice when the size of the encoded result is important. If you have problems with long messages being either lost or truncated, try compressing the files and using BtoA instead of UUEncode. BtoA also includes a simple check to make sure the file hasn't been corrupted, something UUEncode and XXEncode both lack. You have some assurance that if AtoB doesn't complain, the file is correct.

BtoA at a Glance	
Name:	BtoA/AtoB
Use For:	Encoding files for transfer through mail or news
On CD:	Source code for BtoA/AtoB programs; `ecd66win` for Windows

BtoA achieves its size reductions by using more characters in the encoded output (UUEncode and XXEncode only use 64 characters in their output; BtoA uses 85). For this reason, BtoA-encoded files are more likely to be damaged by nonstandard mailers than either UUEncoded or XXEncoded files. If you encounter problems where AtoB can't decode a file that was encoded with BtoA, it might be a good idea to try UUEncode or XXEncode. As I mentioned in the last chapter, XXEncode is by far the most reliable of the three.

How to Use BtoA

The simple Unix versions of AtoB and BtoA simply read a file and convert its contents accordingly. BtoA is used to encode a file for mailing; AtoB is used to recover the file upon receipt.

If you're using a Unix system to send mail, you can use a *pipeline*, feeding the file to be mailed into `btoa`, then feeding the output of that into the `mail` program to be mailed. A typical command line might look like:

```
btoa <filename | mail -s "Subject" someone@host.com
```

It's always a good idea to first send a brief message, so the recipient will know to expect a large mail message, and will know how to decode it.

When you receive such a message, you should save it into a file, then use the `atob` program to recover the original. If you save it into a file called `temp.asc`, you might use the following command:

```
atob <temp.asc >filename
```

How BtoA Works

Another way to explain the operation of UUEncode and XXEncode is to say that they take three bytes as a single number, then express that as a four-digit number in base 64. BtoA uses a similar idea, except that it takes four bytes as a single number and expresses it as a five-digit number in base 85. Of course, this method requires you to have 85 different characters to use as digits, which is most of the ASCII character set.

BtoA collects four bytes at a time from the input, converts that four-byte number into five numbers in base 85, and converts each of those into a single "digit" by adding 33 to get an ASCII character. The encoded output is broken into lines of 78 characters. BtoA has a few extra characters to play with because there are more than 85 characters in the ASCII set. After it reads four bytes for conversion, if all of those bytes are zero (which is quite common in some types of data), it outputs a single z rather than the ! ! ! ! ! which it would otherwise use. This simple compression helps compensate for the expansion caused by the encoding.

The character x is used to mark the beginning and end of the encoded data. BtoA places the line xbtoa Begin at the beginning of the encoded data, and xbtoa End at the end. The xbtoa End line also has several numbers on it, which are used to check for errors. Here's a typical end line:

```
xbtoa End N 8783 224f E c3 S 5613b R c3155fdd
```

The two numbers after N are the file size in decimal and hexadecimal, respectively. At the end of the file, if there are fewer than four bytes left, BtoA pads with zero bytes to get four bytes for its encoding. The file size at the end is necessary so that AtoB can strip those added bytes.[1] The hexadecimal values following E, S, and R are three simple error checks that are used by the decoder to verify that the data wasn't damaged. These error checks include any zero bytes added to the end of the data.

The E check is the exclusive-or of the data bytes. The S check is the 32-bit sum of the data bytes added to the length of the data (including the padding zero bytes). The R check is a 32-bit value computed as follows: For each byte of data, rotate the R value to the left by one bit, moving the high-order bit into the low-order bit, then add the byte. All of these are computed on the unencoded binary data.

---

[1] The authors of BtoA were apparently unfamiliar with the technique of writing fewer than five characters at the end to indicate the correct number of bytes to the decoder without requiring an explicit count.

More Information

Source code for BtoA and AtoB is included with the source code for the compress program, which can be found in Volume 2 of the `comp.sources.unix` archives. One location of these archives is `ftp.uu.net`.

MIME

Programs such as UUEncode and UUDecode work, but they're not particularly easy to use. Over the last few decades, several enhanced mail facilities have been proposed. Many of these, such as the ISO X.400 standard, require dramatic changes to the way mail is delivered and stored, and for this reason, these proposals have been slow to gain acceptance on the Internet. The Internet is a huge collection of computers managed by many different organizations, and major changes at low levels take many years to be deployed.

An alternative approach is to automate the encoding and decoding performed by such programs as UUEncode and UUDecode, so that arbitrary content can be mailed without any special knowledge on the part of the user. The *Multipurpose Internet Mail Extensions* (MIME) standard does exactly this. It defines a standard way that the programs used to read and compose mail messages can encode and decode data without any user intervention. It also provides a standard way to tag the type of data so that the recipient's mail program can display it (or play it through the speaker, as appropriate) correctly.

This chapter is based on an article first published in *Dr. Dobb's Journal*, September 1995.

MIME at a Glance	
Name:	Multipurpose Internet Mail Extensions, MIME
Use For:	Transferring data through mail or news
Reference:	RFC 1521
On CD:	*UUDeview* for Unix and MS-DOS; *WinCode* for Windows

These type indications have been adopted by the HTTP protocol used by the World Wide Web (see page 35) to inform a browser of the type of data being sent. World Wide Web browsers also use this to inform HTTP servers what types of data they can accept.

When to Use MIME

MIME is usually integrated into the mailer program. Many mail reader programs now automatically recognize and decode MIME-format mail. Some can automatically create MIME-format mail; you simply specify an "attachment" to your message and the mail program will automatically encode the file.

This procedure is quite convenient if both the sender and recipient have MIME-compatible mail readers. If not, it's still possible to use MIME, but it is more complex. Several programs, including the metamail program for Unix, can decode MIME-encoded mail. To use them, simply save the received message to a file and process it with the appropriate program. Manually encoding a file into MIME format can be tricky, since you have to specify the content type properly in order for the receiving mail program to automatically recognize the file. It may be better to stick with UUEncode rather than manually encoding a file using MIME.

One complication that sometimes arises is that MIME supports many different types of data. When you decode a MIME-format message, your decoder has only a few options:

- It might have built-in support for that kind of data. For example, many MIME decoders support compound messages directly.

- It might call another program to handle that data. Graphics, sound, and movie formats are usually handled by an external program. You must have a suitable external program and configure your MIME decoder so it will know to use that program.

- It might simply decode the data into a file and tell you the format. It's then up to you to figure out how to view it. In this minimal form, MIME is comparable to UUEncode; it lets you safely transfer binary data through the mail.

The most common source of problems with MIME is not having your MIME software properly configured to use the correct external programs.

How MIME Works

The basic definition of Internet mail is contained in RFC822.[1] According to RFC822, a mail message consists of *header lines* followed by a blank line and a *message body*. While RFC822 describes the syntax of header lines in considerable detail, it is less precise about the body: "The body is simply a sequence of lines containing ASCII characters." MIME augments this definition by adding the five new headers described below. These five headers, among other things, specify the precise format of the message body:

Content-Type   Specifies the type of data contained in the message. For example, a Content-Type of "audio/basic" indicates a particular audio format that the mail reader should decode and play.

Content-Transfer-Encoding   Specifies how the data is encoded into seven-bit text.

MIME-Version   Indicates MIME compliance. This header was omitted from early drafts of MIME, so isn't yet used by all encoders.

Content-ID   Uniquely identifies the body of the message.

Content-Description   Provides an additional human-readable description.

MIME Content Types

MIME specifies the format of the message body in three layers. The first is a broad *type* that identifies the general kind of data. By itself, the type doesn't provide enough information for the reader to do anything useful, but it does help the reader select a default handling for certain classes of messages (for

---

[1]An RFC is a "Request For Comments," a document being evaluated as an Internet standard.

Type	Description
text	Human-readable text, possibly with textual markup. Any file with type text should be intelligible if simply listed to the screen. (Binary word processor formats are *not* text.)
audio	Sound data
image	Still image
video	Movie or animated image
application	Application-specific data file; this type includes script files in certain text languages
message	Wrapper for an embedded message
multipart	Multi-part message. Each part may be in a different format. Subtypes indicate the relationship between the different parts

Table 33.1   MIME Top-Level Content Types

example, text formats might be simply listed to the screen, while unrecognized image formats would not be). The second layer is the *subtype*. The type and subtype together specify the exact kind of data in the message (such as image/gif). The third layer specifies how the data is encoded into seven-bit ASCII.

The Content-Type header contains a type and subtype separated by a / character, followed by a list of *keyword=value* pairs. For example, the type text/plain; charset=iso-8859-8 might be used for a plain text file containing characters in the ISO Roman/Hebrew character set. If the display supported Hebrew characters, the mail reader could (after decoding) display the text as it was intended by the sender.

There are currently seven defined top-level types, listed in Table 33.1. Note that types, subtypes, and keywords are all case-insensitive. Whether or not the keyword values are case-sensitive depends on the particular keyword.

The first five top-level types in Table 33.1 indicate a single data file in a single format. Some subtypes are given in Table 33.2. These basic types are a big improvement over text-only mail, allowing messages to contain graphics, sound, or other types of data. They are also quite easy to support; mail readers only need to parse the Content-Type and Content-Transfer-Encoding headers and decode two simple data formats.

Type	Description
text/plain	Plain text with no special formatting. The `charset` key is used to specify US-ASCII, or one of the ISO-8859 character sets.
text/enriched	An alternate format specified in RFC1563.
audio/basic	A single-channel 8000hz audio file in eight-bit ISDN μ-law format.
image/gif	A still image in GIF format.
image/jpeg	A still image in JPEG format.
image/tiff	A still image in TIFF format.
video/mpeg	A video image in MPEG format. Video images may or may not contain an associated soundtrack.
video/quicktime	A video image in QuickTime format.
application/octet-stream	Binary data of an unspecified format. The `type` key can be used to give additional, human-readable information. The `padding` key can be used to specify up to seven bits of padding that were added to round a bit-oriented file to a whole number of eight-bit bytes.
application/postscript	A PostScript file.
application/mac-binhex40	A Macintosh file encoded with BinHex.

Table 33.2   Simple MIME Data Types

More Complex Messages

The remaining two types, message and multipart, provide a number of useful features that can reduce mail delivery costs and allow single messages to combine different kinds of data.

The message type provides three important capabilities. The subtype message/rfc822 allows another mail message to be embedded within a MIME message. This is useful primarily for mailers that must automatically forward or return messages. The message/external-body type saves on transfer costs by specifying that the actual message body is contained elsewhere. Keywords define exactly how the message body can be retrieved (for example, by anonymous FTP or as a local file). The message/external-body type uses keywords to indicate exactly how to retrieve the data.

The `message/partial` type allows a single large message to be split and sent as several smaller messages. This capability can be useful when dealing with mail systems that limit the size of messages. The `message/partial` type has three keywords: `id` specifies a unique identifier that is used to match different pieces of the same message; `number` specifies the order of the parts (parts are numbered starting with 1); and `total` gives the total number of parts. The `id` and `number` keywords are required on all parts; `total` is required only on the last part.

The `multipart` types allow a single message to contain several pieces, each in a different format. The most common of these types is `multipart/mixed`. This type indicates that the message consists of multiple pieces, each with its own separate `Content-Type` header. A `multipart/alternative` message includes several alternative forms of the same information (such as both plain text and a word processor file with the same content). The parts of a `multipart/parallel` message are intended to be displayed simultaneously (such as an audio recording and a photograph of the speaker). A `multipart/digest` message is the same as `multipart/mixed` except that the default `Content-Type` for each part is `message/rfc822` rather than `text/plain`.

All `message` and `multipart` types allow (indeed, often require) the embedded data to have its own headers. Technically, the embedded data is *not* an RFC822 message (for instance, it may lack a `From` header), even though it has the same general format. For example, if a message has type `message/external-body`, the body contains a series of lines that look like RFC822 headers, including `Content-Type` (the type of the data in the external file) and `Content-Transfer-Encoding` (how the data is encoded in the external file). Like RFC822, a blank line indicates the end of the headers.

Multipart messages must have some way to separate the different parts. The "boundary" keyword specifies a string that *does not occur anywhere else in the message*. The actual separators consist of the specified string preceded by `--` (two hyphens). The end of the multipart message is marked by the boundary string preceded and followed by `--`. Figure 33.1 shows this mechanism in action. This message displays a text message while retrieving and playing audio data from a local file. A minimal MIME-compliant mail reader would show the text part, and inform the user of the type and location of the external file data.

```
From: tim@humperdinck (Tim Kientzle)
To: tim@humperdinck
Subject: A Sample Multipart message
MIME-Version: 1.0
Content-Type: multipart/parallel; boundary=SoMeBoUnDaRy

Any text preceding the first boundary string is ignored
by MIME-compliant mail readers.  This area usually holds
a short message informing a person using a non-compliant
reader that this is a MIME message that they may not be
able to read.
--SoMeBoUnDaRy

The preceding blank line ends the headers for this part.
Since there were none, this is assumed to be plain text
in US-ASCII.  The boundary cannot occur in the actual
text, so that mailers can quickly scan the text to
locate the boundaries.
--SoMeBoUnDaRy
Content-Type: message/external-body; access-type=local-file;
name=/pub/file.audio
Content-Transfer-Encoding: 7bit

Content-Type: audio/basic
Content-Transfer-Encoding: binary

This text is ignored, the actual audio comes from the
file /pub/file.audio.  Both blank lines above are
important.  Also note the different encodings.
The 7bit encoding means that this embedded message is
in 7bit (which is mandatory for message/external-body),
while the actual audio data is stored in binary in the
local file.
--SoMeBoUnDaRy--
This text follows the closing boundary marker above,
and is therefore ignored by compliant mail readers.
```

Figure 33.1   Sample Multipart Message

Encoding	Description
7bit	Unencoded seven-bit text
8bit	Unencoded eight-bit text
binary	Unencoded binary data
Quoted-Printable	Most seven-bit characters are unencoded; other characters are represented as = followed by two hex digits
Base64	Encoded in base 64 using digits A-Za-z0-9+/

Table 33.3   MIME Encoding Types

Encoding

Transparent handling of binary data is one of the primary goals of MIME. MIME uses the `Content-Transfer-Encoding` header field to specify the encoding. The five currently-defined encodings are given in Table 33.3. The first three indicate that the data is unencoded. The `8bit` and `binary` types are used primarily with `message/external-body` and occasionally with mail systems that support eight-bit messages.

The `Quoted-Printable` encoding is intended for data that is primarily seven-bit, with occasional eight-bit values within it. For example, text messages in ISO character sets are often predominantly seven-bit. `Quoted-Printable` allows most seven-bit text characters to represent themselves. The remaining characters are encoded as three-character sequences consisting of = followed by two uppercase hexadecimal digits. Note that = is encoded as =3D.

The advantage of the `Quoted-Printable` encoding is that it allows any part of the data that is in seven-bit US-ASCII to be read without decoding. However, for raw binary data, it can introduce excessive overhead. The preferred encoding for raw binary data is the `Base64` encoding. Each three bytes of binary data is encoded as four characters. The 24-bit value is treated as four six-bit numbers, which are then encoded from the characters A–Z, a–z, 0–9, +, and /. Thus, `the` becomes `dGhl`. The result is padded with = to a multiple of four characters, and broken into 72-character lines. This encoding is similar to the one used by the popular UUEncode utility (see page 257), but avoids using punctuation characters that are lost or altered by certain mail gateways.

In some cases, no encoding is necessary. In particular, the `multipart` type always uses 7bit, as do `message/partial` and `message/external-body`. Under certain circumstances, other `message` types can use `binary` or `8bit`. The remaining types can use any available encoding. The point of these restrictions on `message` and `multipart` is to avoid the possibility of nested encodings, which can unnecessarily bloat the message. Remember that a `Content-Transfer-Encoding` of 7bit for a `multipart` message means that the individual parts have all been encoded for seven-bit transport.

Security

Many projects have used mail to transfer scripts to be automatically executed on the receiving machine. MIME's `application/postscript` is one example, and other such types are being proposed. Any system that allows a received program to be automatically executed is a potential security risk. The PostScript language includes the ability to modify files, and even without that capability, it is possible to crash many systems by consuming excessive memory or disk space. Security-conscious systems may need to restrict the handling of these types. For example, it is usually more secure to send PostScript files to a printer than to interpret and display the data on the host machine.

More Information

The current MIME specification is RFC1521, which is available from the mail server at `RFC-INFO@isi.edu`. Include the following two lines in the body of your message (other RFC documents can be retrieved in a similar fashion):

```
retrieve: RFC
doc-id: RFC1521
```

MIME does not extend RFC822 to allow the use of non-ASCII characters in mail headers. A related proposal, documented in RFC1522, does permit non-ASCII characters in mail headers. An extended text subtype `text/enriched` is described in RFC1563. This replaces the `text/richtext` type proposed in an earlier MIME draft (the name change was to reduce confusion with Microsoft's Rich Text Format).

The complete MIME specification, in both text and PostScript form, and the freely-available *MetaMail* implementation of MIME can be obtained from `ftp://thumper.bellcore.com/pub/nsb`. *MetaMail* integrates well with a number of popular Unix mail reader programs, including Pine and Elm.

The popular *Eudora* mail reader allows users of Macintosh and Windows to access Internet mail on a remote Unix machine. It uses MIME to encode and decode attached documents. (`http://www.qualcomm.com/quest`)

BinHex

The encodings discussed thus far all presume that the file contents are simply a stream of bytes. This is true for Unix and most microcomputer operating systems, but isn't true for some other systems. Most notably, Macintosh and OS/2 both attach databases to each file (Macintosh literature refers to this database as the "resource fork" while OS/2 calls it "extended attributes"). Encoding a file on these systems requires a bit more care. Not only must the file contents *per se* be encoded, but the attached database must also be encoded, and the receiver must be able to separate these two parts of the file.

Apple has defined *BinHex* as a standard way of converting any Macintosh file, including the resource fork, into a single stream of bytes. The text version of this format can be used to transfer Macintosh files through mail. While rarely seen outside of the Macintosh community, it is sometimes necessary to decode such files on another system. Usually, the resource fork has nothing that is usable on another system, so it's sufficient to simply extract and decode the data portion of the file.

BinHex at a Glance	
Name:	BinHex
Extension:	.hqx
Use For:	Encoding Macintosh files for transfer through mail

How to Use BinHex

For Macintosh users, converting files to and from BinHex format can be easily handled by a variety of utilities. Many terminal programs support BinHex, as do many archiving programs. For users of other systems, BinHex files are a little more challenging.

If you're not using a Macintosh, decoding a BinHex file will give you three different output files. These three files hold the data fork, the resource fork, and the Macintosh directory information. Usually, the data fork is the only usable part.

For example, suppose you download a file with the extensions `.sea.hqx` from an archive. The final `.hqx` marks this as a BinHex file. After decoding, you'll have three files, corresponding to the three parts of a Macintosh `.sea` self-extracting StuffIt archive.[1] In this case, the resource fork holds the self-extraction program, and the data fork holds the actual archived data. If you're not on a Macintosh, the self-extraction program isn't useful. You'll need a suitable StuffIt de-archiver to burst the archived data from the data fork.

How BinHex Works

BinHex encoding is performed in three stages. First, the resource and data forks are archived into a single stream of bytes with some error checks so that the decoder can be certain the decoded data is correct. This archive is compressed using a very simple run-length encoding approach. Finally, the data is encoded into a text form.

The archiving step combines the data and resource forks into a single stream of bytes. This is necessary to transfer the file using standard protocols such as ZModem or FTP. This is also necessary to store the file on a Unix archive site. BinHex archiving is pretty simple; it bundles the basic file information with a CRC on each section so the decoder can check for errors. Table 34.1 details the format.

---

[1]The `.sea` extension is used for several different self-extracting archive formats; StuffIt is the most common.

Length	Description
1	Length of filename (1–63)
n	Filename
1	Version (currently zero)
4	File type
4	File creator
2	Finder flags
4	Length of data fork
4	Length of resource fork
2	CRC of previous data
n	Data fork
2	CRC of data fork
n	Resource fork
2	CRC of resource fork

Table 34.1   BinHex Archive Format

Once the file is archived, BinHex does some simple run-length compression. Any sequence of three or more repeated bytes is replaced by a single copy of the byte followed by 144 and the one-byte repeat count. For example, if the value 137 were repeated 23 times, it would be replaced with the three bytes 137 144 23. As a special case, the byte 144 is encoded as 144 0. The zero repeat count means this encodes a single 144, not a repeat of the previous byte.

After compression, you have a single Macintosh file encoded as a stream of binary data. Technically, this intermediate format is called hqx8, but it is rarely used. Instead, BinHex encodes the data into a text format that's suitable for mail transfer. This stage uses a base 64 encoding similar to UUEncode, but using Table 34.2 to convert six-bit values into characters. The final text consists of a leading comment line,

```
(This file must be converted with BinHex 4.0)
```

followed by the encoded data. A colon character (:) is added to the beginning and end of the encoded data, and the result is broken into lines of at most 64 characters.

Code	Char	Code	Char	Code	Char	Code	Char
0	!	16	3	32	J	48	'
1	"	17	4	33	K	49	a
2	#	18	5	34	L	50	b
3	$	19	6	35	M	51	c
4	%	20	8	36	N	52	d
5	&	21	9	37	P	53	e
6	'	22	@	38	Q	54	f
7	(	23	A	39	R	55	h
8	)	24	B	40	S	56	i
9	*	25	C	41	T	57	j
10	+	26	D	42	T	58	k
11	,	27	E	43	V	59	l
12	-	28	F	44	X	60	m
13	0	29	G	45	Y	61	p
14	1	30	H	46	Z	62	q
15	2	31	I	47	[	63	r

Table 34.2   BinHex 4.0 Text Encoding

BinHex Variants

The most widely-used BinHex encoding is known as BinHex 4.0. Earlier versions of BinHex are hardly ever seen. A program from Apple called BinHex 5.0 actually supports an encoding more widely known as *MacBinary*. MacBinary is used by many Macintosh terminal programs to archive the various components of a file so it can be transferred using common file transfer protocols such as ZModem. It's less often seen on the Internet simply because it is a binary encoding, and is therefore unsuitable for use with mail.

More Information

BinHex is supported by nearly all Macintosh archiving programs and many terminal programs and mail readers. If you need a Macintosh program for decoding BinHex files, you'll have difficulty getting it from the Internet because, of course, Macintosh files on the Internet are usually BinHex encoded. In this case, you may want to start by contacting BMUG (see page 12).

Some of the larger multi-format archivers for MS-DOS and Windows also support BinHex. Aladdin Systems, the manufacturer of StuffIt, also has freely available programs for MS-DOS and Windows available from their archive site (`http://www.aladdinsys.com`).

A simple BinHex decoder for Unix and MS-DOS is available from the CTAN archives (see page 75) in the `archive-tools/xbin` directory.

Part Five
Sound Formats

About Sound

Conceptually, digital sound is fairly simple. A sound is carried along a wire as a varying analog voltage. To handle this digitally, you *sample* the sound, measuring the voltage at regular intervals with an *analog-to-digital converter* (ADC). You can then store and manipulate these samples as digital data, and finally reproduce the sound by converting it back into a varying voltage with a *digital-to-analog converter* (DAC). Figure 35.1 illustrates this conversion.

Two important issues affect the quality of the resulting sound. The *sampling rate* is how often you sample the sound waveform. The *sample size* controls the accuracy of the samples. If you increase both the sampling rate and sample size, you'll get better-quality sound, but you'll also increase the amount of data you have to store. Just one second of CD-quality sound (44,100 samples per second, 16 bits per channel, two channels) is 172 kilobytes of data. To

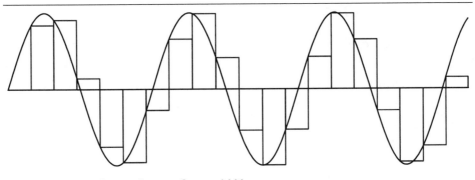

Figure 35.1   Sampling a Sound Wave

determining the best sampling rate and sample size, you must carefully judge the trade-off between sound quality and data size.

Fortunately, it's fairly easy to quantify the effects of these two factors. The sampling rate controls the highest frequency that you can reproduce. A fact known as *Nyquist's Law* says that the highest frequency that you can reproduce is one-half the sampling rate. For example, audio CDs store digital sound sampled at 44,100 samples per second, so they can store sounds with frequencies up to 22,050 hertz.[1] This frequency is well beyond what most people can hear, and helps account for the high perceived quality of CD audio. By contrast, much of the current telephone network uses digital sound sampled at about 8,000 samples per second. Because most human speech lies below 3,000 hertz, this sampling rate works quite well for this application.

The sample size controls a factor known as the *signal-to-noise ratio*. Any method of storing and reproducing sound introduces some random loss, which is heard as noise. For digital sound, the inherent noise is determined by the accuracy of the samples. More accurate samples leave less margin for noise.

Playing Sound

Playing sound requires some way to convert a description of the sound in the computer into a varying voltage that you can feed to the speakers. There are a number of different approaches.

External Synthesizers

The easiest way to play a sound from the computer's point of view is to get someone else to do it. The *Musical Instrument Digital Interface* (MIDI) is a standard way to connect computers to music synthesizers, allowing the computer to simply instruct the synthesizer to play certain notes. More recently, MIDI-capable synthesizers have become available on add-in cards for various computer systems. These cards have essentially the same electronics as their stand-alone brethren, only without a keyboard.

---

[1] Hertz = cycles per second. Hertz is also used for sampling rates.

FM Synthesis

One of the simpler ways to generate sounds electronically is with a technique called *FM synthesis*. This technique is available on a single chip from a number of sources, and is used by many low-end synthesizers and sound cards. FM synthesis chips are controlled by specifying a set of frequencies and a way to combine them. This approach is relatively easy from the computer's point of view, which made it very popular before computers were really fast enough to handle the requirements of sampled sounds.

Sampled Sounds

Both of the previous methods are somewhat limited in that you can produce only a limited set of sounds. Synthesizers only support a limited collection of different sounds, and FM synthesis is also limited in this regard. These methods are also unable to record sound.

The electronics for handling digital sampled sounds are not that complex: An ADC converts an analog sound into a series of digital samples; a DAC converts them back. The problem is that this approach requires the computer to quickly shuffle a lot of data.

The better sound cards have a quantity of dedicated memory for storing sound samples. The computer programs the sound card, then transfers blocks of sound data to the sound card's internal memory. The sound card collects samples from the internal memory and sends them to the DAC at a steady rate, notifying the computer when it needs additional data. With careful programming or a very fast computer, it's possible to perform complex calculations to either create or alter the sound data on-the-fly. The computer has to be able to read a block of sound data, and perform the calculations before the sound card requires that block.

One common use for this type of processing is to combine multiple sounds to simulate a synthesizer playing several notes. Each sound must be frequency-shifted to the correct note, then the sounds are combined. Some sound cards provide memory for multiple sounds. The sound card hardware then reads and combines the sounds automatically; the computer only needs to make sure the correct sounds are loaded into the proper place at the proper time.

Digital Signal Processors

Complex audio effects and sophisticated audio compression can require significant amounts of processing. Doing this processing as the sound is played is simply impossible on many systems. For this reason, high-end sound cards now include *digital signal processors* (DSPs). DSPs are specialized computers designed to perform the type of computation required by sound processing. The computer simply transfers the raw data to the sound card along with a program for the DSP. The DSP then performs the calculations prior to passing the data along to the DAC.

High-Quality Sound on Low-Quality Hardware

Although sound cards are becoming more popular, many computers still lack anything more sophisticated than a single-bit speaker, such as the one built into most PCs. As you might guess, one-bit sound doesn't precisely qualify as "hi-fi." The following trick requires a lot of care but does allow reasonably high-quality sound in this situation.

Pulse width modulation involves turning the speaker on and off extremely fast. Each pulse is translated by the speaker into some intermediate value, allowing the single-bit speaker to simulate a higher-resolution device. While this approach can produce acceptable results, it does require the full attention of the computer to precisely time the speaker pulses.

Storing Sound

The most obvious way to store sound data in a file is to simply write all of the samples, one after the other. This simple scheme is known as *pulse code modulation* (PCM). The fancy name comes from old electrical engineering terminology. Of course, good file formats will also store the sampling rate and sample size in the file, so that different sounds can be recorded in different ways.

Because sound files require so much data, there's a lot of interest in compression. Unfortunately, standard compression algorithms do very poorly on sound. Just as with photographs, low-level noise confounds the standard algorithms.

Simple sound compression schemes were developed by the telephone company many years ago to allow them to pile more telephone conversations on the same amount of wire. The telephone companies have historically only been interested in *fixed-rate* compression, in which all sounds are compressed by exactly the same amount. This approach differs from typical computer compression applications, which don't care if different data compresses by different amounts. However, the predictability of fixed-rate methods is a major asset, which makes this type of compression quite popular with computer sound applications.

Silence Encoding

When people speak, a considerable amount of time is occupied by silence. Simple PCM sound requires just as much storage for ten seconds of silence as for ten seconds of your next door neighbor's favorite loud music. A simple way to reduce the size of many sound files is to replace stretches of silence with a single code indicating the duration of the silence.

μ-Law and A-Law Compression

When you feed sound data to your sound card, the sound card converts each sound sample into a voltage, which is amplified and fed to your speakers or headphones. As the sound samples vary, this voltage varies, and the speakers convert the varying voltage into varying air pressure, which travels through the air to your ears.

What exactly is the relationship between the sound sample values and the voltages produced by your sound card? One obvious approach is to make this relation *linear*, that is, a sound sample of 50 will produce exactly twice the voltage as a sound sample of 25. This approach is not very efficient. The catch is that you want to be able to reproduce a wide range of loudnesses, and our ears don't respond to sound linearly. The difference between 0 and 1 may be too large for quiet sounds, even though the difference between 49 and 50 is too small to be audible.

What you really want is for small sound samples (like 1) to be very small, and for larger sound samples (like 50) to be very large. What works well is to use a *logarithmic* scale. In this scale, a sound sample of 50 will produce more

The μ-Law relation is used primarily in North America and Japan. The following equation converts linear samples m into μ-Law samples y_μ. Here, m_p is the peak sample value and μ is a constant, usually 100 or 255.

$$y_\mu = \frac{\text{sign}(m)}{\ln(1+\mu)} \ln(1 + \mu |\tfrac{m}{m_p}|)$$

A-Law is used primarily in Europe. Again, this equation converts linear samples m into A-Law samples y_A. A is the constant 87.6.

$$y_A = \begin{cases} \frac{A}{1+\ln A}\left(\frac{m}{m_p}\right) & |\frac{m}{m_p}| \le \frac{1}{A} \\[2mm] \frac{\text{sign}(m)}{1+\ln A}(1 + \ln A |\frac{m}{m_p}|) & \frac{1}{A} \le |\frac{m}{m_p}| \le 1 \end{cases}$$

Figure 35.2 μ-Law and A-Law Sound Conversions

than twice the voltage (and sound pressure) as a sound sample of 25. This technique increases the range of loudness without requiring a larger range of numbers.

Two common equations specify the exact relationship. The μ-Law[2] and A-Law relations allow eight-bit sound samples to represent the same range as 12-bit linear sound samples. By changing what your numbers mean, you obtain over 30 percent compression! Figure 35.2 gives the precise relationships between linear, μ-Law, and A-Law sound formats.

DPCM and ADPCM

Another simple fixed-rate compression scheme converts a sequence of samples by storing only the difference between each sample and the previous one. This method, known as *Differential PCM* (DPCM), saves space because the differences are typically smaller than the samples themselves. One of the simplest reasonably effective compression methods for sound is to use Huffman compression (see page 185) on these differences.

To maintain the accuracy of the original samples, you must store some fairly large differences, even though most differences are quite small. *Adaptive*

---

[2] μ is the greek letter "mu." μ-Law is often written as u-Law.

Differential PCM (ADPCM) uses special codes to indicate the scale of the next group of differences. This scaling factor allows a relatively small numeric difference to occasionally represent a large change. ADPCM techniques can compress sound data by a factor of four with reasonable quality.

More Advanced Techniques

More sophisticated compression techniques have been developed to take advantage of facts about human hearing, similar to the way JPEG exploits facts about human vision (see page 157). These methods selectively choose sound data to discard, resulting in fairly impressive compression while retaining high quality. The biggest obstacle to widespread use is that they do require a large amount of computation, and current computers aren't quite capable of performing these complex calculations fast enough to decompress the sound as it is being played.

Some compression techniques were developed for use by telephone systems, including cellular telephones. These methods are based on a model of the human vocal tract. They analyze the sound for specific kinds of patterns that are created by the larynx, throat, and mouth, and convey just those patterns. These methods can achieve impressive compression of human speech.

More powerful schemes have been developed to compress sounds other than speech. MPEG (see page 327) defines three successively more powerful, and more complex, sound compression techniques. Electronics companies have invested significant amounts of money to develop proprietary schemes that allow them to pack hours of music onto compact digital tapes and discs.

Different people are interested in different kinds of sound compression. People with faster computers and DSP chips are using MPEG and other more sophisticated compression techniques, while people with slower systems can't reasonably use these computation-intensive approaches. Because of this variation, many of the current sound-handling systems, including the one in the Macintosh's QuickTime toolbox, support replaceable *codecs* (*co*mpression/*dec*ompression modules). Using replaceable modules allows the same basic software to be easily tailored to specific situations, and also makes it easy to upgrade the software to support newer compression methods and DSP chips.

More Information

The `comp.dsp` newsgroup covers digital signal processing at a fairly technical level. The FAQ has a good (if somewhat dated) bibliography of related
materials. Another useful FAQ is the `audio_fmts` FAQ, regularly posted to
`comp.dsp` and `news.answers`. This is a fairly comprehensive and concise
summary of a number of different sound file formats.

The *Computer Music Journal* archives have pointers to a lot of different music-related resources. They also have a collection of sound files in
different formats. The archives are available on the World Wide Web at
`http://www-mitpress.mit.edu/Computer-Music-Journal/`. They are
also available using anonymous FTP to `mitpress.mit.edu`; look in the directory `pub/Computer-Music-Journal`.

The *utexas mac archive* lists a variety of sound players for the Macintosh
(`http://wwwhost.ots.utexas.edu/mac/main.html`). It's also available
using anonymous FTP to `ftp://ftp.utexas.edu/pub/mac`.

Yahoo (see page 14) has an extensive list of sound files and software. Look
under Multimedia.

AU

36

The *AU* sound file format is one of the most common sound formats on the Internet today. This format is fairly simple. A small header specifies the basic parameters of the sound—sampling rate, sample size, number of channels, and encoding method—and the sound data follows. The major complication is that these files are known as AU files on Sun systems and *SND* files on NeXT. Some further confusion arises from the fact that old Sun AU files lacked a header entirely, and SND is a common extension used by many other formats on other systems.

Despite these minor issues, AU files are common and easy to play on most systems. The most common AU files are 8000 hertz single-channel μ-Law files, although 16-bit linear stereo at 22,050 and 44,100 hertz sampling rates are also common. Many of the sound format codes are used for special NeXT and Sun formats that are rarely seen outside of those platforms.

The 8000 hertz μ-Law format corresponds to the hardware support on several popular Unix-like systems. The /dev/audio device on Sun workstations, Linux[1], FreeBSD[1], and several other systems defaults to this format. On

---

[1] Using the *VoxWare* audio driver and a compatible sound card.

AU at a Glance	
Names:	AU, Sun AU, NeXT SND
Extensions:	.au, .snd
Use For:	Exchanging sound data

Length	Description
4	Magic string: `.snd`
4	Offset of the sound data from the beginning of the file (at least 28)
4	Number of bytes of sound data
4	Sound format

Code	Description
1	8-bit μ-Law
2	8-bit linear
3	16-bit linear
4	24-bit linear
5	32-bit linear
27	8-bit A-Law

Length	Description
4	Sampling rate in samples per second
4	Number of channels
n	Optional text description (at least four bytes)
n	Sound data

Table 36.1   AU File Format

these systems, you can simply dump AU files in this format to `/dev/audio` to play them. A typical command is:

```
cat funny.au >/dev/audio
```

More Information

The *Sunsite* archive has a large collection of AU files available using anonymous FTP from `sunsite.unc.edu`; look in the `pub/multimedia/sun-sounds` directory.

WAVE

With the growing popularity of Windows, the native *WAVE* sound format is increasingly common. WAVE is actually a special type of *RIFF* file, so I'll digress for a moment to discuss RIFF files.

How RIFF Works

RIFF (Resource Interchange File Format) is a file format that allows essentially arbitrary data to be stored in a structured fashion. RIFF files can contain blocks with different types of data in them. They are quite similar to the Electronic Arts' IFF format originally designed for the Amiga. A RIFF file is composed of *chunks*, some of which can contain other chunks in a nested fashion. Each chunk has a four-character identifier and a length, as shown in Figure 37.1.

An entire RIFF file is actually a single chunk. The RIFF chunk serves to collect and organize a group of other chunks. The first four bytes of data in a RIFF chunk are a *form identifier*, as shown in Figure 37.2. The form identifier

WAVE at a Glance	
Name:	Microsoft Windows RIFF WAVE
Extension:	`.wav`
Use For:	Windows sound storage

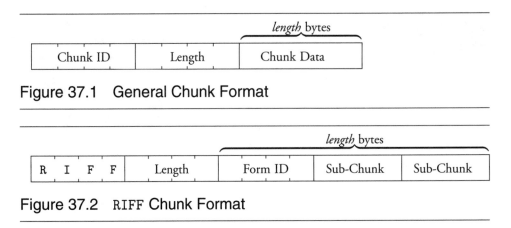

Figure 37.1   General Chunk Format

Figure 37.2   `RIFF` Chunk Format

indicates the type of chunks you should expect. The one we're interested in here is the WAVE form, which stores information about a sampled sound.

WAVE Form

The WAVE form can have a variety of chunks within it, although usually there's only a single `fmt` chunk and a single `data` chunk. In fact, many programs that work with WAVE files assume the rigid format shown in Table 37.1. While this assumption is usually acceptable, programs that only recognize such a rigid format will not be able to handle WAVE files that include optional comment chunks or other data. Properly written programs that deal with WAVE files will skip chunks they don't understand.

The `fmt` chunk, whose contents are outlined in Table 37.2, contains basic information about the sample data. Most of these fields are self-explanatory. Almost all WAVE files on the Internet are PCM format. The number of channels and samples per second are basic sound parameters. The average number of bytes per second is provided to help the player choose appropriate sizes for buffers. Many sound systems buffer one second of sound at a time.

WAVE PCM Data Storage

The actual PCM data is stored in a fairly direct fashion. For concreteness, assume you're dealing with a stereo sound with 20 bits for each sample. Each

Size	Description
4	Chunk type: RIFF
4	Total file size minus eight
4	Form name: WAVE
4	Chunk type: fmt␣
4	Format chunk data length: usually 16
16	Format chunk data
4	Chunk type: data
4	Length of sound data
n	Actual sound samples

Table 37.1   Naïve WAVE File Format

Size	Description		
2	Sample data format		
	Code	**Description**	
	1	PCM data	
	257	IBM μ-Law data	
	258	IBM A-Law data	
	259	IBM AVC ADPCM format	
2	Number of channels		
4	Samples per second		
4	Average number of bytes per second		
2	Block alignment		
2	Significant bits per sample (only for PCM data)		

Table 37.2   WAVE Format Chunk Data

individual 20-bit sample would be stored in three bytes. Because there are two channels, samples appear in pairs; the first sample is for the left channel, the second for the right. A group of samples, one for each channel, is a *block*. The block alignment value in the format chunk specifies the total size of this block (six in this example); this value is specified to help WAVE readers optimize data transfers.

To put your 20-bit sample into those three bytes, WAVE specifies that you add four zero bits to the bottom (least significant end) of the sample to pad

Unsigned Byte	Sound Value	Signed Byte
255	+127	127
254	+126	126
⋮	⋮	⋮
130	+2	2
129	+1	1
128	0	0
127	-1	255
126	-2	254
⋮	⋮	⋮
1	-127	129
0	-128	128

Table 37.3   Signed and Unsigned Eight-Bit Sound Samples

it to 24 bits. This style of padding lets a reader handle it as if it were 24-bit data. Similarly, 12-bit data can be treated as if it were 16-bit data.

You also need to know how to handle positive and negative values. Sound sample data is inherently signed—there are both positive and negative values. One approach for working with signed numbers is known as *two's complement*, which represents a sound value of zero with a byte value of 0. Another is to *offset* the values. For one-byte numbers, you can offset them by 128. This represents a zero sound value with a byte value of 128. Two's complement is often referred to as "signed format," while the offset method is often referred to as "unsigned format." Table 37.3 shows the correspondence between signed sound values and these two formats for eight-bit samples.

WAVE's PCM data format uses unsigned format for sound samples up to eight bits, and signed format for larger samples.

Additional Chunk Types

Although not often used, WAVE does support a variety of additional chunks. The `fact` chunk stores additional information about compressed sound data, such as the total number of samples in the file. The `cue` chunk lets you mark special positions in the sound data stream. This information can be useful when a sound file needs to be synchronized with other events, such as a slide show or movie. The `plst` playlist chunk can specify the order in which parts of the sound file should be played. Other chunks allow text data to be included.

WAVE supports several forms of compressed data, but none of them is frequently used. IBM has registered format codes for μ-Law, A-Law, and ADPCM compression. In addition, PCM WAVE files can replace the single `data` chunk containing the PCM data with a `LIST` chunk. A `LIST` chunk is structured like a `RIFF` chunk, containing a form code and a collection of other chunks. WAVE files use a `LIST` chunk with the `wavl` form code to store silence-encoded PCM data. The sub-chunks are `data` chunks containing PCM data as usual and `slnt` chunks indicating a stretch of silence. The data for the `slnt` chunk is a single 32-bit integer with the number of samples that it's replacing.

Other Formats

While WAVE and AU files are fairly prominent, many other sound and music formats are available on the Internet. This chapter describes a few.

MIDI

The *Musical Instrument Digital Interface* (MIDI) is a fairly old and established standard for connecting a variety of musical equipment. It can be used, for example, to allow a single keyboard to control many synthesizers, or to allow a computer to store keypresses from a synthesizer keyboard and replay them. MIDI can also be used with drum synthesizers and lighting equipment. Indeed, MIDI is one of the technologies that has made some of today's concert special effects possible, by providing a way to synchronize a variety of music and special effects.

It's quite natural that MIDI is an integral part of many music-editing systems. MIDI is based on *packets* of data, each one representing a musical event, ranging from a keypress to a simple time marker. MIDI segregates these events by *channel*. In a complex MIDI environment, there may be many different appliances, each responding to events on a different channel. Alternatively, a single synthesizer may respond to all of the channels.

A standard known as *General MIDI* specifies a method to store MIDI events in a file. This file format has become a standard way to store and exchange music. The advantage of exchanging MIDI files over sampled sound files is that MIDI files are much smaller, because they just store the note names rather than a detailed recording of the sound.

For personal computer users, however, MIDI has two major drawbacks. The first is that it does often require a significant hardware investment. The second is that the MIDI file itself doesn't specify everything that you need to reproduce the sound. MIDI events may specify that channel seven should be playing notes based on the "space warp" sound, but it won't specify in any concrete way what that sound is.

The `alt.binaries.sounds.midi` newsgroup is used to share music files in MIDI format. The associated FAQ provides general information about MIDI files and software.

MOD

Several alternative formats essentially follow MIDI's "note-by-note" data storage approach, but store digitized sound samples to be used as templates for the individual notes. These formats are collectively known as "player modules," and usually use a `.mod` file extension. *MOD* files begin with a set of sound samples, and then specify notes and timing information. Each note is played by using one of the sound samples given at the beginning. Essentially, the final sound is built by copying these template sounds to form a complete piece of music.

MOD files have many of the benefits of MIDI. They are relatively small, and have a note-based structure that makes it easy to edit them using tools that mimic traditional music notation. In addition, they completely specify the sound, allowing them to be played on almost any system, even if you don't have a synthesizer with the "space warp" sound available.

The major drawback is that assembling a high-quality sampled sound from the information in a MOD file is a time-consuming task. At any time, a dozen or more samples may have to be copied on top of each other to simulate simultaneous notes. This intensive data manipulation makes programs to play MOD files rather difficult to write. Because a MOD file can comfortably hold an hour of music or more, it's not feasible to first expand the MOD file into a sampled sound format (such as WAVE or AU) and then play the result. It's necessary to assemble the sound on-the-fly.

The `alt.binaries.sounds.mods` newsgroup is dedicated to the exchange of MOD files. The associated FAQ has information about this format and pointers to software for a variety of platforms.

IFF

The *Interchange File Format* (IFF) was originally developed by Electronic Arts for use on the Amiga. It's currently also used on CD-I. IFF is a structured format whose overall structure is almost identical to RIFF (see page 299).[1]

An IFF file is a single `FORM` chunk, which acts like the `RIFF` chunk shown on page 300. Sound files are stored in an `8SVX` (eight-bit sampled voice) form that contains a `VHDR` chunk with information about the sound and a `BODY` chunk containing the signed data bytes.

The `8SVX` form was designed to hold sampled musical instrument sounds. Because a note can last for a long time, it must be possible for a sound to be extended indefinitely. The `VHDR` chunk specifies two parts of the sound, an initial *one-shot* section that's played only once, and a *repeating* section that can be repeated as often as necessary.

AIFF

The *Audio Interchange File Format* (AIFF) is used on the Macintosh and SGI machines. It's similar to the WAVE format in many respects, but allows both sampled sounds and sampled instrument information (see MOD). The compressed version, known as *AIFC* or *AIFF-C*, is also gaining popularity. More complete specifications are available using anonymous FTP from `ftp.cwi.nl`, in the `pub/audio` directory. The AIFF-C specification is available using anonymous FTP from `ftp.sgi.com`, in the `sgi` directory.

---

[1]The most significant difference between IFF and RIFF is that IFF stores numbers in big-endian Motorola format and RIFF stores them in little-endian Intel format.

Part Six
Movie Formats

About Video 39

Video technology brings together a lot of different disciplines, and will have a big impact on the way we think about and use computers. New applications already feature help files that replace cryptic instructions with animated demonstrations. New games seamlessly intermingle live action with synthesized effects. Telephone, movie, and television companies are eagerly promising a future of interactive movies-on-demand.

One interesting side effect of video technology is that it's also changing the way computer systems are designed. Issues such as compression and time synchronization used to be dealt with separately by each independent program. Because compression and time synchronization are so critical to video, programming libraries designed for video work are finding use in many related areas. A particularly good example is Apple's QuickTime toolbox, which provides developers with a broad collection of tools that are useful outside the specialized realm of conventional video.

Real-Time Compression

Video processing is an example of particularly tough real-time programming. Playing a movie at a modest rate of just ten frames per second requires that the player program retrieve and display each frame in less than one-tenth second. If some frames require more time than that, the motion will appear jerky. If data is being stored uncompressed, a modest 360 by 240 pixel image with 16 bits per pixel requires over a megabyte per second to be read and relayed to the screen. Worse, this data rate has to be sustained for as long as the movie lasts. In ten minutes, over 600 megabytes of data have to transferred, the equivalent of a full CD-ROM.

Because they contain so much data, computer movies are typically distributed on CD-ROMs. Unfortunately, CD-ROM drives are quite slow. A single-speed CD-ROM drive can only sustain a data transfer of about 150 kilobytes of data per second. Even the fastest "6×" speed CD-ROM drives can't maintain the megabyte per second of our modest example. So compression is necessary. But there's a catch. Compression makes it possible to read the data from the disc fast enough, but makes it much harder for the processor, which now has to decompress the data before displaying it on the screen. Smooth video requires just the right amount of compression. If you compress too much, the computer won't be able to decompress the image fast enough. If you compress too little, you won't be able to read the data into the computer fast enough.

In practice, you can achieve this balance in two ways. One is to use specialized hardware to handle the decompression. *Video processors* handle high-speed compression and decompression without bogging down the processor. Some are even capable of applying special effects (such as sharpening, dithering, or fades) as the data is decompressed and relayed to the video display. Another approach is to develop specialized compression methods that can be decompressed very quickly in software.

Compressing in Space and Time

Currently, video decompression hardware is not particularly widespread, making specialized software compression techniques an important part of the video arsenal. Video compression starts with the same techniques used in still graphics. In fact, some of the earliest computer video approaches simply used basic graphics compression approaches on each frame. By looking at more than one frame at a time, though, you can achieve better compression.

The first trick is *differencing*. The easiest form of differencing is to simply subtract one frame from the previous frame and only compress the difference. Frequently, most of the image will be the same, so differencing will reduce large parts of the image to zero. As you've already seen, reducing large parts of an image to zero is a good way to prepare it for compression.

Subtraction is easy to do, but fails to help much in a few common cases. For example, a slow pan across a detailed scene will cause almost every pixel to change with every frame; simply subtracting the two frames gains you very little in this case. A more powerful differencing technique is *motion prediction*. With motion prediction, the encoder looks for blocks of pixels that have moved, and encodes just the coordinates of the block and how it moved. With motion prediction, a slow pan is compressed very well; most of the picture is reduced to a small offset.

Motion prediction is effective and easy to decompress, but it's very hard to compress. Essentially, the encoder has to look at many small blocks of pixels in the first image and see if they reappear anywhere in the second image. As a result, some of the very best video compression algorithms are *asymmetric*. An asymmetric algorithm takes much longer to compress than to decompress, which is usually fine for video. Professional video developers use high-end systems that have the speed, storage space, and additional hardware to do video editing comfortably even without stellar compression. They only compress the video once when it's finished, and they don't really care if it takes hours or even days. All that matters is that the video can be decompressed quickly enough for comfortable viewing on the mid-range systems that their customers are using.

The better video compression methods use some form of differencing in conjunction with typical still-image compression techniques. Of course, the first frame of the movie can't use differencing, so there will always be at least one *key frame*, a frame that doesn't require you to know the preceding frame before you can decode it. The remaining frames are called *difference frames*, since they only encode the difference from a preceding frame, and can't be used on their own.

At first glance, you might reasonably expect only the first frame of a movie to be a key frame, but in practice many key frames are scattered throughout the movie. Some frames are *natural key frames*, frames where the difference from the preceding frame is so huge that it makes sense to not bother differencing it. These frames can happen because of editing; a cut-over from one scene to another will change the entire frame at once. Having regular key frames also simplifies random access. If the user decides to start playing the movie halfway through, she doesn't want to wait while the decompressor starts from the beginning to add up all of the differences.

Frequent key frames also help the decompressors in other ways. A software decompressor on a desktop PC can't always decompress quite quickly enough to keep up. In practice, such a decompressor will keep track of when the next key frame should occur, and will skip ahead to that frame at the appropriate time if it can't decompress fast enough. This trick allows software decompressors to provide reasonable synchronization even on slower machines. Digital video is also starting to be used in broadcasting. Some direct-satellite systems use compressed digital video, and the forthcoming HDTV (High-Definition Television) system will be very similar to MPEG. A digital television will occasionally lose data because of static or a weak signal. If it loses a frame, any subsequent difference frames aren't very useful. The television will probably not be able to resume decoding the video signal until it sees the next key frame. Frequent key frames (several per second) are critical for useful broadcasting.

Rate Limiting

One goal of video compression is simply to reduce the total storage requirements so you can fit longer, higher-quality movies in the same space. You also need compression so you can read the movie data from a hard disk or CD-ROM fast enough. This second concern introduces a new compression requirement. Not only must the compression ensure that the entire movie is small, it must also make sure that each individual frame is small enough. A few very large frames can throw the timing off, even if the rest of the movie is very compact.

Actually, you don't need to make every frame small. In practice, the player program reads several frames at a time before they are needed. Having one frame that's a bit too big can be acceptable as long as the nearby frames are sufficiently small. The process of making sure that the average data rate is low enough is called *rate limiting*.

Rate limiting is frequently done separately, after the initial compression. A separate pass checks the size of the data and tries to address areas where the compression is insufficient. One trick is to replace key frames with difference frames. Difference frames are usually smaller, so such replacement can help smooth out the bumps. You can also deliberately discard some visual data. As I discussed in Chapter 16, throwing out less-noticeable data can significantly improve the compression. Finally, you can simply drop frames, either by duplicating a previous frame (which results in a highly-compressible zero difference) or doubling the duration of a previous frame.

Replaceable Codecs

The most popular video file formats are in a sense merely wrappers around a compression/decompression engine (*codec*). Programs supporting Apple's QuickTime and Microsoft's Video for Windows (VfW) usually allow the actual codec to be replaced. Any codec that meets certain guidelines can be used. This approach allows the general formats (and the software that supports them) to easily adapt to new technologies as they become available. Both VfW and QuickTime were initially released with very simple codecs, but have gradually adopted more sophisticated approaches. Even better techniques are being developed, but the best compression methods currently require too much computation to be efficiently performed by today's mid-range systems. As computers become more powerful and additional hardware becomes readily available, more sophisticated codecs will become generally available.

Replaceable codecs are good for application programmers and end users, but this approach has drawbacks for video producers. Because different users may have different codecs available, it can be difficult for video producers to compress their movie with a single codec that performs well and is readily available. Some video producers provide their own codec with the movie so the end user can simply plug it in to existing software. Other video producers provide their movies compressed with several different codecs, allowing the user (or in some cases, the software) to select the appropriate one. Some producers are simply careful to only use codecs that are widely available.

Audio and Other Data

Silent movies just aren't as popular as they used to be. Most video also includes an audio track, and sometimes additional data beyond that. In addition, the more flexible movie formats can be used for any type of time-sensitive data, including sound, text (for subtitles or lyrics), music notes (as with MIDI; see page 305), or instructions for heavy machinery. For movies, it's sometimes nice to have alternate audio tracks. Imagine watching your favorite Ingmar

Bergman movie with a choice of listening to the original Swedish dialogue, an English translation, or a narrator explaining what is really going on.

More Information

Video and video compression are large subjects. You can read a number of good books for more information.

Nels Johnson's *How to Digitize Video* [JGF94] offers a hands-on look at the theory and practice of creating digital videos with a computer. If you don't know a time base corrector from a dubbing deck, but still want to make high-quality videos, this is one place to start. It includes a summary of the underlying technology.

If you want the real nuts and bolts, A. Murat Tekalp's *Digital Video Processing* [Tek95] dives deeply into the mathematical and engineering theory behind video compression, including a detailed look at television standards ranging from NTSC to MPEG-2.

AVI

Microsoft's *Video for Windows* uses another specialization of the RIFF file format (see page 299 for more information about RIFF). *Audio/Video Interleave* (AVI) files get their name from their alternating chunks of audio and video data. Playing an AVI file requires first parsing a header with various information about the file, including the frame rate and size. The program then pulls in a single video frame and the accompanying audio, passes the audio along to the sound card, and proceeds to decompress and display the video sample.

This simple process is complicated by a number of factors. The computer may not be fast enough to fully decompress a single frame in the required time, which may require skipping one or more video frames to maintain synchronization. It also requires pausing occasionally during the video decompression to retrieve the sound. In practice, AVI player programs retrieve a number of frames at one time so that they can keep the audio playing even if it becomes necessary to drop one or more video frames.

Maintaining a steady flow of data requires attention to many details. CD-ROM drives typically operate most efficiently when data requests always fall

AVI at a Glance	
Names:	Video for Windows, AVI, Audio-Video Interleave Format
Extension:	.avi
On CD:	Video for Windows players for Windows, Macintosh; sample AVI movies

Figure 40.1   LIST Chunk Format

on certain boundaries. Other parts of the computer system have similar requirements, from the sound and video cards to the processor and memory interface. Obtaining peak performance from these different systems requires a great deal of attention.

How AVI Works

As with any RIFF file, an AVI file contains a single RIFF chunk, as shown in Figure 37.2 on page 300. AVI files use AVI␣ as the form ID (the fourth character is a space).[1]

The AVI form contains at least two sub-chunks, each of type LIST. LIST chunks, like RIFF chunks, collect a number of other chunks. Their content is determined by a form ID, as shown in Figure 40.1.

RIFF AVI Form

Figure 40.2 shows the general structure of an AVI file. The RIFF AVI form contains two LISTs. The LIST hdrl comes first, with information about the movie and each of its streams. For example, it might specify that stream zero contains 180×240 pixel video at 10 frames per second, and stream one holds eight-bit PCM audio at 8000 samples per second. The LIST movi holds the actual data. Other chunks may also appear. An idx1 chunk contains an index into the movie data; a junk chunk is padding inserted by the writer.[2] As with any RIFF form, programs should ignore any chunks they don't understand.

---

[1]Note that the form and chunk IDs are always four characters. When you see a three-character ID, the fourth character will be a space.

[2]Padding appears for two reasons. On most systems, data is naturally read in blocks of a certain size. If significant data boundaries match the block size, reading can occur much more quickly. The more important reason for padding is to simplify creating these files. Because data at the beginning of the file requires information such as the length and number of tracks,

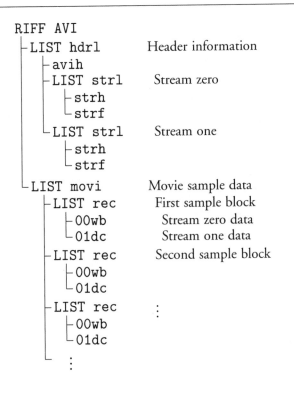

```
RIFF AVI
 ⌐LIST hdrl        Header information
 │ ⌐avih
 │ ⌐LIST strl      Stream zero
 │ │ ⌐strh
 │ │ └strf
 │ └LIST strl      Stream one
 │   ⌐strh
 │   └strf
 └LIST movi        Movie sample data
   ⌐LIST rec       First sample block
   │ ⌐00wb         Stream zero data
   │ └01dc         Stream one data
   ⌐LIST rec       Second sample block
   │ ⌐00wb
   │ └01dc
   ⌐LIST rec       ⋮
   │ ⌐00wb
   │ └01dc
   └   ⋮
```

Figure 40.2   Outline Structure of an AVI File

LIST hdrl **Form**

The LIST hdrl form contains information about the movie. The avih chunk contains general information, while the LIST hdrl forms contain information about each separate stream.

LIST movi **Form**

The LIST movi form contains the actual movie data. This chunk is a sequence of *records*, each one containing a single video frame and a corresponding chunk of sound data.

it's easier to write all of the movie data, then go back and fill in the initial header. If the writer doesn't know the size of the initial data, it may need to insert junk chunks to fill any gap between the header and the rest of the movie data.

LIST rec **Form**

Each record is stored in its own LIST rec form. The record contains one chunk for each active stream. AVI specifies that the sound data is actually skewed three-quarters of a second ahead of the video, so the first several records will typically contain sound but no video. Other points in the movie may lack either sound or video, so those records will have no entry for the corresponding stream.

The chunks containing stream data don't have fixed names. Rather, the four-character identifiers are built from the stream number and data type. For example, 00wb is a chunk containing audio data (wb) for stream zero (00); 01dc is video data (dc) for stream one (01). The streams are numbered in the order they appear in the initial LIST hdrl.

QuickTime

Apple's *QuickTime* is really two different things. For users, it's a uniform way to deal with video, audio, and other sorts of time-varying data. For developers, it's a flexible toolkit that brings together a wide variety of useful technologies.

As a file format, QuickTime is very popular with graphics professionals. The Macintosh has a loyal following among graphics designers and publishers, and many high-end graphics tools are released first on the Macintosh. The companies developing these high-end tools have been quick to integrate QuickTime support into their existing applications and to develop specialized applications for creating and manipulating QuickTime data. The abundance of high-quality movies has made the QuickTime movie format popular on Windows as well.

As a development toolkit, QuickTime provides a standard way for developers to access a variety of useful facilities. These facilities range from low-level tools for graphics and audio compression and timing routines to high-level interfaces that make it easy to include full-motion video and audio editing in

QuickTime at a Glance	
Name:	Apple QuickTime
Extensions:	.mov, .MooV
Reference:	*Inside Macintosh: QuickTime* [App93a]
On CD:	QuickTime player for Windows; QuickTime editor for Macintosh

applications. Even applications that make no direct use of video often rely on QuickTime services for compressing and decompressing pictures and synchronizing multiple events.

How QuickTime Works

The QuickTime file format is considerably more flexible than AVI, so it helps to describe some of the environments that QuickTime supports before trying to evaluate the format itself.

While QuickTime supports movie production very well, it was designed to support any type of time-based information. A QuickTime file can be as simple as a single photograph. QuickTime is commonly used to store audio data. At the other extreme, QuickTime movies can contain multiple video and audio tracks, and there may be a variety of criteria for selecting which tracks to use and how they should be combined. For example, a QuickTime movie may have several parallel audio tracks in different languages. It may also contain time-varying data other than video and audio. For example, you could store a song as two QuickTime tracks, one containing MIDI-style note information (see page 305) to control an external synthesizer, and another containing textual lyrics to be displayed as the song is played.

This last example suggests another QuickTime feature. Not all notes in a piece of music last the same amount of time, and if there are multiple instruments, not all of them change to a new note simultaneously. Similarly, QuickTime does not assume that all events occupy the same amount of time. In an AVI file, a single global frame rate determines how long each frame should display. In a QuickTime file, every event in every track can have a different duration. This feature is useful even with video. Computer-generated animation and some videos contain still images that remain on the screen for long periods of time. Rather than needlessly store copies of the same image, a QuickTime movie can simply store a single copy and lengthen its duration. QuickTime can overlay multiple video tracks; a complex background might be stored as a single long-duration frame in one track, while the foreground action is stored in a separate track.

QuickTime also attempts to provide a flexible environment for editing. Imagine a high-quality video editing system that allows you to combine sequences from laserdisc, computer-generated animation, and recorded video stored on a hard disk. Rather than copy all of this information into a single movie file, QuickTime uses a variety of referencing techniques to allow this melange of data sources to be treated as a single movie, while leaving the actual data in place.

QuickTime uses a three-tier structure. The *movie* specifies the number and type of each *track*, and gives general information about the movie as a whole. The tracks specify the duration, sequencing, and source of each set of data. Finally, the *media* contain the actual data. In this example, you wouldn't need to copy any data from the laserdisc to include it in your movie; the appropriate track would simply specify the laserdisc itself as the media. When the movie was viewed, the appropriate *media handler* software would read the digital image directly from the laserdisc. Editing a movie simply rearranges the references within the track; there's no need to physically copy the frames. Similarly, tracks can be added to and removed from the movie without having to recopy a large quantity of data. Perhaps more importantly, QuickTime allows a single movie to simultaneously play several video and audio tracks. Each audio track can specify a different volume level, and each video track can be independently cropped and rotated before being combined into a single display.

In practice, even when these sophisticated capabilities are used during the production and editing of a video, the final result is "flattened" down into a single file. This single file often exists in a slightly different format on the Macintosh than on other systems. On the Macintosh, the movie is stored in a file's resource fork, while the track and media information is stored in the data fork. The big advantage of this approach is that the movie data is fairly small, and can easily be copied between applications while the much larger track and media data remains in the original file. Other systems, of course, don't support this two-fork approach, so the movie, tracks, and media are all copied into a single large file.

This extreme flexibility is mostly an advantage for video developers, but has benefits for end users as well. For example, a movie might contain four video tracks. The first is the full, high-resolution version of the video. The second track references a single frame from the same media, which can be used as a still-image "poster" for the movie. The third video track is a full-screen preview that selects excerpts from the full version. This third track adds very little to the movie's size, since it references the same media data as the first track. The final track is a reduced-size version for people with slower

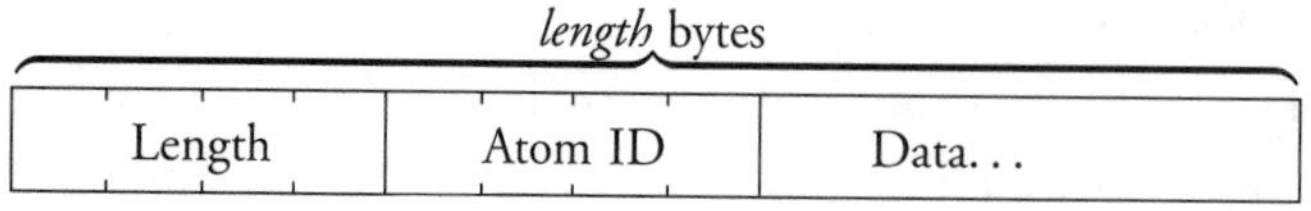

Figure 41.1 Atom Format

computers. Only one of these would be played at a time, of course, but it's convenient to have them all available in the same file. Similarly, a movie might contain several audio tracks in different languages.

Single-Fork File Format

I'll only discuss the single-fork version here. For details about storing Quick-Time data in double-fork Macintosh files or multiple files, you'll need to refer to *Inside Macintosh: QuickTime* [App93a], and possibly other *Inside Macintosh* volumes.

QuickTime files consist of a series of nested *atoms*. Atoms are similar in concept to the *chunks* used by RIFF files such as WAVE or AVI. Each atom contains a four-byte length, followed by a four-byte identifier. Programs reading this format should simply skip atoms they don't understand.

As I described earlier, a QuickTime file has a number of components: a single "movie," several "tracks," and a collection of "media." The media contain the actual video frames and sound data. In a single-fork file, all of the media information is lumped together in a single mdat atom, and the rest of the information is stored in a highly-structured moov[1] atom. Although the media information can appear in any order within the mdat atom, it's best if the video frames and sound samples are interleaved in small sections. This arrangement enables the player program to read and play the data without searching back and forth in the file. As you might expect, the moov atom contains some general information and a collection of trak atoms describing each track. The trak atoms contain mdia atoms, which describe the format and location of the media data in the mdat atom.

One advantage of this approach is the ease with which QuickTime can be integrated with compressed video formats such as MPEG (see the next chapter). The MPEG data stream can be stored in the mdat atom, and can be read

---

[1]Pronounced "moo-vee."

and played directly even by applications that don't understand the QuickTime format. Conversely, the moov atom provides random-access information that is a useful addition to the MPEG data.

moov *Atom*

The moov atom contains a mvhd *movie header* atom and a collection of trak atoms. The movie header lists a number of basic facts about the movie, including the creation time, when it was last modified, which part of the movie is currently selected, which part of the movie can be used as a preview, which single image can be used as a "poster," the volume and visual size of the movie, the duration of the movie, and the *time scale*.

Unlike AVI files, which have a single rate that dictates when each frame will display, QuickTime allows different events (such as frames or sections of audio) to have different durations. Each individual duration needs to be specified. The problem is what units to use. Apple chose to let the video developer specify the units. A time scale of 1 means that all time values in the movie represent a number of seconds, while 1000 means that all time values represent 1000ths of a second. Usually, time scales between 100 and 1000 are used.

trak *Atom*

Conceptually, a movie contains several independent sources of data. Each of these data sources is a single track containing video, audio, or text. The trak atom contains a tkhd *track header* atom describing the kind of data in the track, an edts *edit list* atom that specifies the order in which parts of the track should be played, and a mdia media atom describing how to access the data.

The tkhd atom gives the same basic information about the track that the mvhd atom gives about the movie. Each track can have a different position and size on the screen and a separate volume. This information is used to combine different tracks to create a single audio or video result. In addition, each track can have a different time scale that specifies how the durations given in the track relate to the time scale of the movie as a whole. This information is particularly important for audio tracks, which usually have a much higher sampling rate than video tracks.

The `edts` edit list atom specifies the order in which parts of the track should be played. This atom provides simple editing capabilities, and can help to compress a large movie. For example, it might specify that part of the audio should be repeated, rather than storing the audio multiple times.

`mdia` *Atom*

The `mdia` media atom actually describes the format of the compressed data. Recall that all of the movie data for a single-fork QuickTime movie is contained in a single undifferentiated `mdat` atom. The media atom describes the format of some of that data (by naming a software component that knows how to retrieve it) and where the data is located in the `mdat` atom.

The precise location of a single video frame or audio sample requires understanding several atoms within the `mdia` atom. The `stts` *time to sample* atom specifies the duration of each sample, and is needed to convert a time position in the movie into a particular sample. The `stsc` *sample to chunk* atom specifies which samples are grouped into *chunks*. The `stco` *chunk offset* specifies where each chunk is located in the media data. Finally, the `stsz` chunk specifies the size of each sample. This information allows you to find a sample within a chunk by skipping the preceding samples in that chunk; it also tells you the length of the desired sample.

If this whole scheme seems unnecessarily complex, keep in mind that most of this complexity is provided to allow high-end video tools to comfortably manipulate multiple sources of data. The movie files that are released to end users are deliberately simplified so that they can be read and played as quickly as possible.

More Information

The definitive reference for QuickTime is Apple's *Inside Macintosh: QuickTime* [App93a]. Additional programming information is located in the companion volume *Inside Macintosh: QuickTime Components* [App93b].

Apple also maintains a World Wide Web site devoted to QuickTime, containing software, technical information, and links to other QuickTime resources (`http://quicktime.apple.com`).

MPEG

42

The *Motion Picture Experts Group* (MPEG) was organized by the ISO to develop standards for high-quality video compression. It first met in 1988, and has produced a number of related standards. As a result, a large body of research has been codified into a collection of recommended methods for compressing audio and video. These general methods are now being used by many different video compression products.

The MPEG committee also defined a number of very specific formats for compressed video and audio. These formats vary in the quality of the result and the data rate required.

MPEG-1 The original video format supports television-quality video with a data stream of only 200 kilobytes per second. Its quality is comparable to VHS videotape.

MPEG-2 This newer standard supports high-quality video over higher-speed digital connections (up to 2.5 megabytes per second). It is closely related to *HDTV* (High Definition Television).

MPEG at a Glance

Name:	MPEG
Extensions:	Various, see Table 42.1
On CD:	MPEG players for Windows, Macintosh, Unix; MPEG FAQ

MPEG-4 A forthcoming standard is intended to support lower-quality video over modem-speed data connections. This format is intended primarily for videophone systems.

Layer-1, 2, 3 MPEG-1 defines three different audio formats, which are also used (with minor extensions) in MPEG-2. The three are similar, but with different trade-offs between compression and complexity. Layer-1 is the simplest, but offers the poorest compression, while Layer-3 is the most complex and offers the best compression.

Although the MPEG-1 video format has data rate requirements well within the capabilities of today's CD-ROM drives, it is not yet widely supported by personal computers. The reason is simply that MPEG decoding is very computation intensive. Software-only MPEG decoders are improving, but still have trouble on all but the very fastest computers. However, hardware MPEG decoders are already being widely used in video games and industrial applications, and are starting to find their way into personal computers as well.

How to Use MPEG

Before you try to use MPEG, you should understand a few general facts.

A variety of different data formats are defined by MPEG standards. The MPEG-1 standard defines one format for encoded video, three for encoded audio, and a *system stream* format for combining video and audio. MPEG-2 has the same variety, although you're unlikely to see MPEG-2 video, since it's really intended for broadcast use and isn't a very good match for desktop computers.

This diversity of formats leads to an even wider variety of of file extensions. These extensions often try to specify the particular format, but such attempts are confused by the different numbered parts. For example, a "2" in the extension might refer to MPEG-2 video or Layer-2 audio, or it might mean that the file is audio-only. (The video, audio, and system data formats are parts 1, 2, and 3 of the official standard documents.) Fortunately, the audio layers are somewhat compatible, so many decoders support all three and you don't have to worry about it. Table 42.1 shows some of the extensions you might see.

Extension	Description
.mpg	Various
.mps	MPEG-1 system stream
.mpv	MPEG-1 video only
.mpa	MPEG-1 layer-1 or layer-2 audio
.mp2	MPEG-1 layer-1 or layer-2 audio
.13	MPEG-1 layer-3 audio only
.m1s	MPEG-1 system stream
.m1v	MPEG-1 video only
.m1a	MPEG-1 audio only
.m2s	MPEG-2 system stream
.m2v	MPEG-2 video only
.m2a	MPEG-2 audio only

Table 42.1   MPEG File Extensions

MPEG standards define how the data is stored, but don't specify how to get raw video data into that format. In addition, MPEG is a *lossy* format; encoders can discard data to provide better compression. As you might imagine, these two facts allow for an enormous amount of variation in the compression and video quality of different encoders.

To encode video data into MPEG format as it is received requires dedicated hardware, since no desktop computer is fast enough to handle the computational requirements. If you must use software to compress MPEG data, you'll have to first capture the data in some other format and then compress it separately. Capturing raw video data is clearly the best option, but disk storage becomes a limiting factor. As a result, MPEG movies are sometimes captured in QuickTime or AVI formats and then converted into MPEG. The problem is that the most popular QuickTime and AVI codecs are also lossy. By the time the data reaches MPEG format, it's been through two different lossy compression algorithms, which can severely degrade the quality.

Similar comments apply to decoders. Software decoders can take many shortcuts to improve their speed, but these shortcuts degrade the video and audio quality noticeably. Converting into other lossy formats for faster playback also degrades the image quality.

These cocerns apply to both MPEG video and audio compression, but especially for audio, another concern arises. The audio formats encode blocks of audio data. Any good compressor will have to collect some sound, then analyze and encode it. This procedure causes a short delay between the uncompressed audio going into an MPEG compressor and the compressed audio coming out. For Layer-3 audio especially, this delay can be quite noticeable, which makes Layer-3 audio format a poor choice for interactive applications such as teleconferencing and telephone systems.

Overall, MPEG offers excellent compression and very high quality. Unfortunately, desktop computer systems don't yet have the processing power to handle MPEG well without separate hardware. That obstacle is slowly fading, however, as hardware MPEG decoders become more available and more powerful processors make software decoding more of a possibility.

How MPEG Video Works

MPEG's video formats combine a number of compression tricks that you've already seen in JPEG with new techniques for encoding the differences between successive frames. You should be familiar with the material in Chapter 16 before reading the following paragraphs.

MPEG stores several different types of video frames. *I-frames* (independent) are key frames, which don't require any additional information to decode. I-frames are compressed using a general technique that is quite similar to JPEG compression, but usually provides slightly better compression. *P-frames* (predictive) are stored as a difference from the previous P-frame or I-frame. MPEG uses motion prediction to store P-frames by storing offsets for 8×8-pixel squares. *B-frames* (bidirectional predictive) are stored using differences from both previous and future frames.[1]

Because B-frames can rely on frames that follow them in time, frames do not always appear in the file in temporal order. For example, consider the sequence of frames shown in Figure 42.1. The arrows indicate dependencies; for example, frame 2 requires information from frame 3 before it can be

---

[1]There are also *D-frames*: Separate, low-resolution versions of certain frames intended to simplify browsing. D-frames are rarely used, so I won't discuss them in any detail.

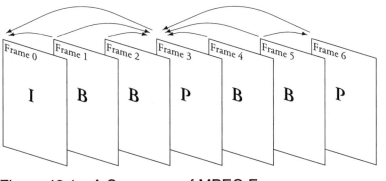

Figure 42.1 A Sequence of MPEG Frames

decompressed. Frames 3 and 6 are P-frames. To decompress frame 3, you need to have frame 0 available; to decompress frame 6, you need to have first decompressed frame 3. The B-frames, however can depend on frames that follow them in time. Before you can decompress frame 1, you must first decompress both frame 0 and frame 3. As a result, the compressed frames do not appear in the file in the obvious order. You have to make sure that when a frame is read, any frames it depends on have already been decoded. In this case, one possible order is 0, 3, 1, 2, 4, 6, 5, although there are other possibilities.

General Issues

MPEG video depends on some of the same facts about human vision as JPEG. It should be no surprise, then, that MPEG uses a color system that separates *luminance* (lightness) from *chroma* (color). MPEG uses the YC_bC_r color system. This system was chosen partly to provide a good start for DCT-based compression and partly because it's the same system used by the PAL and SECAM television standards.[2]

---

[2]The NTSC television standard used in the US and Japan uses the similar YIQ color format. PAL and SECAM are currently used in most of the world outside of the US and Japan.

I-Frames

I-frames are compressed using an approach very similar to JPEG. The primary difference is that MPEG groups four 8×8 blocks into a single *macroblock*, and allows the quantization coefficients to change between macroblocks. By allowing the quantization to vary across the image, MPEG can achieve slightly higher compression than JPEG. It can use an overall lower quality, increasing the quality only where it's necessary, while JPEG has to use the higher quality everywhere. A good MPEG encoder will quantize very busy areas more aggressively, while using more modest quantization on quieter areas where errors are more noticeable.

P-Frames

Like an I-frame, a P-frame is compressed by evaluating 8×8 blocks of pixels. However, a P-frame has more options than an I-frame, because it can refer to data in the most recent I-frame or P-frame, which I'll call the *previous reference frame*. A single block in a P-frame can use any of the following methods to specify its contents:

- A block can specify that it's identical to the same block in the previous reference frame. This method provides very good compression for such images as "talking head" news programs that have an unchanging background.

- A block can specify an offset, indicating that data from another part of the previous reference frame should be copied. This *motion prediction* works well for slowly-moving images.

- In either of the previous cases, the current block may not be identical to the block being copied from the previous reference frame. In that case, the encoder can subtract the two blocks and use a DCT and quantization to compress the difference. The difference will usually be very small and easy to compress. The combination of motion prediction and a compressed difference handles such factors as changes in lighting as an object moves.

- If no part of the previous reference frame matches, the encoder can compress the block independently.

The compression depends heavily on how well the encoder can locate similar blocks in the previous reference. The MPEG standard doesn't specify how the encoder should locate these blocks, and different MPEG encoders will make different trade-offs between speed and compression.

B-Frames

If you lost a few frames from the middle of a long movie, you could use several methods to fill in the gap. You could copy the frame just before the gap. That would work well if the gap was short and there was little motion, but it could throw off the timing. Your next attempt might be to copy the frame before the gap into the first half and the frame after the gap into the second half, on the logic that the missing frames would be most similar to frames close to them. Finally, you might try averaging some existing frames to fill in the missing entries.

B-frames can mix these approaches, copying data (possibly with a compressed difference) from the previous reference frame, the following reference frame, or averaging data from each one. In Figure 42.1, notice that some of the B-frames only refer to one of the previous or following reference frames, while some refer to both. Each block of a B-frame can contain any of four types of data:

- As with a P-frame, B-frames can copy blocks from a previous I-frame or P-frame with or without a difference.

- B-frames can also copy data from the next I-frame or P-frame.

- A B-frame can specify a block of pixels from the previous reference frame and a block of pixels from the following reference frame that should be averaged. A compressed difference can also be included.

- Finally, if nothing in either the previous or following reference frames matches closely enough, the block of pixels can be compressed directly.

All compressed pixel data, including differences, are compressed using the same JPEG-like approach: Each 8×8 block is converted with a Discrete Cosine Transform into frequency information, these coefficients are quantized, and the final values are Huffman compressed.

How MPEG Audio Works

Just as JPEG graphics compression is a big step beyond GIF's lossless approach, MPEG audio is a big step beyond simple PCM or μ-Law encoding. MPEG uses a variety of facts about human hearing to select data to discard. The complete process is too complex to describe precisely, but the following paragraphs should give you an idea of the techniques involved. As I mentioned before, the MPEG standard doesn't specify precisely how to compress data. In the following discussion, I'll refer to what an MPEG "encoder" does, but you should keep in mind that I'm only talking in general terms. Specific MPEG encoders will handle this process in slightly different ways, with corresponding variations in sound quality and compression. Regardless of how the encoder works internally, the resulting data is decoded in the same way.

Noise Floor MPEG's audio compression relies on a simple fact. If you're standing next to a loud siren, you won't hear the whispered conversation taking place across the street. Researchers have discovered that this phenomenon isn't just a matter of your attention being drawn to the louder sound; your ears actually lose sounds that are close in frequency to much louder sounds. This *masking effect* varies with the difference in loudness and frequency of the two sounds.

One of the basic ways to compress sound is to reduce the number of bits used for each sample. Reducing the number of bits is equivalent to adding noise to the sound. MPEG exploits the masking effect to make sure you won't hear the noise it adds. If the masking effect is very strong, MPEG can raise the *noise floor* by reducing the number of bits used for the sound.[3] A weaker masking effect means that the encoder must be more cautious.

Subbands The masking effect depends heavily on how close two sounds are in frequency. An MPEG encoder must be careful to only add noise that is close in frequency to very loud sounds. The audio frequencies are divided into *subbands*, and each range is handled separately. The encoder identifies the loudest sounds in each subband and uses that information to determine an acceptable noise floor for that subband. Better MPEG encoders also compute

---

[3]"Raising the noise floor" is audio-engineer-speak for allowing more noise.

an interaction between subbands; a very loud sound in one subband will have a masking effect on nearby subbands.

Psychoacoustic Modeling This technique relies heavily on models of how humans hear sound. *Psychoacoustic models* are sets of rules used to select which subbands are most important. To compress the audio data as well as possible, some quieter subbands are eliminated entirely, and subbands that are near the center of the human hearing range are preserved more carefully than ones near the edge.

Unfortunately, no neat mathematical formulas precisely specify the optimal noise floor for each subband. Human hearing is a complex process that involves many poorly-understood phenomena. The MPEG committee based much of its analysis of competing audio compression approaches on extensive listening tests, in which expert listeners were asked to compare sounds that had been subjected to various types of compression. Such tests are arguably subjective, but the MPEG committee's final analysis has borne up well under repeated listening tests. Future refinements of these psychoacoustic models will improve the quality and compression of future MPEG encoders.

Fortunately, the MPEG decoders need to know very little about how the data was encoded. The complexity of selecting noise floors for each subband is a process used by the encoder to determine what data can be sacrificed without compromising the quality of the result. The decoder simply takes the data that remains and reconstructs a sound from it. Future MPEG encoders can continue to refine their methods while still retaining complete compatibility with existing decoders.

More Information

The *MPEG FAQ* contains an extensive list of pointers to MPEG software and books and articles about MPEG. It is periodically posted to several newsgroups, including `comp.graphics` and `comp.compression`.

A. Murat Tekalp's *Digital Video Processing* [Tek95] describes the theories underlying MPEG's video encoding in considerable detail. However, he does not discuss audio encoding, nor does he detail the MPEG encoding at a byte-for-byte level.

Appendices

About the CD-ROM

The companion CD-ROM, compiled by The Coriolis Group, contains tools to help you understand and use the files you encounter on the Internet. It is ISO 9660 compliant and can be used on most platforms. There are tools here for MS-DOS, Windows, Macintosh, and Unix that will help you use the formats in this book. This appendix explains how the CD-ROM is organized and provides brief descriptions of some of the applications included.[1]

If you don't see what you are looking for here, there are several places in the book you should check. *Chapter 2: Researching File Formats* indicates some good general Internet resources and large archive sites. In addition, the *More Information* sections at the ends of most chapters give pointers to books, software, and other sources of information.

About Shareware

Many of the programs on the CD-ROM are *shareware*. Shareware is a means of distributing software that allows anyone to copy and test a program without having to pay for it. If you continue to use it, however, you are obligated to pay the original author for the program. This differs from traditional software publishing, where you have to pay money before you can even see how the program works. The shareware system has many advantages over traditional software publishing:

---

[1]This appendix does not discuss everything included on the CD-ROM.

- It allows authors to spend more time developing programs and less time marketing, which results in higher-quality software.

- It reduces the cost of producing software, which allows more people to develop their ideas into useful programs and results in a greater variety of software.

- It allows you to test software before you decide to buy it, so that you can pick the best software for you.

- Shareware authors can release new versions very quickly. (Sometimes, a problem report results in a new version in only a few hours!) This allows shareware authors to be very responsive to their customers.

This entire system depends on honest people paying for the software they use. None of the proceeds from sales of this book go to the authors whose software is on the CD-ROM. The CD-ROM is simply another way for their software to reach you so that you can evaluate it and decide if you want to use it. If you find a program useful, please pay the author.

CD-ROM Organization

The organization of the CD-ROM mirrors the structure of the book. Thus, the contents of the CD-ROM are first separated by format type: text, graphics, compression and archiving, encoding, sound, and video. Most subdirectories correspond to a single format and are further subdivided by operating system. For example, ZIP programs for MS-DOS are found in the `compression/zip/dos` directory. The `apps` subdirectories contain general applications that handle several formats. For instance, `graphics/apps/mac` contains graphics viewers for the Macintosh that support a variety of graphics formats.

For some formats, `spec` and `sample` directories are provided. The `spec` directories contain the format's specifications, detailed information about that format. The `sample` directories contain just that, sample files in that format.

Figure A.1 has a graphical overview of the CD-ROM's directory structure.

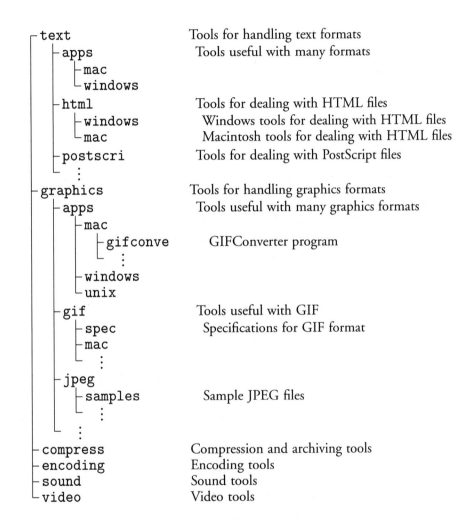

```
┌ text                 Tools for handling text formats
│  ├ apps              Tools useful with many formats
│  │  ├ mac
│  │  └ windows
│  ├ html              Tools for dealing with HTML files
│  │  ├ windows          Windows tools for dealing with HTML files
│  │  └ mac              Macintosh tools for dealing with HTML files
│  ├ postscri          Tools for dealing with PostScript files
│  └ ⋮
├ graphics             Tools for handling graphics formats
│  ├ apps              Tools useful with many graphics formats
│  │  ├ mac
│  │  │  ├ gifconve        GIFConverter program
│  │  │  └ ⋮
│  │  ├ windows
│  │  └ unix
│  ├ gif               Tools useful with GIF
│  │  ├ spec             Specifications for GIF format
│  │  ├ mac
│  │  └ ⋮
│  ├ jpeg
│  │  ├ samples          Sample JPEG files
│  │  └ ⋮
│  └ ⋮
├ compress             Compression and archiving tools
├ encoding             Encoding tools
├ sound                Sound tools
└ video                Video tools
```

Figure A.1   Outline of CD-ROM Directory Structure

Text

Application: MegaEdit
File Formats: Text
Operating System: Windows
Location on CD: `text/apps/windows/megaedit`
Source: `ftp://ftp.cica.indiana.edu/pub/pc/win3/util/megaedit.zip`
Description: MegaEdit is an ASCII text editor, designed to facilitate complex editing tasks involving multiple and/or large files.

Application: Alpha
File Formats: Text, especially TEX and LATEX
Operating System: Macintosh
Location on CD: `text/latex/mac`
Source: `ftp://midway.uchicago.edu/pub/OzTeX`
Description: Alpha is a Macintosh editor that has several features that make it especially convenient for editing TEX and LATEX files.

Applications: HTML editors
File Format: HTML
Operating Systems: Macintosh and Windows
Location on CD: `text/html`
Source: `http://www.yahoo.com/Computers_and_Internet/Internet/World_Wide_Web/HTML_Editors/`
Description: Now that the World Wide Web is several years old, there are many freely available HTML editors for all platforms. These editors allow you to edit and format your document using a WYSIWYG (What You See Is What You Get) interface. The editor saves the file with HTML markers correctly embedded. There are many that we couldn't include, check Yahoo for a more up-to-date listing.

Application: Adobe Acrobat Reader
File Format: PDF
Operating Systems: MS-DOS, Macintosh, Sun, and Windows
Location on CD: `text/pdf`

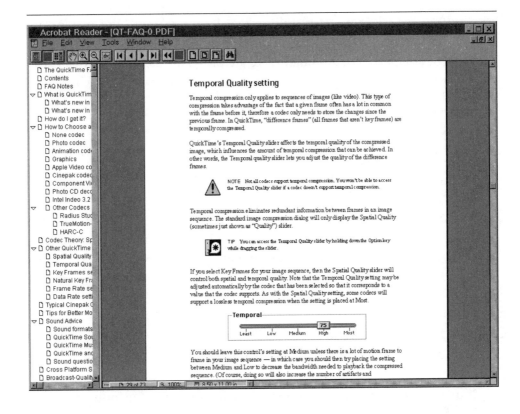

Figure A.2   Adobe Acrobat for Windows

Source: http://www.adobe.com/Software/Acrobat/
Description: Adobe Acrobat Reader lets you read and print PDF files.

Application: ViewPS
File Format: PostScript
Operating Systems: Macintosh
Location on CD: text/postscri/mac/viewps
Description: ViewPS lets you view PostScript documents.

Application: PSUtils
File Format: PostScript
Operating Systems: : Unix, MS-DOS
Location on CD: text/postscri/unix/psutils

Description: PSUtils is a set of utilities to select, rearrange, and manipulate pages of a PostScript file. It assumes the files have correct DSC comments in them (see page 99), although there are programs included that can "fix" the output of several popular programs. Although originally for Unix, they can also be compiled for MS-DOS.

Application: GhostScript
File Format: PostScript
Operating System: Windows
Location on CD: `text/postscri/windows/gscript`
Description: GhostScript can interpret PostScript files and create output for a variety of non-PostScript printers. It can also generate screen output to allow you to preview PostScript documents.

Application: GhostView
File Format: PostScript
Operating System: Windows
Location on CD: `text/postscri/windows/gsview`
Description: GhostView lets you view PostScript documents on the screen. It uses GhostScript (above) to do the actual drawing, but puts up a nice interface that lets you select specific pages, print them, and view the output at various sizes.

Applications: Common Ground viewers
File Formats: Text
Operating Systems: Macintosh and Windows
Location on CD: `text/commongd`
Source: `http://www.commonground.com`
Description: These are viewers for documents in Common Ground Software's DigitalPaper format.

Application: GNU GROFF
File Formats: TROFF, NROFF
Operating Systems: MS-DOS
Location on CD: `text/troff/dos`
Description: This is a complete TROFF and NROFF system for MS-DOS.

Applications: Web2C, DVIPSK, DVILJK
File Formats: TEX, LATEX
Operating System: Unix
Location on CD: `text/latex/unix`
Description: This is a fairly complete TEX system for Unix. It includes the LATEX macros and many other useful packages. The DVIPSK and DVILJK programs convert the DVI output of TEX into output suitable for PostScript printers or the Hewlett-Packard LaserJet printers.

Graphics

Application: GIFConverter 2.3.7
File Formats: GIF, JPEG, PICT, RIFF, TIFF, other graphics, Encapsulated PostScript
Operating System: Macintosh
Location on CD: `graphics/apps/mac/gifconve`
Source: `http://wwwhost.ots.utexas.edu/mac/pub-mac-graphics.html`
Description: GIFConverter, by Kevin A. Mitchell, reads and writes many graphics file formats. It also provides image enhancement, cropping, color table selection, and dithering features. GIFConverter can easily create GIF images with transparent backgrounds, which is especially useful for images that will be used on the World Wide Web.

Application: ImageMagick version 3.6.6
File Formats: JPEG, PNG, TIFF, others
Operating System: Unix
Location on CD: `graphics/apps/unix/imagemag`
Source: `http://www.wizards.dupont.com/cristy/ImageMagick.html`
Description: ImageMagick is a collection of image display and manipulation tools for Unix computers running the X windowing system. It supports many popular image formats. The tools include interactive display and manipulation tools and command line programs for batch image manipulation. ImageMagick works with most Unix systems including Linux. See the README file on the CD-ROM for compiling instructions.

Figure A.3   Paint Shop Pro version 3 from JASC, Inc.

Application: Paint Shop Pro version 3

File Formats: GIF, JPEG, PBM, many others

Operating System: Windows

Location on CD: graphics/apps/windows/psp3

Source: http://www.winternet.com/~jasc/index.html

Description: Paint Shop Pro is a complete graphics program for image creation, viewing, and manipulation. The program features include: painting, photo retouching, image enhancement and editing, color enhancement, image browser, batch conversion, and TWAIN scanner support. It also includes 20 standard image processing filters and 12 deformations. Paint Shop Pro supports over 30 file formats.

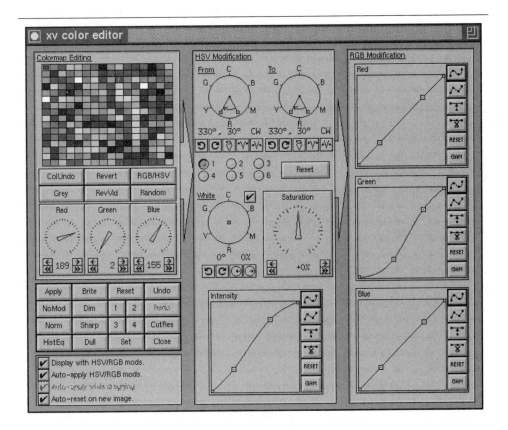

Figure A.4   XV's Color Editing Window

Application: XV
File Formats: GIF, PBM, XBM, EPSF, JPEG, TIFF, XPM, others
Operating System: Unix
Location on CD: `graphics/apps/unix/xv`
Description: John Bradley's graphics viewer program lets you view, crop, and
   manipulate images in a variety of formats.

Application: WebImage
File Formats: GIF, PNG, others
Operating System: Windows
Location on CD: `graphics/png/windows/webimage`

Source: `http://www.group42.com/webimage.htm`

Description: WebImage, by Group 42, is designed to help generate images suitable for use with HTML. It can create GIF images with transparent background, reduce the number of colors in an image, and create the files needed to use an image as an HTML imagemap.

Application: XPaint

File Formats: PPM, TIFF, XBM, others

Operating System: Unix

Location on CD: `graphics/apps/unix/xpaint`

Source: `http://hoth.stsci.edu/man/mann/xpaint.html`

Description: XPaint is a color image editing tool that features most standard paint program options. It allows the editing of multiple images simultaneously. XPaint's user interface has a *toolbox* area to select the current paint operation and *paint windows* to create and modify images. Each paint window has access to its own color palette and set of patterns. XPaint runs on a variety of X displays, though you should be aware that XPaint saves images in the current display type (for instance, a color image edited on a grayscale screen would be saved as a gray image). XPaint has an extensive online help system.

Application: WorldView .9e Pre-Beta

File Format: VRML

Operating System: Windows

Location on CD: `graphics/vrml/windows/wrldview`

Source: `http://www.webmaster.com:80/vrml/`

Description: WorldView is a VRML viewer with integrated networking functionality.

Application: Whurlwind 3D Browser

File Formats: VRML, others

Operating System: Macintosh

Location on CD: `graphics/vrml/mac/whrlwind`

Source: `http://www.info.apple.com/qd3d/Viewer.HTML`

Description: Whurlwind is a VRML viewer that uses QuickDraw 3D. It's a new program that doesn't yet support all of the features you might want; check Whurlwind's World Wide Web site for more current information.

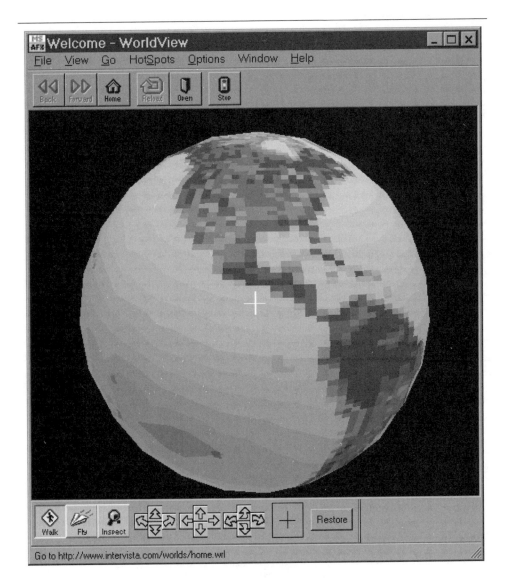

Figure A.5   WorldView Interface

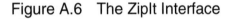

Figure A.6   The ZipIt Interface

Compression

Application: ARC Master
File Formats: Compression
Operating System: Windows
Location on CD: `compress/arc/windows/arcmastr`
Description: This is a shareware graphical compression and decompression program. You can simply drag files into the ARC Master window to add them to an archive.

Application: ZipIt version 1.31
File Formats: Compact Pro, PKZIP, ZIP
Operating System: Macintosh
Location on CD: `compress/zip/mac/zipit`
Source: `http://www.awa.com/softlock/zipit/zipit.html`
Description: ZipIt handles ZIP format files with an interface based on Bill Goodman's Compact Pro. ZipIt comes with an extensive manual that explains how to use all of its features.

Application: WinZip version 5.6
File Formats: Compress, GZIP, PKZIP, TAR, ZIP, (also ARC, ARJ, LZH)

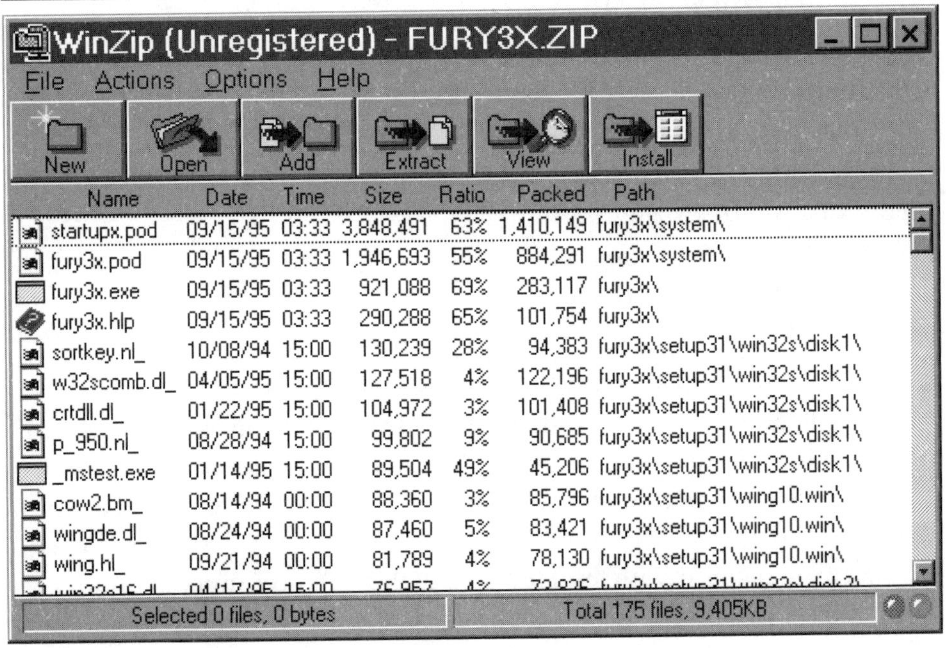

Figure A.7   The WinZip Interface

Operating System: Windows

Location on CD: compress/zip/windows/winzip

Source: http://www.winzip.com/winzip/

Description: WinZip provides a convenient graphical interface for manipulating many types of archives. Support for ZIP, TAR, compress, and GZIP formats is built-in, other formats require you to obtain an external program. WinZip also interfaces to most virus scanners so that you can check compressed files before you run them.

Application: GZIP

File Formats: GZIP, (also Compress, Pack)

Operating System: MS-DOS

Location on CD: compress/gzip/dos

Source: http://andrew.triumf.ca/pub/linux/gzip.html

Description: GZIP is a widely used compression program on Unix systems. The companion GUNZIP program can decompress files created by GZIP, Compress, or Pack. GZIP can be handy for people who also use Unix systems.

Application: StuffIt Expander
File Formats: BinHex, Compact Pro, StuffIt
Operating System: Macintosh
Location on CD: `compress/stuffit/mac/stuflite`
Source: `http://www.xensei.com/ose/utils/tools.html`
Description: StuffIt Expander is designed to decompress any compressed Macintosh file. It fully supports the three most popular archiving formats used on the Macintosh, including files created with the commercial StuffIt Deluxe 3.0 and the shareware StuffIt Lite 3.0. StuffIt Expander also supports files encoded with BinHex 4.0, such as those commonly found on Internet archives and the `comp.binaries.mac` newsgroup. StuffIt Expander requires System 6.0.4 or later.

Encoding

Application: Wincode 2.6.1
File Formats: MIME Base64, UUEncode, XXEncode
Operating System: Windows
Location on CD: `encoding/apps/windows/wincode`
Source: `http://snappy.globalone.net/`
Description: Wincode is a Windows 3.1 program which converts eight-bit binary files to seven-bit ASCII text files for mailing or posting to newsgroups (and vice versa).

Application: UUDeview
File Formats: MIME Base64, UUEncode, XXEncode
Operating Systems: MS-DOS, Unix and Windows
Location on CD: `encoding/uuencode/dos`, `windows`, `unix`
Source: `http://www.uni-frankfurt.de/~fp/uudeview/`

Description: UUDeview is a simple, flexible decoder that easily handles the common encoded formats, including those that have been split across multiple mail messages or multiple news postings. You simply save a group of articles from your mail program or news reader into single or multiple files, then use UUDeview to decode them. Note: The MS-DOS and Windows versions are distributed in binary form, but the source code is identical for all systems, so you can use the Unix source if you need to recompile it.

Application: UULite
File Format: UUEncode
Operating System: Macintosh
Location on CD: `encoding/uuencode/mac`
Source: `ftp://src.doc.ic.ac.uk/computing/systems/mac/umich /util/compression/uulite1.7.cpt.hqx`
Description: UULite is a utility that simplifies UUEncoding and UUDecoding. Includes help files and a tutorial on reading news files and extracting files obtained from a news reader.

Sound

Application: Sound Machine
File Format: AU
Operating System: Macintosh
Location on CD: `sound/apps/mac/sndmachn`
Source: `http://www.znet.com/mac/soundmachine.html`
Description: The Sound Machine will play Sun AU format sound files, the most common sound format used on the World Wide Web. It is the default sound helper for MacWeb.

Application: SoundApp
File Formats: Sun AU, NeXT SND, AIFF, AIFF-C, WAVE, QuickTime audio, MOD, IFF, others
Operating System: Macintosh
Location on CD: `sound/apps/mac/soundapp`
Source: `http://www-cs-students.Stanford.EDU/~franke/SoundApp/`

Description: SoundApp will play or convert AIFF, WAVE, and other sound formats. Simply drop the file onto the SoundApp icon to play. Using QuickTime 1.6 or later, SoundApp can convert audio CD tracks. MOD playback is PowerPC-accelerated on Power Macintoshes.

Application: WPLANY
File Formats: AU, IFF, SND, WAVE, others
Operating System: Windows
Location on CD: sound/apps/windows/wplayany
Source: http://burgoyne.com/vaudio/netsound.html
Description: WPLANY is a compact utility that will detect and play any sound file through a Windows 3.1 audio device. The proper drivers for your sound card (or PC speaker) must be loaded prior to using WPLANY.

Application: WHAM
File Formats: WAVE, others
Operating System: Windows
Location on CD: sound/apps/windows/wham
Source: http://www.netscape.com/MCOM/tricks_docs/helper_docs/
Description: WHAM (Waveform Hold and Modify) is a Windows 3.1 application for manipulating digitized sound. It can read and write Windows 3.1 WAVE files, raw eight-bit digitized sound files and files of several other formats (of which more may be added), and can perform various operations on this sound. WHAM can handle sounds of any size, restricted only by memory.

Application: WinJammer
File Format: MIDI
Operating Systems: Windows, MS-DOS
Location on CD: sound/midi/windows/winjamr
Source: http://www.netscape.com/MCOM/tricks_docs/helper_docs/
Description: WinJammer is a fully featured MIDI player and editor for Windows. The companion WinJammer Player can play MIDI song files in the background, even in MS-DOS.

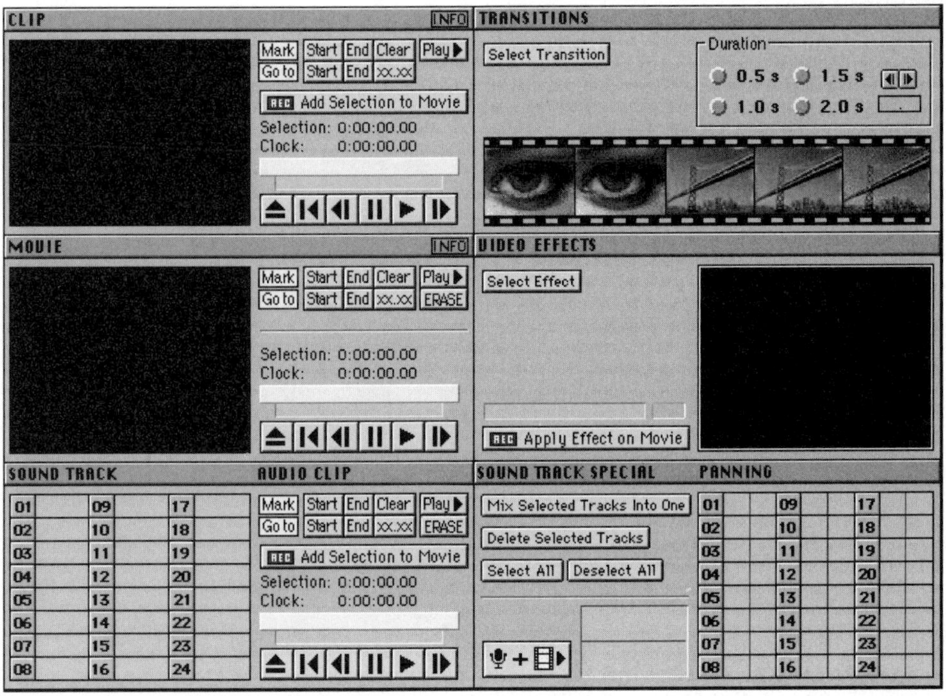

Figure A.8 QuickEdit QuickTime Movie Editor

Video

Application: QuickEdit
File Format: QuickTime
Operating Systems: Macintosh
Location on CD: video/quiktime/mac
Description: QuickEdit is a simple QuickTime movie editor.

Application: QuickTime for Windows
File Format: QuickTime
Operating Systems: Windows
Location on CD: video/quiktime/windows/quiktime
Source: http://quicktime.apple.com/

Description: This is Apple's own player for QuickTime movies under Windows. Note: As this book was going to press, a new version of QuickTime for Windows was being released, so you may want to get the newest version directly from Apple's World Wide Web site.

Application: Video for Windows
File Format: AVI
Operating Systems: Windows and Macintosh
Location on CD: `video/avi`
Description: These are Video for Windows (VfW) players for Macintosh and Windows 3.1. (Windows 95 users don't need this because it's built-in.)

Application: MPEG movie players
File Format: MPEG
Operating Systems: Macintosh, Unix, and Windows
Location on CD: `video/mpeg`
Source: `http://www-plateau.cs.berkeley.edu/mpeg/mpegptr.html`
Description: The CD-ROM includes several easy-to-use MPEG players.

About Files

The seemingly naïve question "what is a number?" was seriously examined by mathematicians at the beginning of the 20th century. This deceptively simple question spawned a huge quantity of new work in logic and set theory, and led to the discovery of basic facts about the nature of mathematics.[1] Exploring the question "what is a file?" is unlikely to lead to any such revolution, but thinking about it carefully will help you to better understand why there are so many different types of files, and how to choose the best file type for a particular purpose.

Definition of a File

Before trying to nail down what files *are*, let's first take a look at what they are used *for*. As any computer user knows, the primary purpose of a file is to save the work you've done. Put slightly more technically, files are *persistent*; they stay around even when the programs that use them are no longer in use.

Files are also the fundamental way that data is transferred from program to program and system to system, that is, files are *portable*. Even when no file is obvious to the user, such as in the *cut-and-paste* or *clipboard* provided by newer computer systems, a file is often being used behind the scenes. (One way to implement cut-and-paste is to have the cut data stored in a file and then to pass the name of the file to the receiving application.)

---

[1]An excellent introduction to some of the apparent paradoxes that arose from this work is Douglas Hofstadter's *Gödel, Escher, Bach* [Hof79].

The fundamental properties of a file are persistence and portability. In fact, you could almost go so far as to define a file as *persistent, portable data.*

I've glossed over an important detail here. So far, I've only discussed the *data in a file.* A file consists of more than just data. The particulars vary from system to system, but usually a file also has a *name, attributes,* a *modification time,* a *creation time,* and sometimes a complete database of *resources, properties,* or *extended attributes.* Throughout this book, I often succomb to the typical practice of using the word "file" to refer to the "data in a file," but you should be aware that there are a few places where the distinction is critical.

What Files Are Made Of

As computer systems have changed through the years, so have the basic units used to store and manipulate files. Mainframe operating systems think of a file as a repository for a database. Each item in a database is a *record,* and so mainframes treat files as a collection of records. Typically, all records in a file are the same size; text is often stored in records of 80 characters each. The development of mainframe operating systems was often driven by the desire to work with large databases, and an enormous amount of work was done to make it possible for programs to find and read or write rapidly any record in a large file.

The development of the Unix operating system in the late 1960s was partly driven by a desire to simplify operating systems for use on much smaller computers. One way in which Unix was simpler than mainframe systems was in how it looked at files. In Unix, a file is a sequence of *bytes.* This restriction simplified Unix in many ways. It made the storage of files on disk simpler—it was not necessary for the disk storage to remember the record size, for instance. It simplified the disk access, since the operating system didn't need complex strategies for dealing with different kinds of records. And, finally, it allowed Unix to treat terminals and printers simply as another kind of file.

Unix was very influential; almost every microcomputer operating system has followed Unix's idea that a file is simply a sequence of bytes. Any more complex structure can be simulated by suitable programming. In particular, fixed-length records can be stored in a Unix file by simply placing the records one after the other.

The previous paragraph holds an important point: Any file, even a mainframe file with a complex structure, can be represented as a *stream of bytes*. Sometimes, the transformation isn't completely trivial, but it can always be done. Byte-stream files have become the basic method of exchanging data between computer systems. When a computer has a more complex file structure (as OS/2 and Macintosh computers do), that more complex structure can always be translated into a stream of bytes and translated back at the other end.

What exactly is a byte? The word *byte* is generally used to refer to the smallest amount of computer storage that can be easily referenced. Modern microcomputers have settled on an eight-bit byte, which is more formally known as an *octet*. However, as with so many things in computer science, this definition isn't universal. Computers exist with a variety of byte sizes. As you might expect, exchanging files between systems with different byte sizes is a tricky topic. Fortunately, the eight-bit byte is nearly universal nowadays, and it's unlikely you'll encounter this particular problem.

For our purposes, then, a file is a sequence of bytes, and a byte is simply storage for eight bits.

How Files Get Around

Portability means that files can be carried from system to system. This "carrying" occurs in many ways: On floppy disk, through networks, over modems. Some files are exchanged directly from person-to-person, while others are essentially made available to the general public through one-to-many "publishing," such as through the World Wide Web. Appendix D gives a little background on the different means for transporting files.

About Text and Binary

I mentioned above that the data exchanged between different programs or different computers is usually a sequence of bytes. It's a fairly natural step to store one character in each byte by assigning each character a particular value.[2] It's also rather natural that the connections between computers evolved so that the byte values not used for characters were either dropped or used for other purposes. As a result, many computer connections, including most mail systems and dial-up connections, only support a restricted set of byte values.

The general terminology is that files that contain only "safe" byte values—values that correspond to the codes for letters, numbers, and punctuation marks—are called *text files*, even if their contents aren't particularly legible. Files containing unsafe byte values are called *binary files*. This distinction is a bit confusing, especially since many word processors (which deal exclusively with text) store information in a binary file format. Similarly, non-text information is often encoded into a text format.

---

[2]See page 20 for a more thorough discussion of *characters* and their relation to *bytes*.

About File Formats

The way in which data is organized into bytes in a file is called the file *format*. To read a spreadsheet file, you have to know which bytes represent which numbers (or formulas or text) in which cells; to read a word processing file, you have to know which bytes represent characters and which represent fonts or margins or other information.

What a File Format Does

Programs can store data in a file however the programmer chooses. However, you often want to share files among several different programs. For this reason, many applications support some widely-understood file format, so that other programs can understand the data in the file. At the very least, large companies (who want to believe that their programs are "standards") often will publish information on the formats they've created for their particular programs so that other programs can use them.

File formats exist so that applications can store information and retrieve it. There are a number of different goals that file format designers might have:

Size   Generally files should occupy as little space as possible. This goal may involve file compression or simply avoiding redundant data.

Fast Writing   Many programs guard against disaster by checkpointing (saving their current state to disk) at regular intervals. Since such data is rarely read, it's not important that it be easy or fast to read, but to avoid interrupting the user, that this information should be written quickly. Saving a file can be slow if the file data is large or if complex transformations must be performed (such as compression or encryption).

Fast Reading   Other types of files are read far more often than they are written, and fast reading is the important goal. Video is one example; additional care while creating the video data can greatly speed the playback and avoid many problems.

Random Access   With large files such as high-resolution graphics or large spreadsheets, the file may be the primary place data is stored while it is manipulated. If all of the data cannot be read into memory, it is necessary to locate and update arbitrary pieces of information within the file.

Portable among Applications   To be portable among applications, file formats need to avoid making assumptions about the internal structure of the program.

Portable among Computer Architectures   Every computer system has its own conventions about such things as the format of floating point numbers, the order of bytes within a multi-byte value, and the organization of complex data structures in memory. For files to be easily portable among different kinds of computer systems, programmers need to avoid the temptation to use system-specific tricks.

These goals are often contradictory. For example, one way to minimize the size of a file is to use a standard compression algorithm to compress data as it is written. The result, however, is significantly slower reading and writing, and you generally lose the ability to randomly access parts of the file on disk. Similarly, portability often requires the use of explicit data conversions while reading and writing, which results in slower file operations. Balancing these requirements is difficult; some applications have multiple file formats that they use for different purposes, a fast but large format that's used purely for temporary storage (often referred to as "virtual memory") and a more compact and portable format used for longer-term storage and exchange with other applications.

Fixed Formats

The easiest way to design a file format is simply to list all of the things that need to be saved and allocate each one a fixed amount of storage at a fixed location in the file. Many early graphics file formats followed this simple approach, using fixed locations to store the palette colors and other basic information and storing the (sometimes uncompressed) pixel data at a fixed location in the file. These are known as *fixed* formats.

While simple, and useful for simple applications, this approach becomes cumbersome when the requirements change. A few simple tricks can help extend the lifetime of these simple formats. The most common trick is to include a version number in the file header and define a certain area of the file as "Reserved." This area of the file is set to zero in the basic file format. When the file format needs to be changed, the version number is changed, and some part of the Reserved area is redefined for the new purpose.

Type-Length-Value Formats

One weakness of a fixed layout is that you cannot define what may be included in the file. For example, a word processor format may need to include font information; if a particular file doesn't need as many fonts, less space in the file is needed. An alternative approach is to build a file from a series of "blocks" or "packets," each one specifying the kind of data in that block and the length of the block. This is known as a *type-length-value* format.

The major advantage of this approach is that it simplifies cross-version file support. Usually, newer files can be read successfully by older applications that simply ignore any blocks they don't understand. Applications can minimize the file size by including only the information necessary for that particular file. This method can also simplify random access; a reading program can scan the file to locate each block and then select blocks from the file as they are needed.

This approach is widely used, and there are many minor variations. One common omission is to not explicitly give the size of the block, relying on the type to implicitly specify the size of the data. This omission makes cross-version support much more difficult, since an application cannot easily skip blocks that it doesn't understand.

Simply skipping an unrecognized block isn't always a good idea. Some formats label each block so the reader can make reasonable assumptions about blocks it doesn't understand. One of the more ambitious approaches is used by the PNG graphics format. PNG files mark whether each block is essential. If a program reading a PNG file sees an "essential" block that it doesn't understand, it should give up; if it doesn't understand a "non-essential" block, it can simply ignore it. Similarly, each block is marked to indicate if it can be safely copied to a different PNG file without being updated. A comment block can safely be copied without being altered, while a block giving statistical information about the picture can't. This type of marking allows simple utilities to make minor changes to a file without understanding every single type of block they might see.

Reading such files is usually both quick and simple. The reader simply reads the type of each block, and either calls a function to read and interpret the data or skips the data. The only point of complexity is that sometimes dependencies exist between the blocks. For example, it might be necessary to know the width and height of a graphics image before attempting to decompress the actual graphics data.

Random-Access Formats

Many programs deal with files by simply reading the entire thing into memory. That's not always possible, though. Sometimes the data is too large to reasonably fit into memory (remember that some systems have only a small amount of memory). Sometimes, even if the file isn't large, you want to quickly identify the particular piece of the file in which you're interested. The result is called a *random-access* format.

A good example of this type of format is the TIFF graphics format. A TIFF file consists of a small header that specifies where an image file directory is located in the file. That directory in turn specifies where the actual picture data is stored in the file. Note that you don't read a TIFF file from beginning to end; you read the header, then follow a chain of file positions to locate additional information.

This indirect arrangement may seem curious for a graphics file until you realize that TIFF was originally designed for use in professional image manipulation. Graphics professionals routinely deal with high-resolution images requiring many megabytes each. The ability to store several different images in one file (such as both low- and high-resolution versions of the same picture) and retrieve any particular image or part of an image on demand is a vital feature for this type of work.

This type of random-access format is also used by some programs that store intermediate data on disk using "virtual memory;" program performance often hinges on how fast data can be moved between disk and memory. Such file formats are beyond the scope of this book, since they're usually intended only for the internal use of that program; they're often deleted as soon as the program finishes.

A drawback of this kind of random-access approach is that it's often cumbersome to simply read the file from beginning to end. For example, PDF is a random-access format used to store electronic documents. Although it has the same graphics capabilities as PostScript, PDF would be a poor choice for sending documents to a printer. It's impossible to make sense of a PDF file until the directory at the very end of the file is available. If you tried to build a printer to accept PDF files, it would have to receive and store the entire PDF file. Contrast this with a PostScript file, which can be readily interpreted as the printer receives it. On the other hand, it's easier for an application to find a particular page in a PDF file than in a PostScript file. For the PDF file, the directory simply tells you where each page resides in the file; finding a page in a PostScript file requires reading the entire file from the beginning.

Stream Formats

One of the benefits I mentioned above for type-length-value approaches is that such files often can be easily read from beginning to end. Being able to understand a file by reading it in this manner is sometimes a desirable property all by itself. One reason is that disk drives and many other computer components are often optimized for handling files sequentially from beginning to end. Another reason is that when files are being transferred, whether over a modem or from one program to another on the same machine, it's convenient if the program reading the data can digest it immediately.

A good example of the latter concern is how some graphics formats (GIF and PNG, in particular) interleave picture data. GIF can store picture data starting with every eighth line, then every fourth line, and so on. A program reading a GIF file can create a low-resolution image using the initial data, then progressively refine the image as more data becomes available. This approach allows people to view pictures as they are downloaded by modem. The person downloading can see a rough overview of the picture very quickly and decide whether or not to bother waiting for the rest of the picture.

This kind of *stream* format requires that the information in the file appears in an appropriate order. The file format designer has to ensure that the reader of such a file will be able to interpret each part of the file as it is read.

Script Languages

The word *interpret* in the preceding paragraph is no accident. The purpose of a file is really to recreate a certain program state. One way to do that is to provide the reading program with a set of instructions to produce that program state. For example, you could store a picture as a set of drawing instructions.

Many applications store information by writing a text script file that can be interpreted by the application. One of the simplest examples is the Microsoft Windows' INI files. INI files can be thought of as simple *scripts* that, when interpreted, define a collection of variables. At the other extreme are full-blown programming languages such as PostScript or TEX. The biggest disadvantage of using script files is that it requires writing an interpreter, which can be a formidable challenge for the application writer. However, because scripting is such a useful part of a large application anyway, program designers often take advantage of this approach.

Text and Binary Formats

Script files, as I described earlier, usually take the form of text. Text files are generally easier to transfer between computers, which explains why the PDF format, which is used to share electronic documents, is a text format. Also, text files are generally much easier for humans to create and understand. The electronic documents used by the World Wide Web are in a format that is easy to create and modify with standard text editors. This format allowed the developers of the World Wide Web to experiment easily, and made it possible for tens of thousands of people to create new HTML documents using standard text editors.

Text and binary formats have many size trade-offs. When they store the exact same kind of data, text formats are almost always larger than the corresponding binary formats. PostScript Type 1 font files can be stored in either a text or binary format; the binary format is typically about half as large as the text format. On the other hand, text formats often allow people to store data in a more abstract (and compact) form. Graphics formats that store a collection of text drawing commands are much more compact than formats that store high-resolution binary bitmaps. Either way, text formats do tend to be marginally slower to read and write, due in part to the additional conversions that must be done to convert data between the text format in the file and an efficient binary format.

These trade-offs are evident in the file format descriptions in this book. Formats that might need to be edited directly by humans, or which need to be shared among many different types of computers, are often text formats. File formats that might be used to store very large amounts of data or for which fast, efficient access is critical are often in a binary form.

About Transferring Files

The portability of files is more crucial than ever in our increasingly networked computer culture. This appendix looks at some of the ways that data gets from one computer to another, and some of the unique features of each approach.

Post Office

Although electronic mail, the World Wide Web, and other such Internet marvels receive a lot of attention, not everyone has access to them. They also require a fair bit of knowledge to use, knowledge you can't safely assume everyone has.

For many years, publishers have been transferring their books to printers electronically by simply placing the entire book—tens or even hundreds of megabytes of data—on a disk, which is then mailed overnight to the printer. Surprisingly, this approach is often both faster and cheaper than using the Internet. With overnight delivery, the printer is likely to have the entire book in an immediately usable form early in the morning. Unless the printer is unusually Internet-savvy, it may require several hours to download, decode, and decompress all of the data. Since human time is expensive, the Internet approach is likewise more expensive. Clearly, as Internet tools become more common, the economics will change, but there will always be situations in which it truly is cheaper to ship a disk than to use the Internet. (In fact, overnight mail delivery of a CD-ROM represents a data transfer rate about four times the speed of today's fastest modems!)

The type of disk to use depends in part on the amount of data and the platform. Graphic artists and publishers often use Macintosh-format removable hard disk cartridges, because of the popularity of Macintosh systems among people in the publishing business and the need to transfer files too large to be comfortably copied onto floppy disks. Magneto-optical disks (which hold anywhere from 128 megabytes to over four gigabytes) are also popular in some circles. On Unix platforms, quarter-inch tape cartridges are the most common way to share data.

For most other purposes, the closest thing to a standard is a 3 1/2 inch floppy disk in 1.44meg or 720k MS-DOS format. These disks can now be read in all new PC-compatibles, most Macintoshes, Atari ST, Amiga, and many Unix systems. The most common platforms that can't read this type of floppy are older Macintoshes and machines that completely lack floppy drives (which includes many new PC and Mac laptops as well as many workstations).

FTP

Most Internet connections now offer access to *FTP* (File Transfer Protocol). FTP is a way of transferring files across the Internet, best suited for publishing; normally files are placed in a special area where anyone on the Internet can access them. FTP can be used for person-to-person transfer, but it requires careful setup to ensure that only certain people can access the data.

The most common FTP client program is `ftp`. While there are many graphical FTP clients, the text-based `ftp` program is often the most reliable.

FTP allows you to log in to a remote computer and transfer files between that computer and the one from which you're running FTP. That part about "logging in" is a bit of a problem; rather than try to create new accounts for everyone who uses an FTP archive, the system administrators usually create a special restricted account called "anonymous." In this way, you can use FTP to connect to a remote site (logging in as "anonymous") and retrieve files. (This is commonly known as *anonymous FTP*.)

A Sample FTP Session

Here's a short example session, which I started by typing `ftp ftp.shsu.edu` on an Internet shell account.

```
Connected to pip.SHSU.EDU.
220 pip.shsu.edu FTP server (Version wu-2.4(4) Thu May 19 1994)
```

The first response was a message from the FTP server (the program at the other end that manages the archive site). Notice that the name it responded with (`pip.SHSU.EDU`) was not the name I specified (`ftp.shsu.edu`). This event is quite common; many Internet hosts respond to several different "aliases." You should stick with the most appropriate one. Today, the archive site is located on a machine called `pip`; tomorrow it might be on a different machine. In any case, the alias `ftp.shsu.edu` will always refer to the machine that contains the archive files. The second thing this response tells you is the program that's managing the FTP site. This particular site is using the `wu` server, which was compiled on May 19, 1994. After using FTP for a long time, you'll begin to recognize some of the more widely used FTP servers; a few offer special features that can help you find specific files. (The `wu` FTP server was developed by the people who maintain one of the largest Internet archive sites, and is one of my favorites.)

```
Name (ftp.shsu.edu:kientzle): anonymous
331 Guest login ok, send your complete e-mail address as password.
Password:
```

This particular FTP site allows anonymous logins under the user name `anonymous`. Just ignore the default name the `ftp` program concocts for you. It's customary to provide your electronic mail address as the password whenever you use an anonymous FTP site. This information helps people who are in charge of the site to help you; for example, if they find out they are getting many requests from your area, they may find someone to "mirror" their site in your area. This mirror will provide you with faster access to those files. Since anonymous FTP is so common, newer FTP programs (including most World Wide Web browsers) automatically log you in as `anonymous` by default, using your mail address as the password.

```
230-You are 33 of 100 users allowed for your class.
230-
230-Please read the file README
230-  it was last modified on Thu Mar 23 06:08:22 1995
230 Guest login ok, access restrictions apply.
```

After you're logged in, the FTP server tells you some things you might need to know. In this case, it draws your attention to a README file that you should download and read to find out more about this site. This server also tells you how many people are using the archive site. This information is helpful because it lets you know what to expect; if there are very many users (say 100 out of 100), things might be a bit slower. Pay attention to this type of information when it's available; the Internet can be exceedingly slow when it's busy, and you can make your online time much more productive if you learn to schedule your usage for quiet times.

```
ftp> get README
200 PORT command successful.
150 Opening ASCII mode data connection for README (1343 bytes).
226 Transfer complete.
local: README remote: README
1375 bytes received in 0.21 seconds (6.3 Kbytes/s)
```

The purpose of FTP is to move files around, and the command you'll use most often is the get command, which copies a file from the archive to the machine running the ftp program. Note that the format of the filename depends on the host; since most server programs run on Unix computers, filenames are usually case-sensitive—README is *not* the same as readme. You should be careful to type the names correctly.

One other thing that you should notice about the previous part of the session: I typed the command to the ftp program running on one machine, which in turn negotiated the transfer with the remote server. When several different programs are running like this, it's sometimes tricky to keep track of who's giving commands to whom. In this case, you give commands to the ftp program, and it gives commands to the server program.

```
ftp> quit
221 Goodbye.
```

Once you've gotten the files you need, you simply exit the ftp program. The ftp program will tell the server you're finished.

More FTP Commands

The example above was deliberately very simple. The common FTP programs allow much more than this. There are even graphical FTP interfaces, but they vary considerably in how you use them and what capabilities they offer; the ones I've used are not as flexible as the basic text-oriented FTP program. I'll go through the most important commands you'll see used:

get I've already briefly discussed the `get` command. On many systems, the `get` command also allows you to specify the name to which the file should be copied, which can be useful if the system you're using has restrictions on the format of filenames. The Unix systems used by many archive sites allow for very long filenames that can include any number of unusual characters. For example, if you're using FTP to copy files from a Unix machine to a MS-DOS system, a simple `get README.uploads` might result in the file `README.UPL`, which is a tad cryptic. It might be easier to `get README.uploads uploads.txt` instead.

One feature of some FTP servers is that they allow you to request a complete directory. The server will automatically archive the directory and send you the archive. Just add `.zip` to the name of the directory to ask for a zip archive of the directory contents, or `.tar.gz` to ask for a Unix-style archive.

cd Just like most computer systems, the files on an archive site are arranged into directories and subdirectories. Usually, there is a `pub` directory, which contains files available for public retrieval.

On most FTP sites (but not all), you can use `cd ..` to tell the server to go to a higher directory. (The catch is that the name after `cd` is interpreted by the server system. While `..` means "next directory up" on Unix, MS-DOS, and many other systems, it's not quite universal.)

dir/ls Of course, all of the above would be much easier if you could see what files were in a directory. The `dir` and `ls` commands work slightly differently; the `ls` command gives you only the names of the files, usually unsorted, while the `dir` command gives you a sorted list, together with such information as the size and date of the files.[1]

binary/text FTP by default assumes that you are transferring text files. If you're transferring non-text files (such as graphics or compressed files), you'll

---

[1]One of my complaints with some graphical FTP programs is that they only give you the names of the files, and not the sizes or other information.

need to tell FTP by giving it the `binary` command. Similarly, the `text` command sets up FTP to copy text files.

`mget`   A FTP archive may have a large collection of files that you want. On some archive sites, you can request an entire directory, and the contents will be automatically wrapped into a single archive file for you. When that approach isn't available, you can use the `mget` command to specify a wildcard pattern; all files matching the wildcard will be retrieved. The kind of wildcards allowed varies by site, but almost all support * (any group of characters) and ? (any single character). For example, `mget README*` would retrieve all of the files starting with README. Again, remember that most FTP archives are case-sensitive.

By default, `mget` asks you before it downloads a file. This step allows you to select only the particular files you want. The `prompt` command allows you to change this behavior, so that you can retrieve large groups of files without answering a Yes/No question for every one.

`put/mput`   FTP also allows you to copy files *to* a FTP site, using the `put` and `mput` commands, which work almost identically to `get` and `mget`.

`lcd`   Being able to switch directories on the archive site is fine, but you might also need to change directories on the local machine, so you can decide where any files you copy will land. The `lcd` command (which stands for "local change directory") does exactly that.

This isn't a complete listing of the commands supported by the FTP program, but these are the commands that you're most likely to use.

Other Ways to Access FTP

The venerable `ftp` program has many competitors. I generally use the `ncftp` program, which has a similar text-oriented interface but offers a number of additional features. Most World Wide Web browsers also support FTP. A graphical browser is a convenient way to find out what's available on a particular FTP site, but I generally prefer a text-based FTP client program to download files. Of course, you may have a different opinion. I suggest you try several different FTP clients and see which one works best for you.

World Wide Web

The World Wide Web was designed to make it easy to request specific pieces of data from different computers. A World Wide Web client (called a *browser*) asks for specific files from other machines. Those files can contain markers indicating the name and address of other small files. A user can read a page of information and simply click on a highlighted entry to retrieve another page with different information.

The World Wide Web depends on three mechanisms. Loosely, these three mechanisms answer the following three questions:

- How do you identify a piece of information?

- How do you retrieve a piece of information once you know its name?

- Once you have the information, how do you make sense of it?

The first question is answered by a *Universal Resource Locator* (URL), which is a notation for describing the location of a piece of information. In essence, a URL is a "phone number and extension" for a file somewhere on the Internet (see page 30). Note that like a telephone number, when the data moves, the URL is no longer valid.

The second mechanism used by the World Wide Web is the *HyperText Transfer Protocol* (HTTP). HTTP is the "language" used by the client program (that runs on your computer) to request specific information from a server program somewhere on the Internet (see page 35). It's possible to use just about any protocol, and there are parts of the Internet that use the FTP protocol as a substitute for HTTP, but HTTP has several features specifically designed for the World Wide Web.

The third piece of the puzzle is the *HyperText Markup Language* (HTML). HTTP can be used to transfer any type of information, and people are experimenting with using it to transfer movies, interactive three-dimensional environments, and sound files, but the bulk of the information currently on the World Wide Web uses HTML. HTML is discussed in more detail starting on page 29, but the the idea is that HTML specifies the general appearance of a text document, and in particular, can specify that certain parts of the document are *links* to other documents. World Wide Web client programs usually highlight those links; when the user selects the highlighted element, the client program retrieves the data from the corresponding URL. In this way, you can follow connections to different data stored all over the Internet. People have assembled vast collections of data simply by taking information that each person had on a separate computer and providing links to tie the individual pieces together into a seamless whole.

Gopher

Gopher is a file transfer method that is similar to HTTP in some respects, but is more limited in the type of data it can support. Gopher is text-oriented, allowing you to browse menus and download files. The menus can contain references to other files (possibly on other machines). To access data using Gopher, you need the name of the machine and the name of the file or menu.

Electronic Mail

The World Wide Web is growing rapidly, but is not suited to all types of data exchange. Primarily, the World Wide Web is oriented towards publishing, making data available to anyone who's interested. Often, you have a file that you want to send to a small number of people, and the World Wide Web isn't particularly helpful in this regard. FTP can be used to transfer files between individuals, but it requires some care to set up for this kind of use.

Electronic mail (email) is often a better option, but there are still some hurdles to overcome. Electronic mail typically only supports text files and can transfer only one file at a time. There are also limits on the size of mail messages.

Overcoming these restrictions requires the use of several programs to package the data you want to send and to convert it into a form palatable to the mail system. The recipient must then carefully unwrap the package to retrieve the original data. The specific steps to send a file are:

1. Archive several files into a single file.

2. Compress the archive to make it smaller.

3. Encode the archive into a text format.

Frequently, a single program will handle two of these steps, and some mail programs (such as Eudora and MetaMail) will handle all of them for you. The catch is that both the sender and recipient must be using compatible software. You'll frequently have to handle each of these steps manually.

Specific programs to handle the first two steps (archiving and compression) are discussed in more detail starting on page 183, and the third step is discussed starting on page 255.

Direct Connect Modems

Often, using mail to transfer files requires that you first upload the file, send it through mail, and then download it at the other end. In this case, it might make more sense to try a direct modem-to-modem connection. The details of how you do this depends on your particular terminal program, but a typical scenario is outlined in Figure D.1. This approach is easier if you can talk to each other on the phone while doing this, but that requires two separate phone lines.

---

1. Both people turn on their modems and start their terminal programs.
2. The callee enables auto-answer on her modem.
3. The caller asks her modem to dial the callee's modem.
4. The modems connect.
5. Both people type to each other to make sure the connection is working.
6. The sender starts sending the files.
7. The receiver starts receiving the files.

Figure D.1   Steps for a Direct Modem-to-Modem Transfer

Getting this method to work can be tricky, but here are a few suggestions:

- Set both terminal programs to 8 bits, No parity, and 1 stop bit (8, N, 1). This configuration is fast, and avoids some common problems.

- To get your modem to auto-answer, type ATS0=1 followed by the Enter key; the modem should answer OK. This setting tells the modem to answer on the first ring. Do this before the caller tries to dial. (Many terminal programs have a menu option or command that takes care of this step for you.)

- Set both terminal programs to use ZModem, and make sure that Automatic ZModem Download is enabled. If both terminal programs don't support ZModem, try YModem (sometimes called "YModem-Batch"), Kermit, or XModem, in that order.

- If you have trouble getting the modems to connect (the modem never says CONNECTED), then first try resetting both modems (ATZ), then read the modem manuals. It's an unfortunate fact that getting some modems to talk to each other can require technical tricks. Sometimes the modem manual will have specific information on how to set it up to talk to particular modems. Sometimes, you can call the modem manufacturer and ask them. Sometimes, you just have to guess.

If all else fails, use freshly formatted floppy disks and an overnight delivery service.

Remote-Access Programs

There are a number of specialized *remote-access* programs designed specifically to simplify the direct connect process. By running one copy on each computer, either person can connect to the other computer and easily copy files between the two systems. These programs can be much simpler than using generic terminal programs, though they tend not to be very standard, requiring each person to have a copy of the same program.

Bulletin Board Systems

If you have the technical expertise (and there are several good books on the market to help you if you don't), you could even set up a *bulletin board system* (BBS). Many terminal programs come with simple bulletin board software that lets you define who can dial into your computer and what files they can access. If you find yourself transferring a lot of data by modem, it may be worth investing in a good BBS program.

A Binary Dump Program

I have written a short program in C that I use to look at the contents of files. To use it, simply type dump *filename*. For example, I typed dump jeff, and the first few lines of output looked like:

```
jeff:

  Addr     0 1  2 3  4 5  6 7  8 9  A B  C D  E F 0 2 4 6 8 A C E
--------   ---- ---- ---- ---- ---- ---- ---- ---- ----------------
00000000   4749 4638 3761 5100 7800 f300 0000 ff00 GIF87aQ.x.s.....
00000010   1010 1018 1818 2929 2939 3939 5252 525a ......)))999RRRZ
00000020   5a5a 7373 7384 8484 9c9c 9cad adad bdbd ZZsss......---==
00000030   bdce cece f1f1 f100 0000 0000 002c 0000 =NNNqqq.......,..
00000040   0000 5100 7800 0004 fe10 c849 abbd 38eb ..Q.x...~.HI+=8k
```

The left column tells you where in the file you are, the middle columns give the numeric values of the bytes, and the right column shows you the characters in those locations (unprintable values are shown as periods). The numbers are all in hexadecimal; don't worry if you don't read hexadecimal—you are usually interested in only the right column. In this case, the first line in the right column starts with GIF87a, indicating that this is a GIF file. Similarly, most binary file formats have the file type somewhere in the first 20 or 30 bytes.

```c
#include <stdio.h>
#include <ctype.h>
char line[80];
long address;
```

```
void puthex(n, digits, pos)
long n; int digits, pos;
{ if (digits > 1) puthex(n/16,digits-1,pos);
  line[pos+digits-1] = "0123456789abcdef"[n%16];
}

void dumpfile(f)
FILE *f;
{ int c,i;
  address = 0;
  c=getc(f);
  while (1) {
      for (i=0;i<50;i++) line[i]=' ';
      for (;i<80;i++) line[i] = 0;
      puthex(address,8,0);
      if (c == EOF) return;
      for (i=0;i<16;i++) {
        puthex(c & 0xff,2, 10 + i*2 + i/2);
        line[50+i] = '.';
        if (isprint(c & 0x7f)) line[50+i] = c & 0x7f;
        if ((c=getc(f)) == EOF) break;
      }
      if ((address % 256)==0) {
        puts("");
puts("  Addr     0 1  2 3  4 5  6 7  8 9  A B  C D  E F 0 2 4 6 8 A C E");
puts("--------   ---- ---- ---- ---- ---- ---- ---- ---- ----------------");
      }
      puts(line);
      address += 16;
  }
}

void main(argc,argv)
int argc; char **argv;
{  if (argc < 2) dumpfile(stdin);
   else {
      while (--argc > 0) {
        FILE *f = fopen(*++argv, "rb");
        printf("%s:\n",*argv);
        if (f) {
          dumpfile(f);
          fclose(f);
        } else printf("*** Can't open %s!!\n", *argv);
      }
   }
}
```

Bibliography

[Ado85]   Adobe Systems Incorporated. *PostScript Language Tutorial and Cookbook*. Addison-Wesley, Reading, MA, USA, 1985.

[Ado88]   Adobe Systems Incorporated. *PostScript Language Program Design*. Addison-Wesley, Reading, MA, USA, 1988.

[Ado90a] Adobe Systems Incorporated. *Adobe Type 1 Font Format*. Addison-Wesley, Reading, MA, USA, 1990.

[Ado90b] Adobe Systems Incorporated. *PostScript Language Reference Manual*. Addison-Wesley, Reading, MA, USA, second edition, 1990.

[Ado93]   Adobe Systems Incorporated. *Portable Document Format Reference Manual*. Addison-Wesley, Reading, MA, USA, 1993.

[App93a] Apple Computer, Inc. *Inside Macintosh: QuickTime*. Addison-Wesley, Reading, MA, USA, 1993.

[App93b] Apple Computer, Inc. *Inside Macintosh: QuickTime Components*. Addison-Wesley, Reading, MA, USA, 1993.

[Bor95]   Günter Born. *File Formats Handbook*. International Thomson Computer Press, London, UK, 1995.

[Con95]   Daniel W. Connolly. "Character set" considered harmful. Published as an Internet Draft, April 1995.

[Cro95]   Lee Daniel Crocker. PNG: The portable network graphic format. *Dr. Dobb's Journal*, pages 36–44, July 1995.

[GIF87]   *GIF Graphics Interchange Format: A standard defining a mechanism for the storage and transmission of bitmap-based graphics information.* Columbus, OH, USA, 1987.

[Gil92]   Daniel Gilly. *UNIX in a Nutshell: System V Edition.* O'Reilly & Associates, Sebastopol, CA, USA, second edition, 1992.

[GMS94]   Michel Goossens, Frank Mittelbach, and Alexander Samarin. *The LaTeX Companion.* Addison-Wesley, Reading, MA, USA, 1994.

[Gra90]   *Graphics Interchange Format: Version 89a.* Columbus, OH, USA, 1990.

[Gra95]   Ian S. Graham. *HTML Sourcebook.* John Wiley & Sons, Inc., New York, NY, USA, 1995.

[Hof79]   Douglas R. Hofstadter. *Gödel, Escher, Bach: An Eternal Golden Braid.* Basic Books, New York, NY, USA, 1979.

[JGF94]   Nels Johnson, Fred Gault, and Mark Florence. *How to Digitize Video.* John Wiley & Sons, Inc., New York, NY, USA, 1994.

[Ker79]   Brian W. Kernighan. *A TROFF Tutorial*, 1979. Reproduced in [USD94].

[Knu86a]   Donald E. Knuth. *The TeXbook*, volume A of *Computers and Typesetting.* Addison-Wesley, Reading, MA, USA, 1986.

[Knu86b]   Donald E. Knuth. *TeX: The Program*, volume B of *Computers and Typesetting.* Addison-Wesley, Reading, MA, USA, 1986.

[Knu86c]   Donald E. Knuth. *The METAFONTbook*, volume C of *Computers and Typesetting.* Addison-Wesley, Reading, MA, USA, 1986.

[Knu86d]   Donald E. Knuth. *METAFONT: The Program*, volume D of *Computers and Typesetting.* Addison-Wesley, Reading, MA, USA, 1986.

[Knu86e] Donald E. Knuth. *Computer Modern Typefaces*, volume E of *Computers and Typesetting*. Addison-Wesley, Reading, MA, USA, 1986.

[Lam94] Leslie Lamport. *LATEX: A Document Preparation System: User's Guide and Reference Manual*. Addison-Wesley, Reading, MA, USA, second edition, 1994.

[Mv94] James D. Murray and William vanRyper. *Encyclopedia of Graphics File Formats*. O'Reilly & Associates, Sebastopol, CA, USA, 1994.

[Nel92] Mark Nelson. *The Data Compression Book*. M&T Books, New York, NY, USA, 1992.

[Oss79] Joseph F. Ossanna. *NROFF/TROFF User's Manual*, 1979. Reproduced in [USD94].

[Pes95] Mark Pesce. *VRML: Browsing and Building Cyberspace*. New Riders, 1995.

[PM93] William B. Pennebaker and Joan L. Mitchell. *JPEG: Still Image Data Compression Standard*. International Thomson Computer Press, London, UK, 1993.

[PRM94] *4.4 Berkeley Software Distribution: Programmer's Reference Manual*. The USENIX Association and O'Reilly & Associates, Inc., Sebastopol, CA, USA, 1994.

[PSD94] *4.4 Berkeley Software Distribution: Programmer's Supplementary Documents*. The USENIX Association and O'Reilly & Associates, Inc., Sebastopol, CA, USA, 1994.

[Smi92] Joan M. Smith. *SGML and Related Standards: Document Description and Processing Languages*. Ellis Horwood Limited, Hemel Hempstead, Hertfordshire, UK, 1992.

[SMM94] *4.4 Berkeley Software Distribution: System Manager's Manual*. The USENIX Association and O'Reilly & Associates, Inc., Sebastopol, CA, USA, 1994.

[Swi26] Jonathan Swift. *Travels into Several Remote Nations of the World, in Four Parts, by Lemuel Gulliver*. 1726.

[Tek95]   A. Murat Tekalp. *Digital Video Processing.* Prentice Hall PTR, Upper Saddle River, NJ, USA, 1995.

[TIF92]   *TIFF Revision 6.0.* Seattle, WA, USA, 1992.

[URM94] *4.4 Berkeley Software Distribution: User's Reference Manual.* The USENIX Association and O'Reilly & Associates, Inc., Sebastopol, CA, USA, 1994.

[USD94] *4.4 Berkeley Software Distribution: User's Supplementary Documents.* The USENIX Association and O'Reilly & Associates, Inc., Sebastopol, CA, USA, 1994.

[vH94]   Eric van Herwijnen. *Practical SGML.* Wolters-Kluwer Academic Publishers, Boston, MA, USA, second edition, 1994.

Index

F

as a replacement for compress, 223

H

halftoning, 119, 160
HDTV (High Definition Television), 314, 327
Helvetica font, 64, 105
Henderson, Thom, 205
hertz, 290
van Herwijnen, Eric, 80
Hobbes OS/2 archive, 13
HSL (Hue-Saturation-Lightness Color
        System), 164
HSV (Hue-Saturation-Value Color System),
        120, 164
HTML (HyperText Markup Language),
        21–23, 26, 29–57, 78, 79, 91,
        125, 126, 170, 174, 367
    anchor tag, 45
    anchor tag attributes, 47
    deprecated features, 54
    elements, 40
    entities, 44–46
    example table, 51, 52
    forms, 38, 48–50
    imagemaps, 39, 48
    input fields, 48
    mathematics, 50–51, 53
    style sheets, 42
    variables, 48, 49
HTML tags, 40–41
    A, 45, 47
    B, 45
    BASE, 42
    BODY, 41
    BOX, 51
    CITE, 44
    CODE, 44, 56
    DFN, 44
    EM, 40, 44
    FORM, 42, 49
    H1, 43
    H2, 43
    H3, 43
    H4, 43
    H5, 43
    H6, 43
    HEAD, 41
    HTML, 41
    I, 45
    IMG, 47, 48

INPUT, 49
ISINDEX, 42
KBD, 44
LINK, 42
LISTING, 54
MATH, 50
OVER, 51
P, 43
PLAINTEXT, 54
PRE, 43
S, 45
SAMP, 44, 56
SELECT, 48, 49
STRIKE, 44
STRONG, 44
SUB, 45, 50
SUP, 45, 51
TABLE, 50
TD, 50
TEXTAREA, 49
TH, 50
TITLE, 41
TR, 50
TT, 45
U, 45
VAR, 44
XMP, 54
HTTP (HyperText Transfer Protocol), 29–31,
        33, 35–39, 41, 57, 272
    URL modifiers, 37
    URLs, 35–39
hue, 120, 164
Huffman compression, 166, 185, 186, 208,
        219, 220, 239, 294, 333
human hearing, 290, 295, 334, 335
human speech, 290, 293, 295
human vision, 123, 124, 158, 163
Hyper-Archive, 12

I

IFF (Interchange File Format), 178, 179, 299,
        307, 354
image compression, 122
Imploding, 215, 218–219
impossibility of perfect compression, 189
including PostScript files, 100
Info-Mac archive, 12, 57, 124, 204
INI file format, 366
interlaced graphics, 54, 131, 140, 146
Internet

Using the
CD-ROM

The CD-ROM contains a variety of useful tools compiled by the Coriolis Group staff to accompany this book. For more information about the CD-ROM and the software it contains, please refer to page 339.

Overall Organization

The CD-ROM is organized to match the book:

- The top-level directories correspond to the major divisions of the book: text, graphics, compression and archiving, encoding, audio, and video.
- Subdirectories correspond to specific formats, such as `graphics/jpeg` for files related to JPEG.
- Within each format are directories for each specific platform.[1] For HTML tools for Windows, look in `text/html/windows`.

Not all files can be neatly classified this way. For example, many of the graphics programs support a variety of formats, and have been placed in the `graphics/apps` directory rather than being duplicated under each format. You'll also find scattered directories with names like `sample` (with sample files in that format) and `spec` (containing official specifications for that format).

---

[1] Many of the Unix archives on the CD-ROM had their original `.tar.gz` extensions inadvertently shortened to `.gz` rather than `.tgz`. We apologize for any confusion this may cause.